ANIMAL PLANET

COMPLETE GUIDE
TO DOG CARE

Everything you need
to know to have a happy,
healthy, well-trained dog

tfh

DIANE MORGAN

COMPLETE GUIDE TO DOG CARE

Project Team
Editors: Heather Russell-Revesz,
         Stephanie Fornino, Mary Grangeia
Indexer: Elizabeth Walker
Designer: Mary Ann Kahn

TFH Publications
President/CEO: Glen S. Axelrod
Executive Vice President: Mark E. Johnson
Publisher: Christopher T. Reggio
Production Manager: Kathy Bontz

TFH Publications, Inc.
One TFH Plaza
Third and Union Avenues
Neptune City, NJ 07753

Discovery Communications, LLC. Book Development Team: Marjorie Kaplan, President and General Manager, Animal Planet Media/ Kelly Day, Executive Vice President and General Manager, Discovery Commerce/ Elizabeth Bakacs, Vice President, Licensing and Creative/ JP Stoops, Director, Licensing/ Betsy Ferg, Design Director, Licensing/ Bridget Stoyko, Associate Art Director, Licensing

©2010 Discovery Communications, LLC. Animal Planet and the Animal Planet logo are trademarks of Discovery Communications, LLC, used under license. All rights reserved. *animalplanet.com*

Printed and bound in China
11 12 13 14 15   1 3 5 7 9 8 6 4 2

Derived from *Good Dogkeeping: Today's Guide to Caring for Your Best Friend,* originally published in 2005

Library of Congress Cataloging-in-Publication Data
Morgan, Diane, 1947-
 Complete guide to dog care : everything you need to know to have a happy,
healthy, well-trained dog / Diane Morgan.
     p. cm. -- (Animal planet pet care library)
 Includes index.
 ISBN 978-0-7938-3712-0 (alk. paper)
 1. Dogs--Care. 2. Dogs--Health. 3. Dogs--Training. I. Title.
 SF427.M744 2011
 636.7'08--dc22

                    2010036227

This book has been published with the intent to provide accurate and authoritative information in regard to the subject matter within. While every reasonable precaution has been taken in preparation of this book, the author and publisher expressly disclaim responsibility for any errors, omissions, or adverse effects arising from the use or application of the information contained herein. The techniques and suggestions are used at the reader's discretion and are not to be considered a substitute for veterinary care. If you suspect a medical problem consult your veterinarian.

Note: In the interest of concise writing, "he" is used when referring to puppies and dogs unless the text is specifically referring to females or males. "She" is used when referring to people. However, the information contained herein is equally applicable to both sexes.

The Leader In Responsible Animal Care for Over 50 Years!®
www.tfh.com

CONTENTS

INTRODUCTION

"WE ARE RESPONSIBLE FOR WHAT WE HAVE TAMED."
—*The Little Prince*, Antoine de Saint-Exupéry

There are more than 65 million dogs in the United States, and every one of them is special. Whether your dog is Westminster-bound or the family pet, you have an awesome treasure. No other creature has so embedded himself in the human psyche and human culture as the dog has. The family dog shares the most intimate secrets of family life. He eats in the kitchen and sleeps in the bedroom. He watches television with his owners and takes his share of the nachos. A disconcertingly large proportion of dog owners shower with their dogs, send them Valentine's cards, and paint their toenails pink. (There is another disconcertingly large number of people who mistreat, neglect, or abandon their pets, but of course, they won't be reading this book. These people should not own dogs.)

Your dog is special. He is probably the most beautiful dog on earth. Or the funniest or most intelligent or most endearing. He charms you. He is loyal and amazingly intuitive. And he is absolutely in your power. You make all the important decisions in your dog's life: what he will eat, when he will go outside, how he will be trained, when he has a bath, when he sees a vet. Your responsibility to him lasts as long as he lives. Your dog will never grow up, move out, go to college, marry, or get a job. Your dog is completely dependent on you to care for him. Your once-bouncy puppy will hang around the house until he is old, tottery, and maybe a bit senile, but he will always be your "boy." Whether you think of yourself as owner, guardian, caretaker, dog mommy, or chum is not important. What is important is that you willingly accept responsibility for making life-and-death decisions on his behalf almost every day.

It's a little scary. Good dogkeeping, like good child rearing, is not intuitive. You don't instinctively know that chocolate is bad for dogs or that plastic dishes can give a dog chin dermatitis or that a wagging tail doesn't always mean a dog is happy to see you. These are things that have to be learned.

This book is designed to help you learn everything you need to know to make dogkeeping a joyful and fulfilling experience. And both you and your dog will like that a lot.

PART ONE

BASIC CARE

FOR YOUR DOG

1

ACQUIRING YOUR DOG

Good dogkeeping begins with getting a good dog. And dogs are such wonderful, adaptable, amazing animals that good dogs can materialize from almost anywhere: responsible breeders, irresponsible breeders, backyard breeders, shelters, rescue organizations, neighbors, newspaper ads, relatives, pet stores, the alley behind the house, or the highway in front of it. Good dogs can be bought, given away, inherited, found, or traded for. They can even follow you home.

BEFORE YOU EVEN START LOOKING

While I believe good dogkeeping begins with a good dog, that's only half true. It also begins with a good owner. Is that good owner you?

Before you even start looking for a dog, please examine your reasons for wanting one. Good reasons include finding a devoted companion, wanting to enrich your life, helping out a homeless dog, and enjoying dog-related activities like tracking, agility, and wandering around in the woods with your best pal at your heels. Bad reasons include teaching your kids responsibility, owning a status symbol, and having a four-legged servant who will take abuse without fighting back.

If your reasons for dog owning are good, it's time to get more specific. Knowing what you want, what you don't want, and what you just can't tolerate will largely determine how successful your dog-owning experience will be. Try this exercise: Take a piece of paper and divide it into three columns.

The first two columns will help you pick the best dog for you. These characteristics can include physical things like size and hair length but should also include personality traits like protectiveness, barking, ability to get along with kids, and so forth. The third column will reveal your attitude and level of commitment toward your dog. The fewer things that you can honestly put in that column, the more successful you'll be as a dog owner. (See chart below.)

Somehow dogs seem to know which owners are committed to them and which aren't. People who have made a mental resolution to keep their dog come what may are likely to have fewer problems with their pets, resolve them more easily, and handle the problems that won't go away than those who take a provisional wait-and-see attitude. In this respect, getting a dog is something like adopting a child. By the way, the same is true for the entire family. Unless everyone is willing to make the commitment, your dog-owning adventure probably won't succeed. Starting off on the wrong foot is a recipe for trouble, and even the smallest puppy will sense that someone does not want him. Inevitably, he will pick that person's shoes to chew on. If not all of you are sure you want a dog, or you don't feel able to deal with the inevitable problems, you may wish to rethink your decision to get a dog in the first place.

Inevitable problems? Yes. As a dog owner, you can expect to deal with the following issues: housetraining mistakes, chewing, nipping, health crises, shedding, digging, and barking. Of course, very few dogs present all these problems, but no dog is trouble-free.

Don't be scared. It's like having a child. Children cause problems, too. If having a dog (or a child) were not ultimately rewarding, no one would have one.

CHARACTERISTICS I WANT IN A DOG	CHARACTERISTICS I DON'T WANT IN A DOG	THINGS THAT WILL MAKE ME GIVE UP A DOG
kid friendly	excessive barking	aggression
active	hairy	allergies
medium size	independent	running away

However, wanting a dog—even wanting a dog very much—isn't enough. Good dogkeeping requires more than wishing—it involves action, resolve, planning, and some sacrifice. (The best things in life aren't free!) Look deep into your own heart. Ask yourself the following questions:

- How long will the dog be left alone during the day?
- Who will take care of him?
- How much time (honestly) are you willing to spend playing with and exercising your dog every day?
- If the dog becomes ill and it would cost $1,000 to make him well, would you be willing or able to pay for the medical expenses?
- If you become ill or for some other reason would be unable to care for your dog, do you have a trusted friend or relative who would take on the responsibility for your pet?

- Would you be willing to take the dog to a professional trainer or behaviorist if he develops problems?
- What kinds of behavior could you simply not tolerate (and would make you get rid of your dog if he developed them): shedding, chronic illness, housetraining mistakes, aggression, barking, running away, digging, destruction of furniture?
- What would you do if you or a family member became allergic to the dog?
- What would you do if your significant other said, "Make a choice. It's me or Fluffy"?
- If you were offered a dream job but would have to move to a place where pets are not allowed, would you go?
- Deep down, would you really rather have a hamster?

Even if everybody in the family is gung ho about getting a dog, you'll need to decide who will be responsible for feeding, watering, walking, training, playing with, and paying the vet bills for the new family member. Naturally these responsibilities can be split up, but the humans in the family all need to know and agree on them. If a child is awarded the task of feeding the dog, an adult still needs to supervise to make sure it gets done, gets done on schedule, and gets done right. It's not fair to make your dog an object lesson in responsibility.

FINDING THE PERFECT DOG

The perfect dog is a magical mix of many ineluctable, never-to-be repeated qualities. You can improve your chances of finding that dog by narrowing your search in the three main categories of breed, sex, and age.

Breed

Setting your sights on a specific breed of dog will help give you an idea of how that dog will look and behave. Collies have one set of looks and

behavioral characteristics, Bulldogs another. Study the breed before you invest your heart and money. No single breed is good for everyone, though it's also not a requirement to get a purebred. Many adventurous people prefer a mixed-breed dog, and with good reason. Every mixed-breed dog is physically unique—you'll have the only one like him in the neighborhood. They also tend to be more versatile, smarter, and healthier than the average purebred. (Purebred does not always translate into well bred.) Crossbreeds often benefit from what we call hybrid vigor, and even completely mixed-up mongrels are often healthier than inbred purebreds. But if you want to show a dog or you have a special passion for a breed, then a purebred is for you. A purebred from working lines is also ideal if you want to enjoy a specific activity for which the dog was bred (Huskies for sledding, retrievers for duck hunting, and the like). If you really want to know the ins and outs of your chosen breed, try to attend that breed's national specialty show. You will not only see the finest

examples of the breed, but you'll be able to attend seminars, meet other fanciers, and perhaps even find a mentor.

Sex

It is hard to generalize about differences between the sexes. In some breeds, the females are gentler, easier to train, and friendlier. In other breeds, it's just the opposite. In no case can we make easy generalizations. However, if you already own a dog and want to add another one to the household, it is often best to select a dog of the opposite sex to the one you own now.

Age

Everybody loves puppies, but they are wrong for many people. Only people willing to put up with the rigors of housetraining and constant supervision should consider one. Older dogs usually come housetrained and are already over their dreaded nipping and chewing phases. Some people think a puppy will bond to the family better than an adult dog, but this hasn't been my experience. Most older dogs, especially those from shelters and rescues, are desperate for a family of their own to love. I always advise people to choose an older dog unless they absolutely have their heart set on a puppy. If you have never owned a dog before, I bet you'll have better luck with an older dog; there will be fewer surprises, including the ones that will be left on your rug.

DOG SOURCES

Now that you've decided what kind of dog you want, all systems are go, so let's look at some of the common sources for finding a dog.

Show Breeder

A show breeder is a person who breeds primarily for conformation (dog shows) or field trials, although nowadays you can also find people whose interest is in obedience, tracking, agility, earthdog trials, or other dog-related events. Show breeders often have older dogs as well as puppies.

Advantages: If you're interested in a show dog, show breeders are your only viable option. They tend to have beautiful dogs whose disposition is well suited to the event the breeder concentrates on. Good show breeders work hard to eliminate genetic defects in their lines. Their dogs also generally get excellent veterinary care and are well socialized as a rule. Simply because a dog comes from a show kennel, however, does not mean that he is show quality. Be sure to tell the breeder what you are looking for. Show breeders also tend to follow up on their puppies closely and provide a lot of support.

Disadvantages: Long waits (sometimes over a year). There are fewer "well-bred" dogs available than there are buyers waiting for them. Dogs from show kennels may not have an appropriate

temperament for pet owners. They need to be "on the muscle"—intense and highly alert—and many pet owners want a more laid-back animal. Some show kennel dogs, because of the intensive line-breeding common in show kennels, may carry genetic defects. Too many breeders put winning ahead of health. In addition, the prices of well-bred dogs may be above what the average person expects to pay.

The X-Factor: Show kennels may be hard to find. (They don't advertise.) Some show breeders aren't as courteous as they should be to novice owners. And some of the larger show kennels should do a better job of socializing their dogs. Show kennels may also expect you to sign a co-ownership contract in addition to the regular bill of sale. This contract may specify veterinary care and housing requirements.

> **If you're interested in a show dog, breeders are your only viable option.**

(See Appendix A for more information about co-ownership.) Don't do it unless you know what you're getting into.

Backyard Breeder

Backyard breeders are usually small-time folks who aren't interested in showing their dogs. In some cases, they're looking to make a few extra dollars. Sometimes the "breeders" simply made a mistake in letting an unneutered male get near a female in heat. On the other hand, some backyard hobby breeders simply like to breed good dogs without getting involved in the political games of dog showing.

Advantages: Most backyard breeders have the mom and dad on site for inspection. (In the case of show breeders, the sire may live in another country. That's not necessarily bad, but you won't get a firsthand look.) Backyard breeders are generally friendly, and most care about their puppies and dogs. Usually, the temperament of their puppies is appropriate for pet owners.

Disadvantages: Some backyard breeders are amateurs in the worst sense of the term. Many don't know anything about genetics, and their so-called breeding program is little more than random mating of whatever dogs they happen to have around at the time. Consequently, these breeders may unconsciously be propagating lethal genes in

their breed. As far as looks go, some backyard-bred dogs bear only a casual resemblance to the breed standard. In addition, the puppies may not have had proper veterinary care or evaluation.

The X-Factor: Backyard breeders are a gamble. Some of them are highly motivated, knowledgeable people who just don't want to get involved in showing. Others are ignorant, greedy, or cruel. I got the best dog I ever had from a backyard breeder—and the worst. This is a case where you really need to take a good look at the puppies and ask the right questions. (See "What to Ask a Breeder" later in this chapter.)

Shelter or Rescue

Shelters and rescues take in unwanted, abused, abandoned, or neglected animals and try to find them permanent homes. Some are publicly operated, but most are small and private. Like show breeders, a rescue will expect you to sign a contract that sets forth your responsibilities to the dog.

Advantages: Getting a puppy from a shelter or rescue is a humane and ethical choice. You are not only getting a dog but also saving a life. All breeds and all ages are available. Many shelters and rescues spay/neuter, temperament test, and vaccinate their animals as well. Shelters, in particular, offer pets for an inexpensive adoption fee. Rescues are often breed specific and have a wealth of knowledge and support to give. Many people have discovered the joys of adopting an adult animal or even more nobly, a senior dog. If you think you'd like to explore this compassionate option, check out www.srdogs.com on the Internet for older dogs. For a list of reputable purebred rescues, check out the national breed club rescue network at www.akc.org/breeds/rescue.cfm. And if you decide to adopt a dog from a pound, shelter, or rescue organization, you'll have the additional satisfaction of knowing you've saved a life. There's no feeling like it.

Disadvantages: People leave dogs at shelters for a reason. Sometimes the reasons are flimsy ("I'm moving," "I want a younger dog"), but sometimes the dog is a biter. Owners of biting dogs may give them up to the shelter because of aggression but don't give the shelter the real reason. And even if the dog was perfectly fine before he came to the shelter, he may not stay that way. In fact, most dogs who have spent any time in a shelter have at least some physical problems (which can range anywhere from skin problems to more serious genetic disorders) or psychological problems (ranging from barking to separation anxiety). Often the problems do not show up until the animal is brought into a home for a period of several weeks, at which point all hell breaks loose.

The X-Factor: Every shelter and rescue agency is different and operates by its own rules. Many rescues operate by a foster home model that will catch many problems before the dog is adopted. The ease (and cost) of adopting a dog from a rescue organization varies a great deal. Not all rescues and shelters are equally responsible.

Newspaper Ad

The newspaper is the first place many people—especially first-time dog owners—look when deciding to get a dog. Many of these ads are

> Getting a dog from a shelter or rescue is a humane and ethical choice.

prefaced by "Free to a Good Home," although the people who place the ads seldom check to see if it's a good home or not.

Advantages: It is a good source to find dogs of all ages, breeds, and backgrounds. A lot of

backyard breeders and commercial breeders advertise here, as well as people who need to give away the family dog. It's a one-stop shop in which you may find the dog of your dreams.

Disadvantages: Many people use the newspaper as a way of unloading a dog with multiple problems, possibly including aggression. Their way of handling the problem is not to train their dog (or themselves). Be careful. You are dealing with complete strangers, most of whom do not even have a business to protect.

The X-Factor: You may find a wonderful dog or a real disaster in the paper—you're taking a big chance. However, sometimes it works out just fine!

Neighbor, Relative, or Friend

Many people get a dog from someone close to them. They often don't even plan to get a dog, but it happens anyway.

Advantages: In most cases, you know and trust the source.

Disadvantages: Most neighbors and friends (unless they are dog breeders) are not experts on the care and raising of dogs. They also tend to

put a lot of pressure on their loved ones to take an unwanted puppy off their hands—even if you are not ready for the commitment.

The X-Factor: If you are truly looking for a dog, don't care about his ancestry or show prospects, and you trust that your friends have taken steps to socialize the pup and get him good vet care, it's a good deal.

Strays

Some dogs really do follow kids home from school or are noticed wandering aimlessly on the road.

Advantages: Nothing is easier than adopting a stray dog. In fact, the dog usually picks you out first.

Disadvantages: The dog may have any number of diseases or behavior problems—and he may belong to someone else. There's nothing worse than finding a dog, spending hundreds of dollars on his care, and then having to return him to his probably negligent owners. Stray dogs can mean heartache.

Newspaper ads are a good place to find dogs of all ages, breeds, and backgrounds.

The X-Factor: Every case is different. Before giving your heart to a stray, make every effort to find his real owners—they may be wonderful people who have been searching for their dog for months. If all your efforts fail, consider yourself adopted.

WHAT TO ASK A BREEDER

If your heart is set on a puppy and you've contacted a breeder, it's time to ask (and answer) some questions. Come prepared to ask the following questions, and don't be shy!

- How long have you been involved with the breed?
- Do you participate in showing or performance events? (While not every reputable breeder is

into the dog show game, many are.)

- How many litters have you had, and when? (Too many litters over a short space will tip you off that you're dealing with a commercial breeder.)
- Are you a member of a local kennel or breed club? (Individuals, by the way, do not belong to the American Kennel Club [AKC]. It's a club of clubs. Only kennel clubs are members.)

The most important step when at the breeder is to check out the appearance and behavior of all the dogs on the premises. They should be bright-eyed, clean, friendly, well nourished, and happy. Their breath should smell sweet. A swollen belly may be a sign of roundworms.

The place itself should be clean, sweet smelling, and have an exercise area available. I like it best if the dogs are raised in the house, although this is not always possible, especially with some giant or northern breeds. Insist on interacting with the mother dog, and take note of her personality. The puppy you choose will probably inherit it. Shyness or aggression on the part of the mother or pups is a bad sign.

Pick up your puppy candidate and cradle him in your arms. He should feel heavier than he looks. A puppy who fights or struggles to get away may be more dominant than you want in a pet. Try looking in his ears and mouth, and see how he responds. Dogs who accept such gestures are more likely to become easygoing adults.

Most good breeders will have already done a temperament test on the puppy, which consists of elements such as social attraction, following, dominant or submissive tendencies, social dominance, elevation dominance, touch

Before giving your heart to a stray, make every effort to find his real owners.

sensitivity, sound sensitivity, sight sensitivity, persistence, retrieving, and activity level. The most famous of these tests, based on research by William Campbell, scores a puppy's temperament from 1 to 6. Puppies who score mostly 1's are considered dominant, easily provoked, and perhaps aggressive. These dogs are not for most people. Puppies who score mostly 2's are assured, dominant dogs who tend to make good working or show dogs. Puppies in the 3's category are friendly and extroverted dogs who work well in most active homes. Puppies who score 4's are more laid back and submissive; 5's are very shy and need a lot of confidence building. And puppies who score in the 6's are aloof, independent, and have little interest in human beings. Different breeds tend to cluster around different numbers. However, there is a caveat here. Several recent studies suggest that these tests are far from reliable. You'd probably do better with close questioning of the breeder and keen observation of your own.

The sire, or father dog, may or may not be on the premises. Some very reputable breeders send the mother dog to a special sire (who may live at a distance) for breeding. Having both parents on the premises is no guarantee of quality. All it means is that the breeder has two dogs of the opposite sex.

THINGS TO LOOK FOR

Whatever your source, some things remain the same about evaluating a breeder or rescue.

- You may consider it an invasion of privacy, but a good breeder or rescue will not just dump a dog in your arms and take a check. They'll ask you many questions about your home situation and may even want to speak with your veterinarian. Some do a home visit. Although these procedures can seem intrusive, a good breeder or rescue coordinator is looking out for the welfare of her dogs.
- A good breeder has a spotless (although perhaps hairy) kennel. In my opinion, it's best if the parents of your prospective puppy are housedogs, where they can be better socialized.
- A good breeder will offer you a contract that clearly outlines both of your responsibilities in regard to the puppy you are purchasing. Be sure to read it carefully and question anything you don't understand before signing it.
- A good breeder has a warm and chummy relationship with her dogs. It's very important that young dogs be introduced to the kind of life and circumstances they will be expected to live under by the time they are four months old.
- A good breeder will happily provide references from former buyers.
- A good breeder is knowledgeable about the positives and negatives of her breed (no breed is perfect). She may show her dogs in conformation, tracking, or obedience.
- A responsible breeder will have had her dogs tested for certain genetic problems and inherited diseases. She will show you proof that your puppy's parents have passed these tests.

The breeder should provide you with a health record of the puppies, including a complete veterinary examination. She should also include a registration with the American Kennel Club (AKC) or United Kennel Club (UKC).

2

SUPPLIES AND EQUIPMENT

Good dogkeepers want to keep their dogs comfortable and in style! To this end, be prepared to acquire the following items:

- crate (and crate divider panel for puppies)
- gate
- collar and leashes
- dishwasher-safe food and water bowls
- comfortable dog bed
- chew toys
- grooming equipment
- dog-friendly cleaning aids

CRATE

The crate is a combination bedroom and housetraining aid. Small puppies should be crated at night so that they don't go wandering around at 2 a.m. getting into all sorts of trouble. However, it's a bad idea to leave your dog in a crate for hours on end—what is he supposed to do in there? Dogs need physical and mental stimulation, just like children.

The size of the crate depends on the size of the dog. It should be large enough for your dog to stand and turn around in. See the chart on page 23 for a rough guide on properly sizing crate depth.

For growing puppies, you must either buy a very large crate now (which can make housetraining more troublesome) or you'll need to "trade up" as your dog grows. One possible solution is to buy a crate with movable barriers so that you can progressively enlarge it. And unless you don't mind dismantling and lugging a heavy crate all around the house, consider getting two crates. You have a wide choice of styles and materials to choose from.

Wire Mesh

Wire mesh crates provide more visibility and ventilation than plastic ones, which is important for heavy-coated and snub-nosed dogs in all weather. They are easy to clean, and the new ones fold up and transport with varying degrees of ease. Be sure to check out how to use it before you buy because some aren't as portable as they claim. Some dogs like their airiness, while others feel somewhat insecure in them. If you go the wire crate route, choose the kind with heavy gauge, epoxy-coated wire. Cost varies with size.

Solid Fiberglass or Heavy-Duty Plastic

These crates provide a cozy, more den-like atmosphere than the wire ones, so many shy dogs prefer them. They keep heat in, which can be

The crate is a combination bedroom and housetraining aid. (below and right)

A gate can serve as a safe barrier that will keep your dog out of trouble. (bottom)

good or bad depending on the season. They are very strong, and most have doors made of metal grating. Many airlines require this type of crate for air travel. Heavy-duty crates can, however, be heavy and difficult to take apart. Cost varies with size and quality.

Aluminum

These are the favorites of many professional handlers. They are sturdy, rust-free, and lightweight (the crates, not the handlers)—a big plus when you're dealing with more than one dog. Some of them even divide into compartments for this purpose, and some are airline approved. They have a pullout floor for easy cleaning, and many are collapsible. The big drawback to these crates is their price—they are expensive.

Collapsible Plastic

Some models come with carrying straps and storage bags. Most of these crates are designed for small dogs. They are a good option if you don't have a lot of room and need to store the crate when not in use. These are usually very affordable.

Fold-Up Portable Nylon Mesh

This is the perfect crate for traveling with your dog. Most hotels require that your dog be crated while in the room—especially if you're gone during the day. These crates are truly easy to move and are an excellent choice for the well-behaved traveler. Choose the kind with water-resistant plastic for easier cleaning. Cost varies with size.

SAFETY GATES

A special dog gate will serve as a safe barrier for your puppy or adult. It will keep him in or out of certain rooms—places where he can get into trouble with the Christmas tree, cat litter box, baby, or Thanksgiving dinner. All of these items fascinate dogs. Many dog owners used to use baby gates, but the ones specially made for dogs are safer because it was possible for some dogs to get their heads stuck in baby gates. Options include extra-wide gates, hands-free gates, pressure gates, automatically closing gates, and more. Your local pet supply store will be glad to help you. (Probably really glad—you'll come home with six of them because you can't decide which is best!)

DOG WEIGHT	CRATE DEPTH
under 25 lbs (11 kg)	24 in (61 cm)
25 to 40 lbs (11 to 18 kg)	30 in (76 cm)
40 to 70 lbs (18 to 32 kg)	36 in (91 cm)
70 to 90 lbs (32 to 41 kg)	42 in (107 cm)
90 to 110 lbs (41 to 50 kg)	48 in (122 cm)
over 110 lbs (110 cm)	54 in (137 cm)

BOWLS

Choose durable bowls made of stainless steel or ceramic, not plastic. Plastic bowls can develop minute cracks that allow bacteria to grow. They can also irritate your dog's chin, causing dermatitis. Stainless steel bowls are inexpensive and keep their looks for years. Ceramic bowls are the handsomest and costliest, but they can break. You can also get nontip and weighted bowls to make spills less likely. For long-eared dogs, there are so-called spaniel bowls designed to keep ears out of the water while the pooch is drinking. Automated bowls that stay full are also available. Please do not buy those raised bowls that at one time were sold as helping to prevent bloat; they do not. In fact, studies at Purdue University show that they have the opposite effect—greatly increasing a dog's chance of developing this fearful condition.

BED

Your dog should have a comfortable place of his own to sleep. Since puppies don't mind where they sleep, you might just want to fold up some old blankets for a temporary bed—your pup will probably chew and rip them up anyway. When he gets over his major chewing stage, you can buy him a sturdy bed of his own. Many beds are completely washable; others have washable covers.

SAFE CHEW TOYS

While dogs can enjoy a number of different toys, most prefer those that encourage their favorite activity—chewing. Dogs love to chew; it's how they experience their world, especially as puppies. Teething youngsters also need chew toys to help set their teeth. If you don't offer your dog safe toys, he'll find his own. And when dogs select their own toys, they generally choose new things, expensive things, irreplaceable things, and dangerous things. However, if you take control of the situation, you have a better chance of saving both your valuables and your dog's life. Choose toys that are durable, washable, and safe. Nowadays toys come in an astounding variety of types—they bleep, burble, gobble, and babble—all of which dogs love.

Give your puppy a comfortable bed in which to sleep.

However, some of these toys are powered by batteries, which if swallowed, can be deadly.

Here are some tips for safe toys.

- Go for variety. Dogs get bored, so rotate your pet's toys. Keep some on top of the fridge until you think he's ready for something new.
- Pick toys of an appropriate size. A Saint Bernard could get a tennis ball stuck in his throat, while the same item might be too big for a tiny Chihuahua. If the ball (or other toy) is small enough for your dog to put the whole thing in his mouth without any of it showing, it is too small for him to play with safely.
- Select toys that have no pull-off pieces like button eyes or the like. The same goes for fringes and strings.
- Give your dog nothing harder than his own tooth enamel, including sterilized bones or cow hooves. These are the number-one cause of broken teeth!
- Rawhide bones and strips are fine for dogs who don't try to engulf them.
- Edible chew bones are very safe.
- Most dogs enjoy pig ears.

- The old stuffed toy is a perennial favorite, but some dogs can chew them to pieces in minutes. If that's the case with your dog, go for a durable toy like a pull rope. Durable toys should also be washable.
- Always supervise! Dogs can get into trouble under the strangest of circumstances. Keep your eye on your dog when he has bones, rawhide, or stuffed toys.

COLLARS, HALTERS, AND LEASHES

Dogs don't wear clothing for vanity's sake, and they don't require their own walk-in closet, but a few items are essential to their well-being and happiness:

- collar (adjustable for puppies)
- head halter
- leash (nylon or leather)

Collars

Collars are essential for dogs. They hold ID tags, and they provide a convenient handle when you need to grab your dog quickly. They also come in such an array of charming colors and styles that

you will easily find one to fit your taste. Your collar choice tells the observer as much about you as it does about your dog.

Flat Collars

Most well-trained dogs do best on a simple flat collar with a buckle. These humane collars do not restrict the neck and come in a variety of materials, including leather, nylon, and cotton web. (You can also get simple cotton cloth, but web is stronger.) Nylon usually outlasts cotton, but it can be irritating to sensitive skin. Polypropylene collars, which are narrow and rolled, combine many of the good qualities of nylon and cotton because they are as sturdy as the former and as soft as the latter. However, dogs who tend to pull can injure their tracheas on a such a narrow collar. A good-quality leather collar is hard to beat, but cheaper varieties smell bad and wear through easily. Some leather collars are colored with a dye that bleeds into the dog's fur and should be avoided.

You can also select a buckle or an easy-snap fastener. Some very large dogs can pop a snap fastener with a concerted lunge, so your best bet may be a sturdy buckle collar.

Martingale Collars

Martingale collars (sometimes called "Greyhound" or "sighthound" collars) are "limited slip" devices especially useful for dogs with long, narrow heads who can easily back up and duck out of regular collars. The limited slip collar tightens up enough to prevent this but not enough to choke the dog the way a choke chain does.

Choke, Prong, and Shock Collars

I lump choke, prong, and electronic collars together because I think they are a bad idea for almost everyone. A case can be made that

Most well-trained dogs do best on a simple flat collar with a buckle.

each has a place if used correctly by a skilled trainer, but since very few people are skilled trainers, they are not a good idea for most of us. Even proponents of choke collars admit that most people do not use them correctly—most people don't even put them on correctly. Because of this, I suggest they not be used at all.

Choke collars and prong collars can damage a dog's trachea if not used properly, and it is possible to actually kill a dog with one. Another problem with these collars is that you can't leave them on dogs without supervision because the danger of catching them on something and choking to death is considerable. And while prong collar enthusiasts insist that the prongs do not really hurt a dog because the correction is distributed evenly around the neck, they are not being forthcoming. Of course prong collars hurt! That's the whole purpose of them. Try one on yourself if you don't believe me.

Shock collars are the worst of all. They work by giving the dog an electric shock, either on a signal from the owner or by some automatic "nudge," such as when the dog barks. Even though they can be tuned down to give only a mild electric buzz, their potential for abuse is so high that I cannot recommend them. Again, they are simply making a statement that the owner is too inept to train his or her dog properly. Dogs are so smart that they know they can do as they like once the collar is off, so they misbehave wildly once it is removed.

The Scruffy Guider Collar

This combination collar is a compromise between a traditional collar and a head halter. (See section below.) It consists of a double nylon collar with one loop that sits high on the dog's neck while the other rests lower. This collar gives more turning control than a conventional collar without evoking the resistance that a head halter usually brings out in a dog (until he gets used to it).

Specialty Collars

There are a variety of specialty collars available in addition to the more traditional ones. Some glow in the dark so that you can see your dog when he's outdoors at night. Others reflect light so that when a flashlight is directed at them, they shine brightly. Check with your local pet supply store for more information on specialty collars.

Head Halters

Head halters may look like muzzles, but they are not. The dog can eat, drink, and even bite. A head halter fastens behind the dog's ears with a strap that goes around his muzzle. The collar works by putting gentle pressure on the back of the dog's neck and nose if the pulls forward—something like a horse halter. This pressure elicits a calming neurochemical response as well. Conventional

Collar Dangers

Collars can prove dangerous to unsupervised dogs, and many experts recommend that a dog not wear a collar when alone. I can't agree with this assessment. If your collarless dog escapes, the chances of a safe return are greatly reduced because the single easiest way to identify him quickly has been removed. While microchipping and tattooing help, it helps even more to have a collar with visible ID. Also, as I mentioned earlier, a collar serves as a convenient "handle" by which to grab a dog during an emergency.

To reduce the risk of your dog being injured by a collar, don't use choke collars (the most likely sort to catch on something). Instead, consider a breakaway collar, at least to hold the tags in place. Make sure the collar is well fitted. Collars that are too tight or too loose pose the greatest risk. Puppies need adjustable collars.

halters can also slip off if not carefully adjusted or if the dog is an escape artist. Owners find that dogs almost always object to the head halter, at least at first. It takes even experienced users several minutes to accustom the dog to the new sensation, and new users (both dogs and humans) can find it a frustrating experience.

GROOMING EQUIPMENT

Buy the best-quality grooming equipment you can afford. In fact, shop the catalogs and buy implements designed for groomers—you won't regret the investment. Things you'll need include:

- doggy shampoo
- dental supplies (toothbrush and dog-friendly toothpaste)
- nail clippers, styptic powder, and nail file
- brushes
- combs

You'll learn more about how to use these tools in Chapter 6.

collars and harnesses, on the other hand, trigger a dog's oppositional reflex, which makes him pull against the pressure. The head halter was invented in the early 1980s by Dr. R.K. Anderson, a professor of veterinary medicine at the University of Minnesota, and Ruth Foster, an obedience trainer from Minneapolis.

Even the head halter is not completely innocuous, however. Pulling the halter tends to pull the dog's head sideways, so a sudden pull could cause damage to the cervical (neck) area of the spine. Head

FLEA AND TICK CONTROL PRODUCTS

Nowadays there's no excuse for flea and tick problems.

Talk to your vet about the best flea and tick control products to use on your dog.

Largely gone are the days of messy dips and dangerous pesticides. Talk to your veterinarian for the best and safest product to use on your dog. If you haven't owned a dog in a while, you'll be astounded at the choice of effective, easy-to-use products available. See Chapter 10 for more on how to control pests.

CLEANUP AIDS

Keep these handy cleaners around for those inevitable cleaning catastrophes:

- pooper scooper (many exciting styles to choose from)
- enzyme stain cleaner and odor remover
- pet-friendly cleaning aids (check the label)

Many common household cleaners can be dangerous to pets. Remember that your dog spends a lot of time with his sensitive nose close to the floor, where he's absorbing those toxic chemicals. Vinegar, baking soda, and natural cleansers are effective, safe products to use.

3

KEEPING HOUSE WITH YOUR DOG

Having both a house and a dog often results in conflicting priorities. If loose hair, muddy paws, chewed furniture, and nose-smudged windows drive you wild, maybe you shouldn't have a dog. Dogs make messes. There's no way around that. To successfully manage housekeeping and dogkeeping, you must be able to tolerate a certain amount of chaos in your life and clean constantly.

Some people try to compromise by setting dog limits. They reserve a particular area where the dog is simply not allowed. The people have their area, and the dog has his. The dog area is bright, roomy, filled with dog toys, and constantly visited by everyone in the family. Yeah, right. Unfortunately, this solution doesn't work very well. What usually happens is that humans gradually relax their guard, and soon the dog has taken over the entire house. This is ideal anyway. If the dog is not to be part of the family, why have one? Sometimes the solution doesn't work out for a different reason. The dog remains in his area and the people remain in theirs. The kids never come to visit, and the dog becomes a lonely outcast, nose forever pressed against the sliding door that separates him from his beloved family.

If you have a dog, please make him part of your family. It's easy—you just need to be prepared. The first thing to do is make up a pet mess kit that includes clean, dry towels, enzyme cleaners, paper towels, and so on. Store the stuff in a bucket, and place it in a handy closet. That way, it will be ready when you need it. Second, cover as much of the house as possible with smooth, wipeable surfaces. Things that aren't wipeable should be washable. Small cotton rugs and furniture throws can help save expensive carpets and valuable antique sofas.

BUT I'M ALLERGIC!

If you suddenly find yourself allergic to your dog, it's not necessary to give him up. A little careful management will usually solve the problem. This is one case where it's important that you seal off a special room—not for the dog but for you. The best choice is usually the bedroom. Install a HEPA (high-efficiency particulate air) filter in every room of the house, use an air purifier, and vacuum like crazy. Well, not you—get someone else to do it because vacuuming stirs up pet dander. Go

shopping while your spouse does the work. Get rid of dust catchers, and trade in that hideous shag carpet for tile. Get someone to wash the dog once a week and have him groomed regularly. You can also apply certain topical products that reduce pet dander, or consider desensitizing yourself with allergy shots (these take three to six months to work), or less dramatically, use over-the-counter antihistamines or nasal sprays.

PROTECTING YOURSELF IF YOU ARE IMMUNO-COMPROMISED

While the advantages of owning a pet are well known, there are some downsides, especially for people who suffer from a weak immune system. Having an immune disorder does not mean you can't have a pet, but it does mean you have to be careful.

If you plan to acquire a pet, choose an older, sedate one. Older pets are less likely to come down with puppy diseases, less likely to nip or scratch, and are simply easier to handle. Besides, it's a kind act to give an older dog a home.

Be extra clean. Wash your hands thoroughly after handling your dog. Keep his living area clean as well. Keep your dog extra clean, too, and keep him on a flea/tick preventive. If you have to

clean up after him, wear rubber gloves as well (and still wash your hands). Make sure your dog gets regular veterinary care. If he gets sick, be prompt in getting him professional help. To avoid being inadvertently scratched, keep his nails short and blunt. Do not feed your dog raw meat; a commercial, high-quality food is safest for you. Keep your dog confined so that he does not run after wild game (and consequently get infested with all sorts of grisly things).

FINDING APPROPRIATE FLOORING

A true dog lover goes into agonies over the right flooring, searching for that perfect combination of looks, comfort, durability, and—not least—proof against urine. To my mind, this eliminates carpeting right away. Sure, it's comfortable and good for traction, but it will hold every odor ever deposited on it. Not to *your* nose, perhaps, but certainly to your dog's.

If you are set on a carpet, buy one in a medium, dirt-covering hue. The best carpets for dog-owning homes are ones made of synthetic fibers, with built-in stain repellent. Natural fibers soak up everything deposited on them, including smelly dog urine and vomit. Choose a textured or multilevel loop, which is easiest to clean and less likely to harbor fleas. Pick one with various shades of the same hue to hide dirt, hair, and stains. Select one that blends in with your dog's fur so it won't show so much during shedding season. And don't spend a lot of money on it, either.

It's much easier to keep house with a hard, impermeable floor like vinyl, composites, hardwood, or ceramic tile. Vinyl flooring is easy to clean, but canine toenails can ruin cheaper grades. Laminates and composites are a better choice; they are made up of several layers, and they're tough and easy to clean. Some even come with lifetime warranties. Hardwood floors are always

Dog Hair Removal

A great way to clean up dog hair is to use a fabric softener mist before vacuuming. Put a little bit of fabric softener in a spray bottle and fill the rest of it with water. Shake well, then mist lightly over any area you want to vacuum. You will get a lot more dog hair out of fabric and rugs! The softener makes the hair release from the fibers, and if you mist the room the right way, you will even have hair falling off the ceiling and the walls. It's a beautiful sight.

popular, especially if the wood is truly hard (like red oak). These floors resist scratching and are easy to maintain, particularly if they're sealed with a protective finish. My personal favorite, however, is ceramic tile. The stuff lasts forever and is very easy to clean.

GETTING STAINS OUT OF THE CARPET

Ah, so you didn't pay attention and the puppy has peed all over the carpet. Don't despair. The important thing is getting to the stain as fast as possible. Grab some old bath towels and throw them down on the carpet. Use paper towels if you must. Then stand on them until you've soaked up as much moisture as possible. Use an enzyme-based commercial cleaner to get the smell out. If you don't have any around (you should, so get some for the future), mix up a teaspoon of dishwashing liquid in a glass of water. Never use an ammonia-based cleaner because ammonia smells like urine to a dog, and he'll be tempted to continue to use that spot. Start blotting from the outside of the stain towards the center, then rinse and blot with a towel. Next mix an ounce (30 ml)

A tile floor is easy to keep clean.

of white vinegar with a glass of water and repeat the previous steps. Put down a dry towel and stand on it some more until the water is taken up. If you have a Shop-Vac, use that to soak up the extra moisture; it works great.

All this works very well, of course, but I'll bet the stain has gone through the carpet and into the padding. That's not coming out. In fact, it will continue to stink, especially during the dog days of summer. (That's why they're called the dog days—just kidding.) At any rate, if the padding gets soaked with urine, you'll have to replace it. (You can just cut out the piece and put something else down, or you can give up and pull up the whole carpet.) Once a dog has started to urinate on a spot, he'll continue to do so, and your carpet will still be host to other stains like mud and vomit that will inevitably happen. Tile. I'll say it again: Tile.

THOSE PESKY BLOODSTAINS

If you have a dog, bloodstains are a part of life. It seems that dogs are always nipping each other, cutting their feet, or suffering from a hotspot. Wiping them off the floor is no problem, but things get trickier when you have to remove them from upholstery. The best way to get rid of

blood is to coagulate it first, using some sudsy ammonia and water (one part ammonia to three parts water). It should smell strongly of ammonia. Spray or pour it on the stain; most of the time it will come right off. Of course, you should test the fabric first to make sure it's colorfast. You may need to use several applications if the stain is an old one.

If the blood is on your clothes, keep the stain wet by soaking it in cold tap water. (Take off the clothes first.) If the stain is old, you'll have to soak it in cool saltwater for several hours. Then soak it in water with ammonia added. An enzyme solution might also work.

DISSOLVING DROOL

Owners of drooling dogs have special problems with flung saliva sticking to the walls. To get rid of the stuff, there are products on the market that dissolve drool on cabinet doors and both flat and glossy paints. The slobber goes—the paint doesn't. (It's not a bad idea to paint your walls the color of the dog slobber. Call the shade Forest Mist or something and you'll set a new trend.) If you're too lazy to clean it off, just wait until it dries and flakes off on its own.

THE BEST MAT

The best mats are not the ones on your dog, but the ones on the floor, so use them. They're portable, cleanable, and you can really scoop up dog dirt on them. Extra mats can go outside all doors, in front of the sink, under the dog dishes, in front of the toilet, wherever. Smart pet owners keep a towel handy and wash off their pets' paws before they come in on a muddy day. There are six-fingered gloves for sale, designed to fit on either hand, backward or forward, that you can use for paw wiping. And remember, the more you groom your dog, the easier your housecleaning will be.

VACUUMING

Your vacuum is your lifeline if you own a dog. Use it frequently. If you have had a problem with fleas or other little critters, you can sprinkle some flea powder on the floor and vacuum it into the bag first. That'll fix 'em. (Some people cut up a flea collar and vacuum it, too.)

Fiddling With Furniture

If you're springing for new furniture (the dog ate the old stuff), select upholstery that is smooth and tightly woven. Anything with an open weave is just begging to be ripped apart or scratched to death. In my own house, we don't have anything with upholstery. It's easier that way. If your dog is a chewer, smear the wooden parts of the furniture with a mentholated product every few days and give your dog something better to chew.

When battling dog hair on the furniture, use some of that clear wide packing tape to take it off. (Do not use directly on the dog, please.)

BEYOND THE HOUSE

Now what should we do about all those nasty urine stains all over your yard? You have several choices. The cheapest and most effective is probably to stand around watching your dog every second and then throw a gallon of water everywhere he urinates, but perhaps you don't have time for that. You'll need to go high-tech. Here are some products that may help.

Saving Your Lawn

Several natural food supplements help neutralize the pH of your dog's urine so that it won't burn or discolor the lawn. (Most dogs have urine that is slightly alkaline, which is what causes the stain.) The products usually include amino acids and vitamins, with yucca and quillaia tree extract to help reduce stool odor. Many of them can be given as a pill or used as spray on food. Grass Saver, Lawn Saver, and Green Grass are a few of the brands available at pet stores and online.

If your lawn is already wrecked (and whose isn't?), there are products that can help get rid of the spots. One is Dog Patch, a special mix of premium seed and granulated mulch made from recycled paper that neutralizes nitrogen from urine. Since grass seed must have continuous moisture in the early growth stages, the mulch helps hold the seed in place and keeps it moist to improve germination. This is a spot treatment, and one box

treats about 50 urine-puddle-sized spots. You can pick it up in a well-stocked gardening center.

Saving Your Dog: Fencing

A fenced backyard is a necessity for a happy dog, but owners must make sure that it is secure. Some dogs are good at digging under, pushing through, and climbing over obstacles. Even if you have a sedentary, unadventurous dog, a low or unsecured fence is no match for a fierce neighboring dog. I have a friend whose gentle, small Poodle was killed by a large vicious dog who broke through the fence.

Apparently, a few misguided people still believe that since it's "natural" for dogs to run free, they should be allowed to do so. Natural it may be, but legal and safe it is not. Dogs who are allowed to run free get lost, poisoned, hit by cars, shot by hunters, and hurt by bigger dogs. They also eat garbage, get into hornets' nests, roll in dead things and tree sap (often at the same time), pick up contagious diseases, and destroy your neighbor's garden. To keep your dog safe and your own life simple, keep your dog in a secure area.

A chain is not a replacement for a fence. Dogs kept on a chain feel vulnerable and scared. They don't get exercise. Furthermore, they are prime picking for dognappers and abusive children. They can also tangle themselves in a chain and suffer serious injury. A brief supervised period on a stake is acceptable, but your dog should not be left unattended.

I knew of a dog who was kept on a chain attached to a steel cable in his yard. The dog got plenty of exercise running back and forth. Everything seemed fine, except that one summer day a thunderstorm appeared literally out of the blue. Lightning struck the cable, passed through the

A fenced backyard is a necessity for a happy dog.

chain, and killed the dog. It's all right to have a cable run for your dog in special circumstances, but your pet should always be supervised while using it.

Preferable to a tether is a sturdy kennel and secure run large enough for a dog or two. For a small dog like a Beagle, the run should be at least 15 feet (4.6 m) long and 10 feet (3 m) wide, with a 6-foot (2-m)-high fence. For a larger dog, the run should be at least 20 feet (6 m) long. The run should be secure, with good drainage and plenty of shade. Trees are a beautiful way of supplying shade, but if you don't have any trees, you can use panels of fiberglass and other materials. It's best if you can divide the pen into two or more areas. That way you can add another dog, move your dog in order to clean one section, and so on.

I like a plain earth floor for a run, but clever diggers might be able to get out. Still, clean dirt gives your dog a comfortable natural footing and

A good fence will help keep your dog safe.

allows him to indulge his natural habit of digging. With a dirt floor, there is always an increased problem with pests and parasites, but keeping your dog on heartworm pills and flea/tick control can reduce or eliminate the problem.

Many people like an easy-to-keep concrete floor. This flooring is simple to clean, helps to keep toenails down to a reasonable length, and will prevent your dog from digging out. But it's cold in the winter, hot in the summer, and hard on feet. Other choices include pea gravel and brick.

Types of Fencing

A standard wood and wire fence provides the best protection for your dog, but other options are available, depending on your financial situation, your aesthetic sense, your local covenants, and the escape artistry of your particular dog. If your fence includes an outside gate, be sure to padlock it to keep out dognappers and thoughtless neighborhood kids who might think it funny to let your dog escape.

The so-called invisible or electronic fence is trendy nowadays, but it has several serious drawbacks. In the first place, dogs need to be correctly trained to heed the fence. This usually means a professional from the company will come and work with you and your dog. Only you, however, are responsible for obeying the instructions. Consider these issues before deciding on an electronic fence:

- Some dogs will brace themselves for a shock and run right through the barrier.
- Clever dogs will know that the power of the fence is connected to their collars, and once the collars are off, they can make a break for it.
- Electricity isn't always as reliable as you might expect. Power outages and natural disasters happen.
- The collars that go with invisible fencing rely on batteries. You need to check the batteries every few weeks.
- Electronic fences rely on pain to work.
- Electronic fences don't keep other dogs out. Neighborhood dogs can get in and bother your dog, who would then have no way to escape.
- Although the electronic shock collar may not keep your dog in the yard if there's a rabbit to chase on the other side of the street, it most certainly will keep him out after he has broken loose.

In short, the best way to think about housekeeping with a resident dog is this: He's not living with you—you're living with him. Somehow that puts it all into perspective.

4

HOUSEHOLD DANGERS

A critical part of good dogkeeping is keeping your dog safe. The contemporary world is full of dangers—cars, thieves, poisons, pesticides, disasters, and other dangers. In this chapter, we'll look at some common hazards of dog ownership and how both you and your dog can survive them.

ANTIFREEZE

Obviously, antifreeze is essential to the health of your car. It protects the engine from extremes of temperature and hinders corrosion and rust. But it can kill your dog, cat, and innocent wild animals that may lick the sweet-smelling, sweet-tasting stuff. It also runs off into streams, where it can poison fish. Ten thousand dogs are poisoned each year by ingesting antifreeze, and most of the incidents occur right around the owner's home. Antifreeze danger peaks in the spring and fall, when people tend to refurbish their car's cooling systems.

The lethal ingredient in most types of antifreeze is ethylene glycol. (This same chemical occurs in air-conditioning coolants, brake fluid, and some color-film processing solutions.) Comparatively harmless in itself, ethylene glycol converts to deadly oxalic acid when ingested. Two ounces (59 ml) of antifreeze is a lethal dose that causes kidney failure. The poison is absorbed quickly in the gastrointestinal system, going to the brain and spinal fluid, then the cardiovascular system, and finally, most dangerously, to the kidneys.

At first, the dog may act as though he's drunk. Other signs include vomiting, excitability, lethargy, and increased thirst. Eventually the dog may go into a coma and die.

If you have the slightest suspicion that your dog is a victim of antifreeze poisoning, call your vet and get him there immediately—no matter what time of day it is. Try to induce vomiting if you believe the ingestion was recent. If not treated within four to eight hours, it is usually fatal. Unfortunately, the first signs may not occur until days after the poisoning. Once at the vet's, the doctor will evaluate your dog with several tests, including a test specifically made to detect antifreeze that works if the ingestion was recent. Your vet may induce vomiting, administer activated charcoal, give fluids intravenously, use peritoneal dialysis, or pump the dog's stomach. She will give oxygen as necessary, as well as an antifreeze antidote, usually 4-methylpyrazole. Your dog will need to spend several days in the hospital.

What You Can Do to Protect Your Dog From Antifreeze

Supervise your pet, lock up the antifreeze, and keep him away from all spills. Obviously, you can't do this if you allow your dog to run all over the neighborhood, which is another reason to keep him at home where he belongs. When you do change your antifreeze, dispose of it properly and clean up any spills using plenty of water. To reduce the risk not only to your own pet but to all wildlife, consider switching to a less toxic antifreeze (like Sierra) that contains prolene glycol as its active ingredient and which provides the same level of protection for your car but is safer if ingested. These safer products don't metabolize into oxalate but may still cause nervous system damage or Heinz body anemia.

BREAD DOUGH

Rising bread dough may seem harmless, but it can be a killer if your dog gets hold of it. Even after being swallowed, the dough will continue to ferment and expand in the dog's stomach. This can lead to severe intestinal gas. In some cases, the dough will expand to such a size that it cannot exit the stomach. Watch your dough! If your dog swallows the stuff, call your vet.

CHOCOLATE

Most people know by now that chocolate is toxic to dogs. It contains theobromine—a substance similar to caffeine—which dogs have trouble metabolizing. However, the level of toxicity depends not only on the amount consumed and the size of the dog but also upon the kind of chocolate involved. The least dangerous is white chocolate, and the most dangerous are cocoa beans. Other types of chocolate (milk, dark) fall somewhere in between. Mild signs of toxicity include vomiting, excessive thirst and urination, and diarrhea. More serious effects are restlessness, hyperactivity, panting, twitching, or even seizures. It is possible for dogs to die from chocolate poisoning.

White chocolate is practically harmless. Mild toxicity occurs at 45 ounces (1.3 kg) of chocolate per pound (0.45 kg) of canine body weight. Thus, a 20-pound (9-kg) dog would need to eat 55 pounds (25 kg) of white chocolate to develop signs of nervous system damage. Your dog is actually in more danger from the fat included in white chocolate than from the miniscule amounts of theobromine in the stuff.

Milk chocolate is more dangerous. Mild toxicity occurs at 0.7 ounces (.01 kg) of milk chocolate per pound of body weight; more serious signs occur at 2 ounces (.06 kg) of chocolate per pound. A little less than 1 pound (.45 kg) of milk chocolate can cause serious neurological symptoms in a 20-pound (9-kg) dog.

Semi-sweet chocolate ratchets up the danger. Mild toxicity occurs at 1/3 of an ounce (.009 kg) of chocolate per pound (.45 kg) of body weight, and severe signs occur at 1 ounce (.03 kg) per pound (.45 kg) of body weight. Six ounces (.17 kg) of semi-sweet chocolate can cause neurological symptoms in a 20-pound (9-kg) dog.

Baking chocolate is so toxic that 0.1 ounce (.003 kg) of baking chocolate per pound (.45 kg) of body weight produces mild toxicity, and severe symptoms occur at 0.3 ounce (.009 kg) per pound (.45 kg). If a 20-pound (9-kg) dog eats two squares of baking chocolate, he can be in serious trouble.

If your dog gets into chocolate, call your vet for instructions.

CLEANING PRODUCTS

Cleaning products—especially toilet bowl cleaners, caustics like drain cleaners, and pine oils—are dangerous to your pet. All bleach and

detergents are unsafe as well. Many of these products destroy tissue on contact, and pine oils can cause severe systemic disease. Keep all containers tightly closed and locked away from your dog. Luckily, most dogs do not find cleaning agents very attractive. If your dog is exposed to cleaning products, flush his skin or mouth with plain water to wash away the remaining chemicals, then call your vet.

DISASTERS AND EMERGENCY EVACUATIONS

Be prepared. Hurricanes, tornados, floods, nuclear meltdowns, terrorist attacks, and other unexpected events may necessitate leaving home. Before disaster strikes, get an emergency kit together. The kit should include several days' worth of food and water, medications, leashes

Natural disasters, like tornadoes, may necessitate leaving home, so it's important to be prepared.

or harnesses, carriers, beddings, toys, and a pet first-aid kit. (See Chapter 11 for things to include in the first-aid kit.) Make copies of your dog's important documents (vaccination records, license, microchip/tattoo number, medications list, and contact information for your vet) and put them in there as well. Before anything happens, make a list of local animal control facilities, rescue organizations, and veterinarians so that you can start calling immediately. During the evacuation, keep your dog on a leash or in his carrier. He should always wear identification, not just so that others can identify him but so that you can as well. (It's amazing how much one Weimaraner can look like another one, especially if there's been some disaster and the dog is covered in dirt or has been grievously injured.) To make things worse, a physically or emotionally traumatized, depressed dog might not even recognize you!

FISH HOOKS

While fishing may be fun for dog owners, dogs can be inadvertently "hooked" as well. The usual cause is when the dog chomps down on the bait intended for the fish, though he might also step on it. If this happens to your dog, do not pull the line! Doing so will "set the hook" and probably make (expensive) surgery inevitable. If your dog ate the hook, tie the line to his collar to prevent him from swallowing any more of it—and call your vet. If he simply caught it in his skin, you may be able to cut off the barb end and pull it through. If that's not possible, you know the drill. Call your vet.

FLOOR WAX

I am too lazy to believe that some people actually still wax their floors, and if you want a good excuse not to, here's one. Some dogs are actually allergic to the ingredients in floor wax. Do yourselves both a favor and skip the waxing.

Keep grapes out of reach of your dog because they can cause kidney failure.

GRAPES AND RAISINS

Grapes can cause kidney failure in dogs, although so far only about ten grape-poisoned dogs have been officially reported to the ASPCA Animal Poison Control Center. The amount of grapes or raisins ingested has been between 9 ounces (.26 kg) and 2 pounds (.91 kg); however, even a single snack-sized raisin package can induce symptoms. Keep them away from your pet. If he does swallow a large number of grapes, take him to the vet—he may need blood tests and intravenous fluids. Your vet may want to induce vomiting, pump the stomach, or give activated charcoal.

GRASS SEEDS

Grass seems like an innocuous substance, but it can be brutal to your dog. Many grasses and weeds have seeds that can stick to your dog's fur. That's bad enough, but there are other smaller, dart-like seeds (foxtail, feathergrasses,

speargrass, buzzard grasses) that can actually invade the body's tissues. Common entry points are beneath the eyelids, in the ear canal, the nose, between the toes, or through the gums. The first sign is a swelling around the entry point, and if the seed is not removed right away, it may burrow farther in. Once these seeds become embedded, surgery may be required—they can migrate several inches (cm) beneath the skin. Results can be devastating—depending upon where the seed enters, a dog may lose vision or develop an abscess (including a life-threatening abscess of the lung). Working field dogs are the most common victims. If your dog is very active outside, try to keep him away from grasses that are obviously seeding. Clipping longhaired pets may also be an option. The fewer seeds that stick to the coat, the less opportunity there will be for seeds to invade. You may also consider an outdoor "vest" for your dog that will afford him some protection.

After an outing, check your dog very thoroughly, especially his armpits, groin, ears, and between his toes. Watch his eyes carefully; seeds have a filthy habit of getting in under the third eyelid. If you cannot remove a seed yourself, call your vet.

HOLIDAY HORRORS

Holidays are made for people, not pets. Dogs don't understand holidays or know why they occur. They usually don't like to dress up in costumes or watch fireworks. They do like stuffing themselves with dropped bits of chocolate, turkey bones, and candy, however, which can be harmful. In short, holidays can be stressful or dangerous to the family dog.

Christmas

The biggest danger to dogs during the Christmas season is the Christmas tree. To ensure a safe holiday, place the tree near an outlet so that you don't have long, tempting electrical cords for the dog to chew. Any visible cords should be taped down. It is best to anchor the tree to the ceiling or wall with hooks and clear fishing line so that the dog doesn't grab it and start pulling it around the house. For some reason, dogs who ignore trees outdoors (except to pee on them) can't get enough of them if they are inside. Some decorations, including angel hair, flocking, and artificial snow, are all somewhat toxic as well. Remember to attach ornaments with a bit of ribbon or string rather than hooks. And place tempting chewable ornaments (or glass ones) well out of reach. No ornament is completely safe if it can be swallowed. Tinsel and garlands can be especially dangerous; dogs tend to swallow them, and they then get stuck in the intestine, which means dangerous and expensive surgery. Use bows instead, and spray everything on the

Holidays can be stressful or dangerous to the family dog.

tree with a safe dog-be-gone product. Always sweep up pine needles because they can irritate the mouth and perforate a dog's intestines.

Tree preservatives, which are sugar based and therefore tempting to dogs, are also dangerous. There's no telling what else may be lurking in the tree water (bacteria, fertilizers, insecticides, and flame retardants are all possibilities). Cover the tree stand with a skirt and supervise your dog.

As for presents, dogs will sniff out and eat even food that's in a wrapped box. The only food present safe to leave under the tree is fruitcake. Even dogs won't eat that.

Halloween

According to the American Pet Products Manufacturers Association (APPMA), Halloween is getting increasingly popular among pet owners. We dress them up, photograph them, and even take them out trick or treating. We have turned Halloween into Howl-o-ween, and now there is even dog-safe candy on the market, which is a good thing. Breath mints and cheese and beef "candy" will appeal to your dog and won't harm him (as chocolate or macadamia nuts will). This is the time to remind the kids that sharing candy with the family pet is not a good idea. Even the foil or cellophane candy comes wrapped in can play havoc with your dog's digestive system. And while costumes are fun, please don't dress up your dog if the costume will obstruct his movements, restrict his vision, or stress him out. Never leave a costumed dog unattended. He will almost certainly attempt to escape the costume (possibly by eating it) and could injure himself in the process.

Halloween is also a time to remember to decorate safely. Real candles are an obvious fire hazard, especially if they are placed inside real pumpkins (which naturally attract the attention of the always hungry, curious dog). Candles can also

be overturned by over-enthusiastic tail wags.

Halloween revelers can often get crazy, so please do not

To keep your dog safe, make sure that he's not underfoot for Halloween celebrations.

leave your dog outside alone, even behind a fence. You never know what kind of mischief will pop into a child's head. Don't tempt fate—your dog belongs close to you on such a busy night.

Another kind of Halloween danger comes from the children knocking at the door. This is the perfect chance for your dog to charge out into the night (and Halloween is a very bad night to be a lost dog). Even normally phlegmatic dogs get excited by the constant ringing of the doorbell and arrival of weirdly dressed little visitors, so it might be a good idea to secure your dog in another room during Halloween havoc time. If you have an exceptionally nervous dog, either turn off your porch light so that the kids don't show up at

other items saturated with cooking meat. When permitted, they gorge themselves on high-fat table scraps, which places them at risk for pancreatitis. Watch your dog carefully, and lock away the trash.

LAWNS AND GARDENS

Most chemicals you spray, pour, and shake on your lawn are harmless to you. That's mostly because you don't roll around in the stuff. Small dogs have a much more intimate relationship with your yard than you do (which may be the reason nasal cancers are so common in dogs). They roll in the grass and then lick themselves. They eat the grass and rub their faces in it. Do not allow your dog to play in an area that has been recently treated with chemicals. Most lawn treatments contain crabgrass treatments, broadleaf weed control, insect controls, and fungicide treatments. All have the potential to hurt both humans and animals.

Choose organic products for your own lawn, and fight to get your community to switch to healthier alternatives in public places. If you suspect your dog has been wading through such an area, wash his feet afterward. Avoid walking your dog through recently treated areas.

To help keep your lawn weed-free organically, mow frequently but at the highest setting. That keeps the grass strong but kills the weeds. Don't use a bag to catch the cuttings; instead, let them fall back into the lawn to refurbish the soil, and water deeply and infrequently. Grass likes that. If you want, check with your local nursery about organic fertilizers.

If you garden, stay away from cocoa mulch. Dogs love the smell and taste, but then they ingest it, and it is akin to eating a huge amount of chocolate. The most commons signs of cocoa mulch poisoning are vomiting and muscle tremors. If you suspect your dog has eaten this stuff, call your vet.

all, or provide your dog a quiet place well away from the action. Some dogs are comforted by the presence of radio or TV in their private area. Just don't show any scary movies.

> **Keep your dog indoors or on a leash if there are going to be fireworks in your neighborhood.**

Independence Day
Every year, thousands of dogs suffer through scary, ear-splitting fireworks. More than a few jump the fence at the first boom and are never heard from again. Keep your dog indoors or on a leash if there are going to be fireworks in your neighborhood.

Thanksgiving
While this is a great feast day for human beings, dogs can get very sick on this holiday. They search out and swallow foil, plastic wrap, strings, and

Insecticides also present a risk to your dog. Most of these poisons are either organophosphates or carbamates. Both of these disrupt normal nervous system function. Use organic insecticides like pyrethrin, which come in the chrysanthemum plant.

LEAD

Lead poisoning can occur when dogs ingest fishing weights, lead shot, or batteries. Some paint, caulking, and motor oils also contain lead. Lead affects both the gastrointestinal and neurological systems, so look for a combination of signs that include vomiting, constipation, diarrhea, depression, circling, incoordination, muscle tremors, and even blindness. Obviously, you'll need to call your vet.

LOST DOG!

Nobody ever plans to lose a dog, but it happens every day. The American Society for the Prevention of Cruelty to Animals (ASPCA) estimates that of the millions of missing pets across the country, fewer than 2 percent of cats and 20 percent of dogs are ever returned to their owners. Sometimes dogs just run off because they are curious about what lies beyond the backyard. If this happens to you and your dog, you need to maximize his chances of a safe return. The first step in keeping your dog safe is to keep your dog from running away.

However, the truth is that even the best-kept dog occasionally goes missing. The worst can happen. Someone leaves a gate or door open, a tree blows over and knocks down a portion of the fence, the dog charges out of the car, or someone steals him. If this happens to your dog, you want him back—and soon.

The easiest step is also the most important. Put an ID tag on that collar, and make sure the information stays current. This is your best chance of getting your dog back. Do it today (or the instant you get your dog). The ID tag should have your name, telephone number (including area code), and address. Also get a license and put that number on the collar—it's probably the law in your area anyway. You can even get your phone number embroidered right on the collar, write it on yourself using a plain old laundry marker, or buy a riveted ID plate if you want to go more high end. But do something. And check the tag frequently to make sure the writing is still present and legible.

You may want to go high tech and get a microchip implanted. The chips began to be widely used in the early 1990s and have helped return more than 173,000 pets to their owners nationwide. This simple procedure can be done by a veterinarian or trained technician. The identifying chip goes between the dog's shoulder blades; it's not very expensive and it doesn't hurt. Equally important, the chip stays in even when the collar comes off. There are several brands available, and your veterinarian can recommend a good brand commonly used in your area. As with collar IDs, it is important to keep the information current—the microchip company knows only what you tell them.

Another option is an identification tattoo for your dog. You can have his belly tattooed with your phone number as long as you're sure you're not moving anywhere. However, even if your dog

Microchips

For years, animal control advocates have been pushing to make microchipping your pet mandatory. Not only do chips help reunite owners and their dogs, they also save precious taxpayer money by reducing shelter costs.

background. Another should be a close-up shot of his head. If the worst happens, you'll need those photos on flyers.

If you have a website, include a series of photos showing different views; your lost dog posters can direct people to your website. You may also need to prove the dog is yours, so keep any ownership records you have—registration or adoption paperwork, vet bills, and so on. None of these will prove to the authorities that the dog on the paperwork is the dog you are looking for, but it helps. Your best bet may be a clear picture of you and the dog together in happier times.

It also helps to keep all your dog's medical records easily available. This includes his vaccination records (especially rabies certificate), as well as a list of medications your dog may need, allergies he may have, or special diet he requires.

If you do lose your dog, make up flyers immediately (don't wait even an hour) and place them on every legal place within a square mile (1.6 sq. km) of your home. (Roaming dogs travel about a mile [1.6 km] a day.) The flyer should contain the dog's photo, description, and your phone number in big letters.

Go door to door in your neighborhood and talk to everyone. (Don't go by yourself unless you really know your neighbors.) Give everyone a flyer. Put ads in the newspaper. Offer a reward, as much as you can afford. That will start kids looking, and they are creative lookers! Check with every vet, animal shelter, and rescue organization in the area. Keep checking. Go there personally and repeatedly and eyeball the captive dogs yourself. (Although they are well meaning, some shelter volunteers can't tell a Poodle from a Pomeranian.)

Look everywhere, including roads and roadsides. If your pet has been hit, he may be alive on the

is microchipped or tattooed, you must still put a collar and tags on him. If you are worried about

A lost, roaming dog travels about 1 mile (1.6 km) per day.

the collar getting caught on a bush or tree, use a breakaway collar with a Velcro clasp to carry information. The chances of the dog being choked or caught on a regular collar are much less that his being lost forever if you have no visible tags on him. When you travel, keep temporary "travel tags" on your dog as well.

No matter what kind of ID you choose, always keep recent photos (both color and black and white) of your dog in your files. The pictures should be clear and focused. One should show your dog from the side against a plain side of the road. If he has been killed, you need to know—it will bring closure. You may also contact your local department of transportation to see if any dead animals were picked up. If your dog has been injured, he may hole up in places you would not ordinarily think of, so bring a good flashlight and use it. Consider your dog's personality. Friendly dogs will most likely seek out human beings; shy dogs or loners are more likely to be found in less populated places.

An old hunting trick is to put out some old, unwashed clothes that carry your scent. This is especially useful if your dog has disappeared from a place that he is not familiar with. Check the area frequently—you may find him lying on your clothes.

Be careful. Some unsavory people use "found pets" as a ploy to extract money from you. If someone claims to have your dog, meet her in a public place and take a friend with you.

One of the latest services to help owners find their lost animals is the Pet Protector System, a 24-hour, nationwide emergency system similar to Medic Alert for human beings. Here, all vital information about your pet is immediately available to the company's emergency operators, including: numbers where you can be reached, alternate contacts, and your dog's medical history. If your pet gets lost or needs emergency assistance, whoever finds him can call a toll-free number located on a special tag on the collar. A trained operator is there to coordinate the assistance. You can even leave your credit card on file in case there is a veterinary emergency.

In any case, if you are lucky enough to find your precious lost dog, please let the people who helped you know, and pick up the flyers you distributed.

OVER-THE-COUNTER MEDICATIONS

Never use human over-the-counter medications for your dog unless directed to do so by your vet. Not only are many human medications toxic to dogs, but even nontoxic medications can be harmful, because pound-for-pound (kg for kg) doses for animals are often not the same as those for people. Your dog may also have a medical condition that contraindicates the medicine you are considering. Always check with your dog's veterinarian first. Bad medications for dogs include aspirin, ibuprofen, phenylbutazone, and naproxen—all pain relievers that decrease mucus production in the stomach and increase the likelihood of ulcer formation. Acetaminophen is especially dangerous to both cats and dogs, since they don't make enough of the enzyme needed to process it. Signs of acetaminophen poisoning include salivation, vomiting, weakness, and abdominal pain. If your dog eats any of your pills, get him to a vet.

PESTICIDES

Pesticides have largely brought benefits for both humans and dogs. Take the use of pesticides in controlling mosquitoes, for example. Everyone knows that mosquitoes carry heartworms, West Nile virus, and a host of other diseases. Dog owners, however, need to be aware of the dangers that can occur to pets while we are trying to control the mosquitoes! Mosquito control products can be deadly, so follow these guidelines to keep your dog safer.

- Know when pesticides are going to be sprayed in your community and keep your dog inside during those times. Old, sick, and asthmatic animals are at the highest risk.
- Bring in any pet dishes and pet toys as well—you don't want them covered with the stuff.
- While spraying is occurring, close your windows and turn off window air-conditioning units.

If you think your pet is reacting to a pesticide, call your veterinarian right away.

POISONOUS PLANTS

Here are some plants likely to grow in your garden or live in your home. All are more or less toxic; however, adult dogs are not likely to chomp down on them. Puppies are more at risk.

- Amaryllis (*Amaryllis* spp.)
- American bittersweet (*Celastrus scandens*)
- Azalea (*Rhododendron*)
- Autumn crocus (*Colchicum autumnale*)
- Burning bush (*Euronymous alatus*)
- Christmas cactus (*Schlumbergera or Zygocactus*)
- Christmas rose (*Helleborus niger*)
- Chrysanthemum (*Chrysanthemum morifolium*)
- Daffodil (*Narcissus pseudonarcissus*)
- Dumb cane (*Dieffenbachia*)
- European bittersweet (*Solanum dulcamara*)
- Foxglove (*Digitalis*)
- Holly (*Ilex* sp.)
- Japanese yew (*Taxus cuspidus*)
- Jerusalem cherry (*Solanum pseudocapsicuni*)
- Mistletoe (*Phoradendron* spp.)
- Poinsettia (*Euphorbia*)
- Thanksgiving cactus (*Zygocactus truncactus*)

Philodendrons, rhododendrons, and the nightshade plants are also deadly. If your dog ingests any of the plants, call your vet immediately.

PORTABLE HEATERS AND FIREPLACES

Portable heaters are convenient and fireplaces are romantic, but both are dangerous to dogs. Screen all fireplaces and place portable heaters out of their reach. Dogs can suffer burns and shock from these devices; this is an emergency that requires veterinary treatment.

RODENTICIDES

These poisons are meant for rats and mice, but unfortunately, they work perfectly well on dogs, too. These poisons can be very attractive to dogs.

Amaryllis (below), daffodils (right), and pointsettias (bottom) are just some of the plants that can be poisonous to dogs.

Many are anti-coagulants and will cause the victim to bleed to death internally. Veterinary care is essential in case of ingestion.

SNAKEBITES

Poisonous snakes in the US include copperheads, cottonmouths (water moccasins), rattlesnakes, and coral snakes. Most snakes are nonpoisonous, but even a "harmless" bite can become nasty and infected. Nonpoisonous snakes in the US have small teeth, not big fangs. One exception, the poisonous coral snake, does not have fangs. The good news is that even poisonous snakes don't always use their poison, especially if they are just trying to frighten a predator. Fanged snakes tend to have hemotoxic poison, which destroys the blood. Coral snakes produce neurotoxic venom, which attacks the nerves.

Poisonous snakes in the US include rattlesnakes.

To keep your dog safe, keep him on a leash in snake country, and don't let him stick his nose down interesting holes—they may turn out to be more interesting than either of you would like. Stay on open paths, and keep your eye on the ground. If your dog is bitten, try to identify the offending snake by carefully noting his size and coloring. And look for rattles—those are a dead giveaway. Check the dog for fang marks. (The snake may have bitten more than once—they're quick.) If the bite is on a leg, wrap a constricting bandage (you can rip off a piece of your shirt), not too tightly, around the wound. Keep the dog as quiet as possible, and head for the nearest animal hospital. Do not put a tourniquet on the leg, and for heaven's sake, don't try to suck out the venom.

SPIDER BITES

Dogs are forever sticking their noses into spider hideouts. Nearly all spiders are venomous to some degree, but most don't have strong enough fangs to penetrate human or animal skin. In North America, two kinds of spiders are dangerous to people and pets: the five species of black widow spider, which are found all over the country, and the brown recluse or fiddleback spider, which is found mostly in the southern states. Either of these

spiders can deliver a painful bite that can be fatal. If your dog appears with any suspicious lesions, contact your veterinarian.

SUN

While all life needs the sun to keep going, there can be too much of a good thing. The ultraviolet light from the sun can cause reddening of the skin, hair loss, skin thickening, rough patches, blackheads, secondary infections, blisters, scabs, lesions, aggravation of autoimmune disease, and skin cancer. Yes, like people, dogs can get skin cancer, and the primary cause is catching too many rays. Certain breeds, such as Rottweilers and Cocker Spaniels, are more susceptible than others to cancer caused by the sun, as are dogs with thin or white hair. The following breeds seem particularly photosensitive:

- American Staffordshire Terriers
- Australian Shepherds
- Beagles
- Boxers
- Bull Terriers
- Bulldogs
- Chinese Cresteds
- Cocker Spaniels
- Collies
- Dalmatians
- Great Danes
- Greyhounds
- Italian Greyhounds
- Rottweilers
- Shetland Sheepdogs
- Whippets

To keep your dog free from sunburn, keep him out of the sun, especially between the hours of 11 a.m. and 4 p.m. in the summer. If your dogs has to be outside, put on some protective clothing to block the sun. You can even use made-for-children sunscreen. Another great idea is to put a cap on your dog's head, if he will stand for it.

WALNUTS

Fresh walnuts are fine, but once they get moldy, throw them out. They can contain toxins that cause tremors and seizures.

WINTER WOES (IT'S COLD OUT THERE)

Cold and wind chill affect pets as well as people, and wet weather is especially dangerous, even when it's not freezing. Here's how wind chill can actually make your dog feel.

At 35°F (1.7°C)

- with 10 mph (16 kph) winds, feels like: 22°F (-5.6°C)
- with 20 mph (32 kph) winds, feels like: 11°F (-11.7°C)
- with 30 mph (48 kph) winds, feels like: 5°F (-15°C)

At 25°F (-3.9°C)

- with 10 mph (16 kph) winds, feels like: 16°F (-8.9°C)
- with 20 mph (32 kph) winds, feels like: 4°F (-15.6°C)
- with 30 mph (48 kph) winds, feels like: -2°F (-18.9°C)

Cold Weather and Calories

Cold weather requires extra calories! Even if your dog is at his proper weight, you may need to up his intake during the coldest weather. Of course, if your dog is lying around the house more, feeding him more won't be necessary.

At 20°F (-6.7°C)

- with 10 mph (16 kph) winds,
  feels like: 3°F (-16.1°C)
- with 20 mph (32 kph) winds,
  feels like: -10°F (-23.3°C)
- with 30 mph (48 kph) winds,
  feels like: -17°F (-27.2°C)

Even short exposure can be deadly. Elderly, very young, sick, and underweight animals suffer most. The most vulnerable parts of your dog include the feet, nose, and ears. And the wetter it is, the worse it is. It is very dangerous if an animal does not have room to move around and get his blood circulating; dogs who have previously suffered from a cold-related injury like frostbite are most vulnerable. (This all applies to human beings as well.) To find out how to care for a dog with hypothermia, see the section on first aid in Chapter 11. The best cure, however, is prevention!

In addition to the damage cold can do, de-icers are paw irritants. They contain lime rock salt or calcium chloride salt that can be poisonous if licked off. Wash and dry your dog's feet, including between the toes, as soon as he comes in from the outside. Or you may decide to outfit your dog with doggy boots. If he won't tolerate boots, try slathering his feet with petroleum jelly to protect them.

ZINC POISONING

While zinc is a trace mineral necessary for life (it is a component of more than 200 enzymes and a cofactor in the synthesis of DNA, RNA, and protein), in large doses it can cause a serious kind of poisoning by destroying red blood cells. How can your dog get poisoned by zinc? By swallowing pennies—a practice rather common to curious

Poisoning

In case of poisoning, you can also call the ASPCA Animal Poison Control Center. Their hotline is open 24 hours a day, seven days a week, at 888-426-4435, for a fee of $45 per case. You will speak to a veterinarian who is an expert in poisoning cases. You'll also be asked to provide your name, address, phone number, and credit card information.

Be prepared with the following information:

- the name of the poison your animal was exposed to
- the amount and how long ago it was ingested
- the species, breed, age, sex, and weight of your pet
- the symptoms the animal is displaying.

puppies. In 1983, the US government started minting pennies made of zinc coated with copper rather than pure copper. Other zinc-containing household items include nuts and bolts and creams containing zinc oxide (sunscreen and diaper rash cream). Signs of zinc poisoning include vomiting, diarrhea, red urine, and yellow mucous membranes. Get your dog to the vet immediately; she may be able to see the object on an X-ray and remove it. Researchers are still working on a substance that will "bind" the zinc to render it harmless as it passes through the body.

5

FEEDING AND NUTRITION

Nutrition is a cornerstone of good health. It affects the way your dog looks, feels, and behaves. When dogs were wolves, they managed to find proper (although sometimes inadequate) nutrition on their own. Nowadays, they totally depend on you. Your nutritional choices for your dog largely determine how healthy and happy he will be. This is not a responsibility to take lightly.

COMMERCIAL FOODS

The majority of dog owners feed their pet a commercial food. In fact, the pet food industry pulls in billions of dollars every year worldwide, so you know somebody's eating this stuff.

Dry Versus Wet

Despite the money pouring from our pockets to theirs, we still, after all these years, have only two basic choices in dog food: canned or dry (although there are some more rarely used alternatives). Both can be either high or low quality. Let's compare two high-quality versions of canned and dry food. If you ask your dog, he'll choose canned food—which, not incidentally, tends to contain higher-quality protein (animal based) than most dry foods. Dry foods, also known as kibble, tend to be higher in fiber (good for diabetic dogs) but also contain a lot of carbohydrates—some as much as 40 percent. No dog needs that much, and there may be a link between such foods and diabetes.

Mold contamination is another worry for owners who feed kibble. In 1999, there was a major recall of mold-contaminated kibble, but more than 20 dogs died anyway. There has also been a strong link noted between the feeding of an all-kibble diet and the development of bloat, a deadly disease affecting many large dogs.

Canned foods seldom contain preservatives—the canning process ensures that they are not needed. However, canned food is more expensive than dry, and you're paying for a lot of water (though this may be just the ticket for dogs with kidney trouble). Dry food is more convenient, less prone to spoilage after it has been opened, and cheaper. If you have several dogs, dry food may be your best option.

Deciphering the Label

Reading dog food labels is almost an art. The package contains several labels, each of which provides different information.

- The principal display panel tells you the brand name of the food (e.g., Purina) and the name of the product (lamb). It names the intended recipient of the food (dog) and how much food is in the package.
- The information panel gives you the guaranteed analysis, which gives the minimum amount of crude protein and crude fat and the maximum of crude fiber, moisture, and ash. It also contains the nutritional adequacy statement, which usually tells you that the food is complete and balanced for dogs of a certain age or condition, such as pregnancy. The information panel also lists the ingredients in decreasing order of weight.
- A third label provides feeding instructions that tell you how much food to feed a dog per day according to his weight.

Unfortunately, few manufacturers actually list the calories contained in the food in a way a normal person can understand, like calories per cup. At

the very minimum, choose a food that carries the AAFCO (Association of American Feed Control Officials) label, preferably one that has been tested by feeding trials rather than nutrient profiles. (This appears on the nutritional adequacy statement.) This tells you that the dog food has actually been fed to dogs for six months before being put on the market and that they survived on it. Because the processing of pet foods destroys many nutrients, most manufacturers add extra vitamins, minerals, and other nutrients. But even this can be problematic—the AAFCO sets only minimum profiles for nutrients, and some studies have shown that manufacturers have actually over-supplemented with some minerals.

There are strange, esoteric rules associated with dog food labeling. For example: the 95 percent rule. If the label reads "Farkleberry's Beef Dog Food," then 95 percent of the named ingredients must be beef. If it reads "Farkleberry's Beef and Sawdust," then the combined beef and sawdust must account for 95 percent, with more beef than sawdust because beef is named first.

Then there's the dinner rule. If the label reads "Farkleberry's Milk Dinner," then between 25 and 94 percent of the food must be milk. (Other dinner-like terms include "entrée," "platter," and "formula"). Let's slide down to the with rule. Here, if a product reads "Dog Chow WITH Cheese Sticks," then at least 3 percent of the food must be cheese sticks. The last one is the flavor rule. Here the food doesn't actually need to have any of the named ingredient. "Farkleberry's Dog Food with Smoked Rhinoceros Flavor" need not have

> ## Food Labels
> While dog food labels tell you what additions or supplements may be included, they don't tell you how much—to find out, you will need to call the company at the phone number listed on the package.

any rhino in it at all. It just has to taste as though it does. (There are canine testers assigned to this task, by the way, but not Beagles or Labradors—they'll eat anything.)

It is impossible to provide an evaluation of every dog food and flavor on the market. Nor is there one best dog food for every dog. However, a few guidelines can steer you away from the worst foods and toward the best ones.

- Chose a food with the AAFCO guarantee.
- Avoid dog foods that contain by-products. Meat by-products are the part of the animal not deemed fit for human consumption, and while a few by-products are healthy and tasty to dogs, many more are not. Since the label doesn't tell you exactly what the by-products are, you're better off not getting foods that contain them. Grain and cereal by-products are the part of the plant left over after the milling process; they are technically called "fragments" but appear in many guises on the label. Any carbohydrates in food should be from whole grains. Many dogs are allergic to soy; stay away from it.
- Generic or grocery store brands are generally much lower in quality than named brands.
- Good food should not contain sweeteners, artificial flavors, colors, or artificial preservatives. The best dog foods are preserved naturally with vitamin E (tocopherols) or vitamin C. At one time, dog food manufacturers used ethoxyquin, a rubber hardener and pesticide, to preserve food. Few manufacturers use it anymore.
- Choose a food with the specific name of a meat (beef, chicken, turkey) as the first ingredient, and avoid foods that just say "meat"

or "poultry." Unfortunately, just because a product has "beef" as the first ingredient doesn't mean that the product is mostly beef. Some companies engage in a practice known as "splitting." If they can possibly do so, they will divide the cereal products up into separate categories, like "rice" and then "brown rice." Added together, there may be more rice than beef. But because the manufacturers are allowed to list them separately, beef can be listed as the first ingredient.

Another complication is that although the label declares the amount of protein in a food, it doesn't say where the protein comes from. Some kinds of protein are much more usable than others. Plant proteins are much lower in quality than animal-derived protein, but it's not possible to tell where the protein comes from by reading the label. Bone has a lot of protein as well, but it's not very digestible.

Improperly stored food can become loaded with molds, fungi, and other deadly toxins, so be sure to use the freshest foods available. If you use a commercial food, check the manufacturing date. Do not buy in bulk—it may save you some money, but it's dangerous for your dog. Smaller bags get used more quickly and stay fresh longer.

Varying the Diet

Don't get trapped into feeding your dog only one food, even a good one. Here's why:

- It's unnatural. Dogs are hunters and scavengers by nature and are designed to feed upon a wide variety of foodstuffs.
- It's boring. Dogs don't like the same food day in, day out any more than we would.
- It may be unhealthy. Studies have not been done long enough, on a large enough number of dogs, to guarantee that any single food is completely adequate by itself.

Feed your dog a variety of foods to keep him healthy and happy.

- It may cause allergies. Researchers believe that one of the best ways for your dog to avoid a food allergy is to consume a wide variety of foods from puppyhood on.
- It may be impossible. What if your dog becomes allergic to something in the food, or the company goes out of business, or they change the formula, or you are vacationing in Upper Horse Pasture Gully where Fifi's Special Braised Cuts of Hippopotamus With Sauce is not available?

Don't feed your dog kibble alone—add broth, soup, or some other moistener to help reduce chances of bloat.

Testing Freshness

Commercial food can provide adequate nutrition for your dog as long you purchase high-quality fresh food from a reputable retailer. To see if it's fresh, check the expiration date on the package. The best companies include a "Best if used before" date on the label. Buy an appropriately sized package; it's false economy to buy in bulk if most of it will turn rancid before it's fed. Always check bags for rips and cans for bulges. Good food should look good and smell good. If it smells bad, don't feed it to your dog. Throw it out or take it back to the point of purchase for a refund. Dog food should be stored in a dry, cool area in a sealed container that's designed for dog food storage. Don't use a plastic garbage can, even a clean one. These containers are often made of plastics that exude offensive or dangerous vapors, and temperature fluctuations can result in condensation that may lead to the development of mold or toxins.

To reduce the buildup of mold, clean out the old food before you put fresh food in the container; don't just pile it on top or mix it in. Leftover canned food should be resealed with a plastic lid and refrigerated for up to three days.

HOMEMADE DIETS

Somehow dog food companies have managed to imprint the American dog-owning public with the mantra "Never, ever give your dog table scraps." If what they mean by table scraps is rancid fat and a leftover chocolate bar (as if anyone ever has a leftover chocolate bar), I agree with them. But the message they are not so subtly selling is "Don't make your dog anything to eat at home. Go out and buy kibble instead. You can pour some water on it if your dog absolutely won't eat the stuff." Most people have noticed by now that dogs don't really like kibble. Some of them have to be bribed or starved to eat it. And despite manufacturers' claims, all but the best of it is made up of slaughterhouse and mill leftovers, which are a lot worse than anything left over at home, believe me.

It's quite possible to make a highly palatable, well-balanced meal for your dog at home. It's not rocket science. The best diets maintain nutritional balance by offering a rich variety of foodstuffs. Neither dogs nor humans need to have 100 percent of every nutrient at every meal. It's more important that we receive a diet high in variety and overall quality. If you wouldn't want to eat a boring, packaged, "complete" food for every meal, even if it were nutritionally perfect, don't do it to your dog. Eating should be a pleasure, not a task. Anyone who claims that dogs don't appreciate variety has a very dull dog.

A good homemade diet can be more expensive than a cheap commercial dog food. This is especially true if you purchase human-grade, organically grown meat for your dog. But nutritionists who specialize in homemade diets say that what you spend in the food market, you'll make up for in savings at the vet's office. And where would you rather put your money? You can also save if you buy in bulk and freeze what you don't need. Preparing a healthy meal is more time consuming than plunking down a bowl of kibble, but there are ways to save time, such as cooking your dog's food at the same time

Homemade Food

Homemade food does not mean stuff that has gone bad or is ready to be thrown out. Bad food goes in the garbage. Good food goes in your dog.

you cook your own meals or making up individual dinners and storing them in single serving, self-sealing plastic bags for future use.

The greatest advantage of a homemade diet is that the power belongs to you, the dog owner. You control the ingredients. This is a great advantage for people who have dogs with health problems or multiple dogs with widely varying needs. If you decide to go the homemade route, be sure the diet provides the following:

- An animal-source protein. Unless your dog is allergic to all animal protein, a vegetarian diet is not normal and is not advised.
- A fat source that includes EFAs (essential fatty acids).
- Adequate minerals, especially calcium, with calcium and phosphorus in correct balance—approximately 1.2:1.
- A supplement to provide vitamins and trace elements.
- A carbohydrate source if you like. It isn't necessary or natural but will probably not hurt your dog. If you add carbohydrates, they must be cooked; they're simply not digestible for dogs otherwise.

RAW FOOD DIETS

While the raw food diet has become rather trendy in recent years, I no longer recommend it. With salmonella becoming an increasing problem, I do not believe the meat supply is sufficiently safe. Dr. Link Welborn, President of the American Animal Hospital Association, writes, "While raw food diets are becoming increasingly popular among pet owners, there is a growing body of information showing that these diets pose a health risk not only for the pets that consume them but to their owners as well." Commercial food has its own dangers, but the answer is not raw food. If you want to develop a home diet plan for your dog, cook the meat. Palatability studies have shown that dogs actually prefer cooked meat anyway, just as we do.

VEGETARIAN DOGS?

Although dogs are classified anatomically as carnivores (based on tooth structure rather than eating habits), they are really omnivores and thrive on a wide variety of foods. However, dogs usually do best on a meat-based diet. (There are few cases on record of dogs being allergic to all kinds of meat and who have been "forced" to adapt to a vegetarian lifestyle.) If you insist, it is possible to feed your dog on a vegetarian diet, especially if you include eggs and dairy—otherwise it's difficult to get the high-quality protein dogs need. Some companies do manufacture balanced vegetarian diets for dogs.

THERAPEUTIC DIETS

Diet can be used to fight disease, and a therapeutic diet is a prescription diet formulated to feed dogs with specific conditions. There are kidney diets, urinary tract diets, cardiac diets, and joint health diets. There are diets for diabetes, diets for good teeth, diets for old dogs, diets for allergies, and diets for gastrointestinal disease; they are not meant for normal, healthy dogs. Some, for example, are lower in protein than is advisable for a normal animal. The largest maker of therapeutic diets is Hill's Pet Nutrition; however, Eukanuba, Purina, and Waltham all produce them, too. Today, there are more than 50 special diets available, which come in both dry and canned formulations.

YOUR DOG AND MAD COW DISEASE

Dogs are not known to contract "mad cow" disease, although cats may (rarely) come down with a wasting syndrome that resembles it. While the use of brains and spinal tissue in cattle feed has been banned for cattle, sheep, and goats

since 1997, the US Food & Drug Administration's Center for Veterinary Medicine says it does not plan to expand its ban to include food for dogs, cats, pigs, and poultry, at least not right now. They believe these animals are not likely to get mad cow disease. No one is likely to get mad cow disease. (It is quite rare but always fatal.) This is a blatant play to the cattle industry, which can't think of anything else to do with this tissue other than feed it to pets. Cattle brains and spinal cords—the dangerous parts of the animal that can spread the infection—are in fact a regular part of the rendering mix that goes into dog food, especially dry dog food. The normal process of cooking dog food at a high temperature that gets rid of bacteria does absolutely nothing to destroy the protein-like culprit (called a prion) that causes mad cow disease. Since the cause of mad cow isn't alive, it's impossible to kill.

Pigs and chickens get this same food as well. Since the regulations regarding this issue are constantly being updated, please check with the FDA before assuming any commercial dog food is free of possibly contaminated material. You can find out what's new at http://www.fda.gov/oc/opacom/hottopics/bse.html.

HOW OFTEN?

If possible, feed your dog two or more meals a day rather than feeding him just once or free feeding him, in which you set a bowl of dog food down and leave it there. Feeding a dog only once a day has been linked to bloat and other digestive problems, while free feeding may pose a storage problem or encourage the dog to eat too quickly. In addition, if you have more than one dog, you don't know who's getting most of the food. Monitoring intake is important.

SUPPLEMENTING YOUR DOG'S DIET

It is an axiom that if a healthy dog is getting good food, supplements are not needed. While this may be true, even canine nutritionists aren't completely sure what comprises "good" food. In addition, not all dogs are completely healthy. In any case, it may make sense to add a little something extra to your dog's diet.

Do not supplement minerals like calcium or phosphorus except at the direction of your veterinarian. Supplementing the carefully balanced minerals in your dog's food can lead to trouble. The same is true of certain fat-soluble vitamins like A and D; these vitamins are stored in the liver and can be toxic in large doses. (Vitamin E, another fat-soluble vitamin, does not appear to have toxic effects and may be supplemented if desired.)

However you may feel about supplements, they are not all equal—even when you consider the same supplement. Before you buy, check out the source. Use a product that was designed for animals, even if it uses human-grade ingredients, as it should. The best supplements carry the Good Manufacturing Practices Certificate (GMP) and the ConsumerLab (CL) seal of approval. In addition, if the product has been produced according to the United States Pharmacopoeia (USP) Guidelines, the label will say so. Look for organically grown herbs where possible.

The following supplements may be valuable for your dog's health.

The B complex vitamins: is a group of all the B's plus biotin; they are energy boosters that help to turn carbohydrates into energy. They are especially important for dogs on kibble, which contains a high percentage of carbohydrates. Since these are all water-soluble vitamins, they are completely safe to use.

Vitamin C: is a water-soluble vitamin, so it's hard to overdose on it. Dogs can make their own vitamin C, so theoretically they don't need any added to their diet. (Most animals, with the exception of primates and guinea pigs, manufacture their own.) However, dogs are less efficient at this than any other animal that makes its own vitamin C. (Perhaps they've been hanging around us too long.) Holistic veterinarians recommend it as a supplement, especially for sick or stressed animals. You can safely add 200 to 400 milligrams per day to your dog's diet.

Vitamin E: is a fat-soluble vitamin and a powerful antioxidant that is sometimes used to preserve foods. In combination with vitamin C, it boosts the immune system and may slow the growth of certain cancers. Holistic veterinarians also like to use it against epilepsy and allergies. The recommended supplemental dose is 450 to 500 IU per day per kilogram of food.

Acidophilus: is a powdered form of the

bacterium *lactobacillus*. It can be added to the diet if intestinal function has been impaired from sickness, stress, or antibiotics. In these cases, friendly bacteria that help digest food are often killed and replaced by bad bacteria that result in gas and diarrhea. The lactobacillus bacteria help prevent overgrowth of these bad, undesirable bacteria but allow the "friendly" bacteria to reproduce. Follow the directions on the container for dosage.

Alfalfa: these sprouts supply protein, vitamins, and minerals. They are also said to be helpful to the kidney and the immune system. They can be added to your dog's food bowl.

Amino acids: are the building blocks of protein; they can also function as antioxidants. One of the most important ones, which canine practitioners are just coming to appreciate, is taurine. (Its benefits for cats have long been known.) Supplements of 200-500 milligrams, depending

Certain supplements may be valuable for your dog's health.

minutes before eating. Dogs using chitin should be supplemented with fat-soluble vitamins if the supplement is used long-term. Side effects may include cramping and constipation. Chitin may interfere with calcium absorption or with the friendly bacteria in the intestine. It should be taken with plenty of water. Follow the directions on the container.

Coenzyme Q10: or ubiquinone, is a nontoxic, fat-soluble vitamin-like substance that occurs naturally in mammals, although amounts in the body decrease with age, especially in the heart, kidneys, and liver. Supplementing it in the diet, however, is excellent for dogs with heart disease, especially cardiomyopathy. It may also boost the immune system of older animals and it seems to increase the exercise tolerance of older animals. Depending on your dog's size, you can add 30 to 80 milligrams a day. Brewer's yeast may increase the absorption of Coenzyme Q10.

Echinacea: is the Latin name for the coneflower. It appears to inhibit viral and bacterial breakdown of cell walls (which those evildoers need to do before they can start replicating). It may also slow tumor growth. For maximum effectiveness, use echinacea for only short periods, and do not use it with animals suffering from immune disorders. Follow directions on the container for dosage.

Enzymes: Some dogs are apparently deficient in certain digestive enzymes. Sometimes this is a matter of breed vulnerability (Boston Terriers seem prone to this), or sometimes it's a matter of age (seniors have fewer digestive enzymes since the pancreas becomes less efficient), or sometimes it could be the result of a disease such as pancreatitis. Dogs low on digestive enzymes typically exhibit symptoms such as gas, diarrhea, constipation, or even nonseasonal shedding. Proponents of enzyme supplementation suggest they also help halitosis, curb vices like feces or

on the size of the dog, twice daily have proved to be helpful for large-breed dogs with heart conditions.

Bioflavonoids: are water-soluble plant-based compounds that help to prevent fat oxidation and inhibit the production of histamine, thus helping to control the symptoms of allergies. Follow the direction on the container for dosage.

Brewer's yeast: a single-cell fungus, contains B vitamins, zinc, and proteins. Yeast improves coat quality and may stimulate the immune system. It does not repel fleas, no matter what you may have heard.

Chitin: is a dietary supplement made from a starch-like substance found in the skeleton of certain shellfish. Currently it's being studied as a weight-loss supplement. Chitin is not digested when eaten but passes through the intestines unabsorbed. It works by binding with fat that is eaten in a meal and must be consumed 30 to 60 grass eating, and help allergies and colitis.

Garlic: has long been used as a flavor enhancer and blood purifier, and it may also aid circulation, digestion, and the nervous system. However, large quantities can cause an upset stomach and may also increase the risk of bleeding. (It contains natural coumarin, an anti-clotting agent.) While it has long been rumored to repel fleas, it doesn't. You can add very small amounts to food to improve flavor.

Green-lipped mussel: is an edible shellfish found off New Zealand. It is high in protein, glucosamine, chondroitin, glycosaminoglycans (CAGS, major components of cartilage and synovial fluid), and lipids. Originally tested as an anti-cancer drug, researchers found instead that it helps arthritis. (It turned out that the coastal New Zealanders who ate the mussels regularly had extremely low incidences of arthritis compared to the folks who lived in the interior.)

Milk thistle: is native to the Mediterranean; it grows wild throughout Europe. This is an excellent supplement for liver problems; it aids in the detoxification process. It is also an antioxidant more potent than vitamins C or E. Follow the directions on the container.

Seaweed, kelp, and algae: are sea vegetables with great sources of minerals, especially iodine, iron, and potassium. They also contain highly digestible protein, which most veggies lack. Of the lot, kelp (brown algae) is the most nutritious. You can buy it commercially to sprinkle on your dog's food, although many high-quality dog foods already contain it. Red algae is sometimes used to absorb toxins and carry them from the body. Green algae is an excellent source of iron and also contains

Supplements

The supplement industry is big—there's no doubt about it. In the past few years, the market has grown 3,000 percent.

cesium, which binds with carcinogens to remove them from the digestive tract.

Selenium: is a trace mineral that helps the thyroid function. When used in combination with vitamin E, it is also a powerful antioxidant. It can be supplanted in a dose of 0.221 milligrams/kg in the diet. Be careful with selenium supplementation, however. Toxicity may result from an amount that is not much greater than the dose recommended for supplementation.

Omega fatty acids: The Miracle Ingredient. Dietary ingredients with multiple positive effects are the omega-3 and omega-6 fatty acids, which

are kinds of polyunsaturated fat. (The differences between the two are based on their chemical structure.) Your dog needs both kinds of fatty acids in his diet. Dogs can produce some fatty acids themselves; the ones they cannot produce are called "essential" because they must be added in the diet. (What is essential for one species is not necessarily essential for another.)

Most dog foods used to be deficient in omega-3, which is hard to obtain from common sources; however, that situation is being corrected in better dog foods today. Manufacturers are now feeding cattle and poultry more omega-3 fatty acids, which in turn produces meat and eggs that are higher in these fatty acids. In the future, the use of these products in pet food may help to optimize the omega-6 to omega-3 ratio in the diet.

Supplemental fatty acids are used to help treat allergies, inflammation, and auto-immune conditions. They also improve a dull, brittle coat. Diets containing these fatty acids also help treat yeast infections of the ears and may help the heart and strengthen the eyes.

TREATS

Treats are a part of every well-loved dog's daily ritual. Your job is to make them healthy as well as fun. Some dedicated people enjoy making their own dog treats, others use healthy bits of carrots or apples, while still others pore over the delicacies offered at pet supply stores. If you're into buying treats for your dog and want top-notch stuff, look for treats with whole food ingredients rather than meat by-products or grain fractions. Some healthy treats have no preservatives; others are preserved with vitamins C and E. I'd also avoid food with sweeteners. Dogs have enough tooth problems without adding molasses. Avoid treats with artificial preservatives, artificial colors, and propylene glycol. As for packaging, treats that come in zip-lock-type bags are very practical.

Remember that treats contain calories, and if you use positive-reinforcement training, you'll probably end up using a lot of treats. You may have to cut back on meals to adjust. If you do use treats to train, use the tiniest size you can. (Besides, dogs have a hard time thinking and chewing at the same time.)

WATER

Water is the basis of good nutrition. Fresh water should be available at all times, even in the winter, when you might get tricked into thinking dogs don't need as much. Remember that winter homes are dryer, which increases a dog's water requirement. Wash the water bowl regularly; even dogs don't like drooly water.

OBESITY

Like most mammals, dogs are programmed to be hungry pretty much all the time. This stems from the old wild days when actually catching game was a chancy business. If one waited until one was actually hungry before hunting, it might still be several days before mealtime. Then one would be too weak to hunt. So a dog's rule is, eat as much as possible whenever possible because you never know when starvation days are coming. Unfortunately, this plan, while workable in the wild, has turned America's dogs into fatties—about 40 percent of the nation's dogs are overweight. Dogs who are exercise intolerant may also be obese.

Omega Fatty Acids
Omega fatty acids are delicate substances that can be destroyed by overcooking or improper storage.

If you aren't sure whether your dog is obese, check him out. You should be able to feel (but not see) his ribs. From the side, you should note a tucked-up abdomen; from the front, you should observe a definite waist. If your dog weighs 15 percent or more over his ideal weight, he is clinically obese. Fat dogs aren't always happy ones—statistics show that the fatter your dog is, the shorter his life span tends to be. Maintaining a healthy weight on your dog is more important than all the supplements on earth. Fat dogs have a higher risk of arthritis, diabetes, heart disease, liver disease, orthopedic problems, respiratory trouble, and even neurological disease. Cut back the calories, increase the exercise, and your dog is on the way to a healthier life.

While the actual number of calories a dog needs to maintain weight is variable from individual to individual (just like people), a few general rules apply. Large dogs, neutered dogs, and older dogs burn fewer calories pound for pound (kg for kg) than their smaller, unneutered, younger cousins. Also, dogs burn more calories in the winter.

Of course, lowering calorie intake does not mean a crash diet. In the first place, crash diets don't work. (The dog will tend to regain weight when the diet ends.) Second, it puts tremendous psychological stress on the dog; he has no idea why you are suddenly starving him. And third, crash diets are potentially dangerous since they often lack important nutrients in sufficient amounts.

Start out by consulting your veterinarian. Your dog's extra weight may stem from a medical problem such as hypothyroidism or Cushing's disease. Even psychological problems like stress can cause obesity. These and similar problems need to be ruled out before weight loss is attempted. At that point, the vet may suggest a

high-fiber diet, which tends to make the dog feel full or a special commercial lean or low-calorie formulation. Do not simply cut back on your dog's meal portions, since this can result in nutritional deficiency, especially with nonpremium, marginal brands of dog food.

Exercise can also help in weight loss, although it must usually be accompanied by diet change. (You have to run many extra miles (km) to lose even a pound.) Still, exercise is a good displacement behavior. While the dog is running or playing, he's probably not concerned about eating. Exercise also produces more serotonin in the brain, which reduces appetite, among its other benefits.

FASTING

It won't hurt—and will probably help—your dog to fast him for a day once a week or so. This mimics a dog's natural diet. Zoos put all their carnivores on a one day a week fast. Unlike a cow's, the canine digestive system isn't programmed to work constantly. Fasting also gives his body a chance to flush out toxins. Some experts even think occasional fasting is a good bonding tool. It's amazing how even the most independent Scottie becomes quite glue-like when he thinks you've forgotten to feed him.

FOOD ALLERGIES

While food allergies are comparatively rare in dogs, they can occur. (To diagnose a food allergy, the dog must be put on a food elimination diet.) Here are the main culprits, roughly in order of occurrence: horsemeat, beef, pork, lamb, eggs, dairy, corn, soy, and preservatives and dyes. Many dogs are allergic to rawhide chews, which may contain many of these.

FOOD DANGERS

Onions, chocolate, macadamia nuts, grapes, or raisins in large amounts are all toxic to dogs. High-fat meals are also implicated in pancreatitis. Please do not feed your dog treats containing these items.

Bones can also be dangerous to dogs. While bones are an excellent source of calcium and phosphorus, inappropriate bones can cause cracked or broken teeth, choking, and intestinal blockage and perforation. So-called sterilized bones are especially hard on teeth. One solution may be to grind the bones or at least choose bones that are more appropriate, such as beef knuckles, beef tails, and raw chicken necks. Avoid sharp or sawed bones, and always supervise your dog while he is enjoying his bone. Throw the bones away after a couple days of use and then get new ones.

6

GROOMING

Good grooming is essential to your dog's health and happiness as well as to the cleanliness of your home. Grooming is not just for Lhasa Apsos and Poodles! It serves a multitude of purposes:

- It keeps your dog sleek and handsome.
- It's a mini health check, letting you notice fleas, lumps, and other skin conditions.
- It's a training session.
- It's a moment of quality bonding time.

For grooming to be successful, the dog must accept it. This may mean working with your new dog or puppy to get him to stand (or lie) still while being attended to. That is half the battle.

Start grooming your new dog as soon as possible—the more often, the better. Your careful attentions to him not only assure him that he is important and cared for but also establish you as the pack leader as you gently move him about and ask him to lift his feet. Total acceptance may not come all at once, and older dogs may be more resistant to being handled. Some dogs never enjoy being handled. It's very important not to lose your temper during the process, especially with a puppy, or you will reinforce the impression that grooming is a terrifying experience. If your puppy is quite young (and small), in the beginning it doesn't hurt to hold him in your arms while you are doing the grooming. Later you can put him up on the grooming table. Sometimes it's easier for puppies to get used to one thing at a time.

GROOMING TOOLS

Good grooming doesn't just make your pet look better; it's important for his health as well. It is also a pleasant way to help you form a bond with your dog. The equipment you need to groom him properly depends first on his coat type. You need a brush that gets through hair down to the skin and not one bit more. You certainly don't want to give your dog a rash! Shorthaired dogs like Dalmatians, Dobermans, and Pointers need nothing more than a hound mitt or a soft bristle brush. A soft brush is a little gentler on your dog than the mitt. A thorough brushing will remove dead hair and skin and also distribute the oils evenly through the hair, making it shiny and soft.

More heavily coated dogs like Saint Bernards, Collies, and Siberian Huskies benefit from an initial going-over with a slicker brush (the kind with metal

Equipment

Get the best equipment you can afford. It makes a big difference. Clean your tools with a soft cloth after each use, making sure to remove all the hair. Scissors need to be oiled and professionally sharpened every once in a while.

pins set into a rubber backing); this helps pull out the loose hair of the undercoat. Then you can use the softer brush.

Breeds with long coats like Afghans and setters must be brushed every day to keep them looking their elegant best; otherwise, you will have a matted, miserable dog on your hands. Use a mat rake or shedding comb for regular maintenance, and follow with a slicker brush. If you've neglected grooming, however, and the mats go all the way to the skin, you may have to clip the dog. Longhaired dogs also benefit from oil conditioner, which keeps them looking great.

Some breeds, like Poodles and terriers, need to be clipped. If this is the case with your dog, start by getting him used to the clippers. Many good breeders run clippers (without blades) close to their puppy's faces when they are only three or four weeks old to get them used to the sound. Never yell or even raise your voice to a puppy while he is being groomed—doing so will only make him fear grooming.

To get your puppy used to clippers, you can keep a pair running while you dole out special treats. Soon he'll associate the presence and sound of the clippers with something delightful. If you have a small dog, you might want to consider using a human beard trimmer or even an electric razor around the face rather than big scary animal clippers. Also be careful around the ears, feet, and tail, and give the clippers time to cool down because they can overheat and cause clipper burn.

BRUSHING, COMBING, AND HAIR CARE

Hair is made up of protein called keratin. It grows from follicles, each of which has an oil gland to help keep the hair soft and smooth. Dogs have not one but three kinds of hair—a downy undercoat (most abundant in northern breeds), stiff guard hairs that protect the skin from cold water and wind, and of course, those endearing whiskers. For owners, dog hair poses two basic kinds of problems. First, when the hair is actually on the dog, it can get dirty, matted, and full of burrs. Second, when it is falling off the dog (shedding), it requires endless grooming to keep it from engulfing the house.

Every little hair on your dog's body has its own life cycle preprogrammed into it:

- anagen phase: hair is actively growing
- catagen phase: hair has stopped growing; it just stays there
- telegen phase: hair falls out to be replaced by new hair

Hair growth occurs in definite cycles, which are controlled by the length of day or photoperiod. When the days start to change, the dog starts to shed his undercoat. This can result in massive sheds twice a year. Presumably, equatorial dogs do not experience a seasonal shed, partly because most have no undercoat.

Hair grows to a specific length that is dictated by the dog's genetic heritage. When the hair reaches its predestined length, it will fall out. The main purpose of hair is to keep the animal warm, but it also serves to protect against injuries to the ears, feet, and even the eyes. In addition, the condition of the coat tells us a lot about the dog's health.

A clean, beautiful coat starts with a clean environment, followed by regular brushing and shampooing and plenty of exercise.

When brushing, go slowly. If grooming seems to make your dog nervous, start with the hindquarters. (Dogs react best when they can't exactly see what is going on.) Most important, however, is to develop a pattern of grooming. Dogs learn to expect what comes next, and that gives them confidence. Doing things in a regular way also makes sure you won't skip any important parts.

After brushing, you can comb your dog if he needs it. Don't neglect those tricky areas behind the ears and elbows where mats tend to collect. The hair between the pads of the feet can also collect debris and get tangled. If you do run across a mat, try separating the hairs as carefully as possible. You might spray it lightly first with a detangler, mink oil, or coat conditioner. Separate the mat as much as possible before attacking it with the comb. Comb a bit, and then try separating again.

To prevent mats from forming in the first place, brush right down to the skin, but be careful not to brush the skin itself, which can become irritated. If you irritate the skin, the dog will come to hate being groomed. If he hates grooming, he'll be more unpleasant to work with. This will make you avoid the task, and the coat will get steadily more matted. At that point, you will need to take him to the groomer, where most of the coat will be shaved off. Now you have a shaved dog who hates grooming, and the whole process will begin again. The lesson? Groom your dog regularly and gently.

STRIPPING

Wire coated dogs look their best when they are hand-stripped rather than clipped. All show dogs with this coat type are hand-stripped, but it's a little much for most pet owners. Stripping requires taking a densely packed slicker brush and running it rather firmly from the shoulder to the tail. Pluck out the dead hair that is raised up. After this treatment, bathe your dog in cool water to help close the pores. Finish off by brushing the coat in the direction of growth.

TRIMMING

You may decide to trim your dog's hair yourself. If you do, remember to use sharp, high-quality scissors. Use scissors designed for hair (not

Good grooming doesn't just make your pet look better; it's important for his health as well.

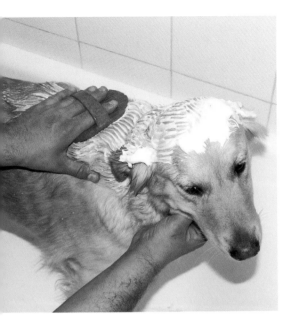

has dry skin—or any skin problem, for that matter. If your dog ends up with a bad case of frizzles, it's a sign that his hair is too dry. (Also be careful that the dryer isn't too hot.) You can apply a conditioner or hot-oil treatment.

You might also consider a finishing spray after bathing your dog, but use it sparingly. These sprays contain silicone and seal the hair shaft, making it lie flat. This makes coat care between baths a lot easier.

Before you start, get your equipment together.

- Start with a dog-safe shampoo, and include eye ointment to protect those tender orbs and cotton balls for the ears.
- If you do not want to get soaked yourself, get a waterproof apron.
- A spray attachment for the faucet is also a necessity.
- To keep a headstrong dog in place, try a grooming noose. You can get one with a suction cup that attaches to the wall of the bath.
- Put a non-skid rubber mat on the floor of the bathtub.
- Use a washcloth for the face, and be careful not to get water in the ears.

paper or cloth), and when they get dull, have them professionally sharpened. Clean them with a soft cloth after each use, taking care to clean out all the hair that's collected in the joint. You can wash them in lukewarm water if you are careful to dry them thoroughly—you may want to put a spot of alcohol on the joint to aid this process.

BATHING

A great deal of nonsense is talked about frequent bathing stripping your dog's skin of its natural oils and that sort of thing. Perhaps this would be true if you were washing your dog in detergent, but a gentle shampoo with conditioner is good for your dog's skin. Shampoo designed to enhance specific coat colors and types can be purchased from your pet supply store. Too-infrequent bathing creates many more problems than the other way around. I bathe each of my dogs once a week and would do it more frequently if I had the time. Not one of them

Skin and Hair Color

The color of the skin and hair is determined by the amount of melanin produced and the specific genetic codes for color, including codes for black or red dapple. Dog hair colors are black, brown, red, yellow, white, or agouti (a "wild" color in which each hair has bands of different colors). The brightness of the coat is determined by something called dilution factors in the genes. A dog's undercoat may be a different color than his guard hairs.

Now you're ready to start. With a small dog, a kitchen or utility sink is the perfect place—otherwise, it's the bathtub. When you run the water, test it carefully. Too hot or cold will make the experience doubly unpleasant for your dog. Bathing a dog is not very tricky, although it is important to wet him right down to the skin, which can be difficult with a heavy-coated dog. After your dog's coat is thoroughly wet, apply the shampoo according to the directions on the bottle. Rinse the suds out thoroughly, and follow with a cream rinse if desired. Afterwards, rinse the coat very carefully again. If the rinse or soap is left in the hair, it can irritate his skin. It will probably take twice as long to rinse the dog as it did to wash him. Towel-dry him thoroughly, using plenty of towels. You can buy chamois-type towels that really soak up the moisture. If the dog's coat is very thick, use a handheld dryer on a low or medium setting to dry him. (You can get him used to the sound of the dryer the same way you get a dog used to the sound of clippers—run it in front of him on a day you are not bathing him, and reward him with treats.) There are several dryers on the market that are designed just for dogs.

EAR CLEANING

Clean ears are essential to your dog's good health, but they must be cleaned correctly. Improper

cleaning, such as shoving cotton swabs in the dog's ear, can result in a ruptured eardrum. Unnecessary vigorous cleaning can cause your dog's ears to become red and inflamed. The frequency of cleaning depends on the general condition of your dog's ears

First collect your materials, which should include:

- Cotton balls, paper towels, or moistened gauze sponges.
- A commercial ear cleaner or a combination of vinegar and water (if you can handle the smell). Vinegar does a good job in killing many varieties

Begin ear cleaning by cleaning the earlobe and then proceed to the cartilage.

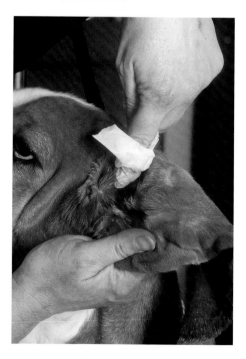

Most dogs do best if their nails are clipped every two or three weeks.

of fungus, but it's not an especially good cleaner. Avoid products with alcohol because they sting.

While most dogs tolerate having their ears cleaned, those who don't may need to be restrained by having their body wrapped in a thick towel (for small dogs) or getting a helper (for large dogs).

Begin by cleaning the earlobe, removing the dirt, wax, and debris. Don't use cotton swabs; you're better off with thin wipes. Then proceed to the cartilage. The ear canal is shaped like an L, so you will not be able to manually clean the entire ear. It's safest to just clean the parts you can see. Use a paper towel to dry the ears afterwards—you do not want the dog to go running around shaking his head, causing trauma to the inside of the ears. Repeat the procedure on the opposite ear. Then give your dog a nice treat to reward him for his "pawfect" behavior.

Certain breeds, such as Poodles, have hair growing down into the ear canals. While some people pluck this out, I don't advise it. It is true that hairy ear canals are more likely to become infected than clean ears, but there's a downside to plucking the hair. First of all, it hurts. Second, it can lead to infection. Third, it takes up too much time. You can prevent infection by simply cleaning instead—so leave the hair in there.

NAIL CARE

Maintaining your dog's paws and nails is essential to his good health. Long nails are a danger to the dog, the furniture, and your leg when he paws you. Some people who show dogs overreact and clip their dogs' nails too short, thus depriving them of traction. Use common sense. The nail should not click on the floor, but it should be usable. Overlong nails not only make for ugly feet, they splay the toes, impede your dog's movement, and cause pain and limping. I personally know a dog who broke his toe because his nails had not been cut short enough. But because many people fear nail clipping, they avoid it. Consequently, the dog becomes increasingly reluctant to have anyone touch his feet. Most dogs do best if their nails are clipped every two or three weeks, although some lucky city dogs manage to wear their nails on the pavement naturally. Vigorous regular exercise will also help keep your dog's nails in good trim, but always check his feet afterwards for cuts.

Handle your dog's feet frequently, even when you're not planning to clip his nails. Examine the nails frequently for toe or nail infections. (There's even a kind of cancer that can occur there.) That way, he won't make an immediate association between having his feet touched and getting his nails clipped.

If your breeder has done her job, your puppy will already be used to nail clipping by the time you bring him home. Chances are, however, that the animal has either never had his nails clipped or else has had a negative experience. In that case, extreme patience is your best ally.

Pick a time when your dog is most relaxed and comfortable. After exercise is often a good time. Gently pick up his foot, and praise him as he relaxes it in your hand.

You can use either pliers-type clippers or guillotine-type clippers, whichever you prefer. In either case, make sure they are sharp. Many people also like to use an electric nail grinder. And oddly, dogs seem to prefer them as well, once they get used to the noise. (Be careful not to use them for too long a period, however, since they can heat up.)

Begin cutting the nails, but do not cut the nail all the way down. Dogs have a blood vessel in the nail, the quick, which will bleed and cause pain if cut. The quick is easy to see in a light-colored nail—it shows up as a dark line in the nail. Strong, heavy, dark nails are the worst to clip, since you can't

Grooming your dog will help him bond with you.

see the quick. Clip the nails at the same angle as the natural curve of the nail, not straight across. Use adequately sized clippers for hard nails, and if your dog has extra-long hair around the feet, scissors and clippers will help keep it in check. If the nails have grown too long, don't expect to cut them back all at once. The quick grows along with the nail, and you don't want to injure the dog. Just in case, keep some styptic powder or gel on hand to stop any bleeding.

TEETH AND GUMS

One of the simple ways to check the health of your dog's mouth (and possibly the rest of him) is just to smell his breath. Bacteria associated

The Skunked Dog

There's no mistaking it—the odor of skunk. It's bad enough to catch a whiff of the stuff on a mild summer evening, driving along with the windows rolled down, but when it's sprayed on your own dog, it's truly a horrendous challenge.

Skunk spray is an oily yellow discharge secreted from the skunk's anal scent glands. The bad smell comes from stuff called mercaptan, which has sulphur in it. Skunk spray is really a sort of urinary by-product, and skunks have control over when to release it—usually when they are defending themselves. If your dog smells like skunk, believe me, he has done something to deserve it. Skunks are pretty good with their aim (usually going for the face), and they are accurate up to 10 feet (3 m) but have a total range of about 16 feet (5 m). Dogs might not mind the smell itself (who knows?), but the spray also causes a temporary burning in the eyes and nausea. It's also nauseating for the owner who has to smell the dog, too.

Okay, your dog has been skunked! Now what? Most commercial products have one or more strategies to eliminate the odor. Some try to neutralize the smell by combining a couple of smells to create a third, more pleasant smell. Some try to bond the odor by changing the chemical structure of the actual odor particles, which usually has only a temporary effect. Others work by absorbing the odor; the active ingredient in the product actually swallows up the smell.

Some viable home remedies include bathing the dog using a mixture of 1/4 cup hydrogen peroxide, 1 cup baking soda, and 1 teaspoon of nice-smelling liquid soap. Wash your dog and then rinse him. Douche powder works, too! Just scrub it in and rinse it off. Keeping your dog in at night from now on is an easy "remedy" as well.

with periodontal disease can cause bad breath (halitosis). Other causes may include eating foul food, diabetes, uremia, respiratory diseases, and gastrointestinal problems. If a simple tooth brushing doesn't clear it up, check with your vet. Antibiotics, dental surgery, or treatment for another underlying cause may be necessary.

To brush your dog's teeth, you'll need:
- Dog toothbrush or cloth
- Canine (not human) toothpaste

Never use human toothpaste on a dog; it's not designed to be swallowed, and swallow it he will. (However, you can use a human toothbrush.) Put the canine toothpaste on the cloth or your finger and allow the dog to sniff it. This may encourage him to permit you to slide the cloth into his mouth and start brushing. Personally, I use a washcloth rather than a brush because it works just as well.

While brushing is the best way to keep your dog's teeth in good order, it also may help him to have chew toys and tartar-removing food. You can also rinse your dog's mouth with an oral rinse, or you can use dental wipes every day. You can find these in a pet supply store, but your best bet is simply to brush your dog's teeth—with or without toothpaste. And do it often! Bacteria are attracted to the tooth surface within hours of cleaning. Within days, the plaque becomes mineralized, producing calculus, which in turn can develop into periodontitis (bone loss).

ANAL SACS

Beneath your dog's tail, at the four and eight o'clock positions, are the anal sacs. These sacs are filled with a smelly fluid that is normally released onto the feces during defecation. It can also be released spontaneously when the dog is nervous or startled. While the sacs don't appear to be useful to the dog, they can certainly cause a fair amount of trouble for owners and dogs alike. One or both sacs can become impacted, infected, or abscessed, and each of these conditions can lead to even more serious problems.

Small dogs seem to be more likely to have problems with their anal sacs than larger breeds. No one is sure why this is, but it may be related to the fact that small dogs are more likely to be fed a canned, low-fiber diet than big dogs. This makes the dog's stools softer and less able to exert sufficient rectal pressure to express the sacs during normal defecation.

Typically, a dog with anal sac problems scoots his behind along the ground, which is also a sign of worms, vaginal or uterine infection, perianal adenoma, or other tumors. Sometimes scooting takes care of the problem. If it doesn't, the anal glands may need to be expressed. Although this is a smelly operation, you can learn to do it easily at home. First find the anal sacs, which will feel like two peas. Don a pair of latex gloves and grab a tissue. Stand a little to one side. Press the sacs gently together and upward until the fluid inside is released. It is neither necessary nor desirable to express the dog's anal sacs as a matter of regular grooming procedure. No point in fixing something unless it's broken.

If your dog has chronic anal sac trouble, your veterinarian may recommend having them surgically removed—a fairly safe operation. Since your dog doesn't need the sacs in the first place, this is probably a good idea.

CHOOSING A PET GROOMER

There's nothing embarrassing about getting your dog professionally groomed. Some breeds, such as terriers and Poodles, practically demand it. If your veterinarian has a grooming service, you may want to go there, or you may ask friends for recommendations. Some groomers offer pickup and delivery services, which is a real boon for busy people.

It's a good idea to actually visit the shop before you take your dog there. The facility should look and smell clean. (Tables should be wiped down with sanitizer between each dog.) It should not be so packed with dogs that you can't hear yourself think—this is extremely stressful for everyone, including your dog. Good groomers are friendly and polite. Look for a groomer who has lots of experience or who is a graduate of a certified

condition—or be prepared to (literally) pay the consequences. Detangling and clipping take up time, and time is money. Don't forget to inquire about the cost, which varies widely from area to area. Cost also depends on the size of your dog and the complexity of the job. Poodles will cost more than Pointers. My groomer charges "combat pay" if he needs to muzzle a recalcitrant dog.

To learn more about dog groomers and grooming, go to the International Society of Canine Cosmetologists (ISCC) at www.petstylist.com, or the National Dog Groomers Association of America Inc. (NDGAA) at www.nationaldoggroomers.com.

A professional groomer should treat each pet with consideration.

grooming school. Groomers should treat each pet with consideration. A little observation will tell you how much they really like animals and enjoy their job. They also shouldn't promise the world—your backyard-bred mix will not look like a Westminster winner no matter what groomer you go to. Most places require proof of vaccination, so be sure your animal is up to date on shots, including bordetella (kennel cough), the most frequent problem for kennels and groomers. And it's only polite to potty your dog before you arrive.

Professional groomers are not dog trainers, so it's your responsibility to teach your dog to put up with being handled by strangers. If your dog starts thrashing around, he is a danger to himself and others. If your dog has any bad habits or medical problems, be sure to tell the groomer. It is also your job to keep your dog in reasonable

PART TWO

CARING FOR YOUR

DOG'S MANNERS

7

SOCIALIZATION

Dogs are social creatures and are not meant to live life tied on a chain or relegated to a doghouse in the backyard. Most people who own dogs want them to be family members and take great advantage of the dog's inherent sociability. The exact parameters and intricacies of such relationships, however, can sometimes be daunting.

DOGS AND KIDS

It is well known that pets positively influence the mental and physical health of children. Take allergies, for example. We now know that exposure to cats and dogs during the first year of life can significantly reduce risks of allergic reaction and asthma later on. Pets also serve as comforting companions to bored, anxious, and lonely children.

However, no matter how much children and dogs seem meant for each other, their play needs to be supervised at all times. Puppies can nip in play or even snap in frustration. They can easily run off if not watched. Kids can pull tails, scream, kick, and do other inappropriate and even cruel things when you're not looking. Unless you trust your child alone in the house without an adult present, don't trust the child or dog alone with each other.

Children can also benefit from a training course where they will learn the best way to interact with their dog. Helping to train the family dog will also awake in kids a sense of understanding and attachment that is essential to their development as good pet owners.

IF A BABY COMES

Dogs can develop a jealous streak, so it's important to get your dog and the new baby off to the right start. Since you know in advance that a baby is on the way, you can acclimate your dog ahead of time. This is a good time to review all obedience commands with your dog. It's important that he will reliably sit, come, stay, and lie down on command.

Your baby will undoubtedly take up a great deal of time previously allotted to the family dog. If you wait until the baby shows up at the house to make the change in your attentions, your dog will certainly pin the blame on the child. If your dog has been the center of family attention all his life, gradually cut back. This seems mean, but the new baby is bound to cut back on the attention spent on the

Socializing your dog involves introducing him to new people, places, and things.

smells, and if you have selected a name for the baby, use it frequently around the dog. You may decide to keep the child's room off limits, and if you do, start right away by using a strong baby gate. If he's a friendly dog, allow him to meet babies. Of course you'll always want to keep him on a leash! If you have friends with babies, ask them to visit with the baby so that the idea of a child will not be a totally new one to the dog.

To ensure the health of baby and dog, take the pup for a complete vet checkup before the baby arrives. If your pet is not neutered, he probably should be before the child comes home. Trim your dog's nails and keep them trimmed. Any behavior problems should be corrected now; otherwise they may get worse with the arrival of a new family member and the stress attendant upon such an event.

It's best if you can plan to have the dog visiting with a friend or neighbor when the baby arrives. When he does come in, the child is an accomplished fact, and the dog may be more likely to accept her as a bona fide family member. It may help if the dog can sniff an empty but used baby blanket first.

Make sure introductions are gradual, with the dog on leash. Of course, you should never force your dog to meet a baby, and never, never allow them to be together unsupervised. Your dog may not understand that a baby is a human being and part of the family—there's no telling what he may think it is.

dog anyway. You don't want the dog to associate the new baby with the attention withdrawal, so it's best to get him used to it now. However, do it gradually—you have time. If the expectant human mom is the light of the dog's life, see if another family member can take over part of that role. Perhaps an older child (if you have one) can start feeding the dog, walking him, and playing with him more. Or call in the services of the spouse.

This doesn't mean that you'll give your dog no attention. In fact, after the baby arrives, try to set aside some time for working with and cuddling your pal—with the baby present. In this way, the dog gets the idea that when a baby is in the room, treats and playtime come with her. This makes him more favorably disposed towards the child. Keep a short leash on the dog while he's in the baby's presence, just in case something untoward happens, and keep them a safe distance apart.

Let your dog see what babies look, smell, and sound like. Prepare for the baby's arrival by letting the dog see the baby's carriage, crib, blankets, and other paraphernalia. Sprinkle yourself with baby cream or powder to get him used to the new

YOUR DOG AS CO-HOST

All sorts of problems can arise when company comes. Part of it may be due to the guest who may (1) dislike dogs; (2) be afraid of dogs; (3) be allergic to dogs. In any of these cases, it's probably wise to separate guest and canine (while you think about how you can get rid of the guest as quickly as possible). It may be possible to lessen

or eliminate your friend's fear if you have a gentle, quiet, friendly dog. In some cases, you might even convince a dog hater that dogs are pretty cool. And possibly your allergic friend will start getting desensitization shots, all for the love of you. None of this is very likely, but it can happen.

If it is a serious case of hate, fear, or allergy, you'll just have to keep the dog in a separate, safe room. (Ideally, you will have trained your dog to be alone for a while without going crazy.) In other cases, even with dog lovers, you must teach your dog to be a good citizen, which means no jumping, barking, or begging. The best way to handle this is to ignore him while he is exhibiting any of these unwanted behaviors. But the training needs to start well before the guests arrive, which will be discussed in the next chapter. Do not allow guests to give your dog treats in situations where you don't (i.e., begging at the table) or let the dog jump on them (no matter how much they like dogs). You must also ensure that your guest will treat your dog well—certainly you should not allow them to chase or frighten your dog. Children especially need to be watched, since they are not always the precious little angels their parents would like you to think they are.

YOUR DOG AS GUEST

It is even more imperative that a guest dog be well behaved. Before taking your dog visiting, make absolutely sure he is invited and welcome. Even if you know your dog is welcome, ask anyway; it's only polite, and circumstances may have changed. (Perhaps one of the kids in the house has developed an allergy.) Bring your dog's crate with you, even if you think it won't be necessary. You just never know.

Know the house rules before you go, and stick to them. (If you think they stink, leave Fido at home.) Ask your hostess specifically what your dog will be allowed and not allowed to do. Will he be free to move about the house, or must he stay in a crate? Can he sit on the couch? Sleep in the bedroom? Know before you go.

Be honest about your dog's own habits (especially those that concern nipping, chewing, and housetraining). If your dog is not quite perfect in the housetraining department, your hostess may not want the dog on her Oriental carpet. Chewers should not be left alone with the Queen Anne chair. A friend came to visit me once and never mentioned that her dog was a great jumper. While we were at

Stick to a Schedule

When your new addition comes, adhere to a regular schedule as much as possible, particularly in regard to the dog's feeding. He'll appreciate that.

the movies, the dog simply leaped over the garden fence into the fish pool and managed to flip several goldfish out of the pond (and to their deaths).

Be particularly honest about your dog's tolerance for children. If you aren't sure, supervise constantly. In fact, even if you think you are sure, supervise anyway. As we know, the children of others are never as nice as your own.

DOGS AND DOGS

One big concern multiple dog owners have is the problem of dogfights. Nearly all inter-dog aggression occurs over resources: food, toys, sleeping places, or attention. Much of the time it sounds a lot worse than it really is (lots of snarling and snapping but no contact), but occasionally you get a dog who has no bite inhibition, in which case other dogs or even you can get hurt.

Breaking up the dogfight is only a short-term solution.You need to find a way to prevent the problem from occurring in the first place. The first thing you need to do is to figure out what triggers the attacks. If this is predictable, it's a simple matter to remove the trigger—if it is chew toys, don't let the dogs have chew toys. If it is food, feed them in separate rooms, or at least in separate corners of the kitchen, facing away from each other.

If you can't figure out what triggers the attacks, you simply have to separate the dogs, at least until you can consult with a veterinary or certified animal behaviorist. In some cases, it's helpful if you can determine which dog is the "dominant"

It's important to prevent dogfights from occurring in the first place.

dog and support that dog's status. But the canine dominance hierarchy is a complex thing, and upholding what you perceive as the dominance structure may be exactly the wrong move; it may actually exacerbate the situation.

Here's a typical situation involving a "bully dog": A member of our Basset rescue organization wrote, "My Chinese Shar-Pei died recently. Since then, my Shepherd mix (Chelsea) and Basset Hound (Sadie) have not been getting along. The Shepherd pushes the Basset around, makes her lie in corner, and won't allow her to eat. I have been feeding them separately, then reuniting them after dinner, but is there any way I can stop Chelsea from bullying Sadie?"

My friend and fellow dog trainer Laura Hussey responded as follows: "It sounds like you are doing a great job with the situation. It often happens that when the family dynamic changes, quarrels break out. Chelsea is trying to hog all the resources (and you are a resource to her). Here are a couple of ideas that I use with my own dogs:

1. No dog ever gets a treat unless both dogs get a treat. In other words, from Chelsea's point of view, Sadie getting a treat is a good thing because it means she will get one too.

2. No dog gets petted by me unless both dogs get petted. If one dog growls or tries to hog me, I quietly get up and leave the room. They learn fast that trying to hog me means no dog gets my attention. While this might seem to be punishing Sadie, believe me, in the end, it will help her (and dogs usually catch on to this pretty quick).

3. If I drop something in the kitchen, like part of something I am cooking, all the dogs get some, even if they weren't there when I dropped it. This makes it less important to be the only one standing there and to keep the other one away.

4. I don't gush over one dog in the other's presence. I schedule time alone with each

Dog-Dog Aggression
Here's a quick fix for dog-dog aggression: Direct Stop, a citronella spray that is strongly distasteful but harmless to dogs. It works so well that it is effective against trained attack dogs. But this is only a short-term solution.

somehow and give them special attention that way; it doesn't have to be every day or exactly equal, but I make a way to have an individual relationship with each one."

I believe that in cold weather, dogs have a natural instinct to be more protective of valuable resources, such as food and sleeping places. Let's face it, when it's cold and damp, who wants to lie on the throw rug in front of a drafty door (which might have been a perfectly acceptable sleeping place in warmer months)? The number of cozy sleeping places is smaller in this kind of weather, which means that dogs may be willing to fight to protect one they have claimed as theirs. Also, food and items that dogs perceive as food (like rawhide chews) are more valuable in cold weather, and dogs may be more willing to fight over them.

Cold weather exacerbates some painful conditions such as arthritis and hip dysplasia. Dogs with these conditions (and that would likely include any middle-aged and older dogs to some degree) may be more irritable, especially with bouncy youngsters.

To the extent that inclement weather causes school cancellations and other changes in the routine, it disrupts what for many dogs is a pleasantly predictable daily schedule. Even if Rover loves having everyone home for some extra time, change to routine is inherently stressful for most creatures (including humans). In fact, if the inconveniences of arranging child care for kids home from school, dealing with horrible commutes, and other problems we face during winter weather cause you to be stressed, you probably communicate that stress to your dog, who absorbs it like the sponges that dogs are.

Working in Bad Weather

So what can you do if you find yourself with some testy dogs in this weather? First, try to arrange for some kind of exercise. If walks or normal outdoor play are out of the question, try playing some games with your dogs in the house. Many dogs love a few minutes of hide and seek with their owners. Make up your own rules, but just get the dogs moving for a few minutes! Or if your dogs play well with other dogs, try a dog park or dog day care (although not all dogs do well in those settings)

Second, pay special attention to having a sufficient number of warm, cozy places for your dogs to relax. You may need to have more dog beds (or just folded up blankets or old pillows) than you normally like on the floor in bitter weather, or you may need to put blankets over your special piece of furniture, but lying on the cold hard floor is just not pleasant, and dogs will fight over a dog bed or the couch. If you don't believe me, put shorts on and walk around barefoot, and see what it feels like at dog level: It's cold!

Lastly, be mindful that the conditions may cause dogs to be more likely to spark tiffs. Head off disagreements by removing contentious objects like rawhides, and keep a closer eye on your dogs. If your dogs do get into a fight, it isn't necessary to punish either of them, although you can firmly tell them to knock it off. Separate them for a little while to let tempers cool down, and refrain from adding to the tension by making a bigger deal about it than it is. Thankfully, most fights between

About Cats

Unfortunately, dogs are just crazy about cat food and cat feces. The careful dog and cat owner must be creative about keeping cat bowls and especially the litter box away from the dog! This may mean putting the litter box in a closet with a cat door too small for the dog.

well-adjusted dogs result in only minor (if any) injuries, providing the dogs are fairly matched in size and neither is handicapped by injury or physical limitations.

DOGS AND CATS

"Fighting like cats and dogs" is largely a myth. Most cats and dogs can learn to get on well together, and many become inseparable friends. Cats and dogs do have different body language, however, as Lewis Carroll's Cheshire Cat noted in *Alice in Wonderland*. The famous cat remarked that dogs wag their tails when they are happy, while cats do the same when they are angry. He then deduced that if dogs are sane, cats are mad. We should probably conclude, however, that they are just different. For example, to dogs, rolling over indicates playfulness or submission, but to cats, it's a fighting posture that allows them to make full use of teeth and claws. (Sometimes it is a play fighting posture, but with a cat, you can never be sure.) Dogs have to learn all this by trial and error.

When introducing a young cat and an old dog, the kitten may be the first to approach; otherwise, the dog will almost certainly make the first move. Cats are notably conservative in their social interactions.

8

BASIC TRAINING

Trained dogs are safe, pleasant to be around, and happy. An owner is much more likely to spend time with a dog who is pleasant to be around, which in turn makes the dog happy. It's a cycle that works for both the dog and the owner. Dogs are eminently trainable—the only thing left for us to do is train them. The first step towards training them is to understand them, and that means learning their language.

BODY LANGUAGE

We consider our dogs well trained if they can learn our language: "Sit!" "Come!" "Stay!" However, training gets easier if we can learn to read their language, too. While dogs do have distinct vocal sounds, most canine meaning is carried through body language.

In general, confident, alert dogs stand tall, with raised heads and erect, forward-pointing ears. Their eyes are wide and their mouths are closed or only slightly open. They stare intently. They may wag their tails slowly at half-staff. If feeling aggressive or threatened, they may raise their hackles and growl. When meeting such a dog, it is best not to stare directly back, which the dog may regard as a threat. However, a cringing attitude on your part will give the dog the wrong impression, especially if it is your dog! The best plan is to gaze aloofly at the tip of the animal's ear. This shows that you are not threatening but that you are a grandiose creature too far above his limited ability to influence (even if this is not strictly true). However, a stiff-necked position on your part also constitutes threat; bend it a little.

Fearful dogs tend to lower their heads and tuck in their tails in an effort to appear smaller. They avoid direct eye contact, and in severe cases, may "leak" urine. Other fear signals may include sniffing the ground (this is an appeasement sign where the dog is saying, in effect, "Hey, look, I'm not bothering anyone, no siree, just minding my own business, that's all"); turning the head away or holding it to the side; and glancing quickly to the side. Treat fearful dogs as you would aggressive ones, since fear can turn into aggression. Approach slowly at an angle, and look away from the dog. Fearful dogs, especially black ones, may also lick their noses. (The

> Fearful dogs tend to lower their heads and tuck in their tails in an effort to look smaller.

theory here is that the pink tongue against the black fur is an especially visible sign.) Yawning is also a sign of stress, but if you yawn back at your dog, especially an older dog who is used to you, it may calm him down.

Friendly dogs wag their tails gently or in an excited, happy way. They tend to have an open, relaxed mouth and may bark in short, excited yips.

Many dogs' signals are very subtle and sometimes appear mixed. If you are having trouble understanding a dog's signals, the safest thing to do is to assume the dog is aggressive or anxious and back off.

TRAINING AND PUNISHMENT

When it comes to training and behavior modification, avoid punishing your dog. Punishment simply doesn't work very well

for animals. If you want your dog to behave well, he needs to internalize good behavior. Punishment makes this difficult or impossible, because punishment is pain (either physical or psychological), and pain sets up barriers to internalization. For example, let's say a dog does something you don't like, such as snapping at a visitor. Yelling at or striking the dog creates an immediate unpleasant association in the dog's mind between the stimulus (the visitor) and the punishment. He will associate visitors with pain, and that will not make him like them any better. If this doesn't convince you, here is a simple example: taking a bath. Presumably your dog does not like taking baths. (Most dogs don't.) If you hit the dog when he shows reluctance to get into the bath, he will not suddenly decide that taking a bath is a good idea because the consequence of reluctance is being beaten. Instead, the dog will just become increasingly fearful and soon generalize his fear to other situations. (Dogs,

contrary to what some people say, are terrific generalizers—they are too good at it, in fact. They can, however, be poor discriminators, which in the long run may amount to the same thing.)

To get a dog to do as you want without inciting a bunch of other "bad" behaviors means getting him in the habit of performing a desired behavior. In other words, motivate him. Of course, this is not always possible; most dogs never learn to like baths or getting their nails clipped because those experiences are inherently unpleasant. In such cases, you will need an external enforcer—but not punishment, which makes the experience even worse. Instead, try rewarding your dog, which, if the reward is great enough and the experience tolerable, will work. Rewarding is an external motivator, which if performed correctly may eventually get the dog to internalize desired behavior. (Truly internalized behavior, such as sexual desire or the drive to chase a rabbit, is instinctive. It's very hard to overcome these passions.) If an experience is sufficiently terrible, no reward will work and you may have to use "force" (e.g., carry the dog to the tub), but if you have built a relationship of trust between you and your dog—accomplished by not punishing him— he will acquiesce. Although he may never really understand why you are doing whatever it is you are doing, he will trust you. (I am assuming here that you are not actually hurting the dog.) A dog may not understand the difference between pain inherent in a certain activity and pain as punishment.

Most dogs equate height with authority. In play, dogs often try to gain a height advantage by climbing on furniture, over other dogs, or by trying to mount their opponent. (It has nothing to do with sex.) In some cases, your tall presence

You must motivate your dog to perform a desired behavior.

is worrisome and threatening; if you sit down next to the dog, it's more relaxing to the animal. However, children should never attempt this around dominant or threatening dogs; in fact, it's best to keep them away from the dog altogether.

HOUSETRAINING

While people have different expectations of what being "trained" is, everybody includes "housetraining" under that definition. Your dog may be able to sit, roll over, shake hands, or ride a bicycle, but if he is not housetrained, he's not trained in the way that really matters.

The good news is that dogs are naturally clean animals; they want to keep their "den" clean. All you have to do is teach them that their den includes the entire house. This leads to my nonpatented system of housetraining.

C: Containment and Consistency

Get a crate to housetrain your puppy as a way of establishing his "den." The crate is not a babysitter or place of punishment but a vital tool in orienting your puppy to the idea that some places are okay to eliminate in and some are not. Dogs seldom dirty their own beds, so you're working with his natural instincts here. However, if your puppy came from a pound or pet shop, he may not have been allowed out of his crate long enough to eliminate elsewhere and had no choice but to use the crate.

Use the crate consistently. Use it whenever the puppy is not eating, playing, exercising, or interacting with you (which should be often). This does not mean hours and hours of sitting in a crate. That is very bad for the puppy, partly because it is unutterably boring for a growing mammal and partly because by doing so, you are setting the dog up for failure. A puppy cannot "hold it" for a long time; you need to make sure that you keep an eye on him and take him out often.

R: Reward and Resolve

Reward your dog for doing the right thing. You can use a tasty treat, praise, walks, or playtime! Let him know that going outdoors to eliminate can be rewarded with quality time with you. If you simply take him out to "do his business" and then haul him in again, he'll delay "going" as long as possible because of the inherent reward of being out there. In this regard, show resolve. Keep him outside until he is successful—and then reward, reward, reward!

A: Attention and Attitude

Pay attention to little signs of needing to eliminate. Your dog can't tell you, "I have to go out now." He may (if you're lucky) go the door or whine, but he's just as likely to yawn, circle, or shift nervously. Once you know your dog's signs, you should be able to get him outside in time, or at the very least, catch him in the act. (In this case, grabbing the puppy and tucking his tail between his legs as you charge out the door with him usually works.) Nowhere is timing more important than in the housetraining department. Catching a dog in a mistake two minutes after the fact is too late to correct it. Remember that prevention is much better than cure. In fact, prevention is the only cure.

Crate Training

It is critically important for your dog to learn to use a crate. He'll need it when he travels, for instance, or if he is injured and needs to have his movements restricted. You can get one that is easy to store when not in use. Crate training a puppy when he is most amenable to the idea is a kind act as well as a smart one.

Reward your dog for doing the right thing when housetraining.

P: Patience and Praise

Despite all those books that tell you how to housetrain your dog in an hour or a day or week, it's not likely to be that easy. Puppies younger than 12 weeks (at the earliest) have poor sphincter control and tiny bladders. A child isn't reliably toilet trained until the age of two or so, so don't expect miracles from a dog. Praise him lavishly whenever he is successful, and he'll get the hang of it.

S: Supervision and Scheduling

When the puppy is out of the crate, he must be in your field of vision. Not only will this make housetraining easier, it will keep him safe.

That's why supervision is the absolute number-one (pardon the pun) ingredient in successful housetraining. If your puppy is properly supervised, you will notice when he needs to go out or at the very least get him out in the midst of his error. But don't get angry or upset when he makes mistakes. Take him where you want him to "go" and reward him!

The scheduling part means, first of all, make sure you feed him on a regular schedule—don't just plunk down a whole day's supply at once. (He'll eat it all at once and get sick anyway.) You should take your dog out immediately after he eats, and keep him out for 15 minutes or so. If you get no results, bring him in and put him in his crate for another ten minutes and then try again. If you succeed, stay out with him just a bit longer and play with him. It's also a good idea to feed your dog a high-quality puppy food, which will result in fewer, firmer stools.

Scheduling also refers to your "scheduling" a special spot for elimination, which can have enormous benefits. Pickup will be simpler (fewer little surprises under your shoe), the yard will stay greener, and your pup will soon learn to associate that special area with a certain activity. Stay outside with your dog the entire time; putting the dog out while you stay in will not allow you to see what has been accomplished. It will also convince your dog that he is being punished somehow (by being separated from you) and to begin to dislike the whole notion of housetraining. A doggy door, if it is practical for your house, can be a great asset both during and after housetraining. Your puppy will benefit from the freedom of using the door and will have fewer accidents as he matures.

Some people prefer to paper train their dogs. This method takes longer and requires more work on the part of the owner; however, small urban dogs who don't get to go out much can often benefit from it. In fact, dogs can be trained to use litter boxes just as cats do naturally. The trick to successful paper training is finding the substrate you want to your dog to use. This can be tricky, because once a puppy starts using a particular surface, he'll tend to stick with that surface. If you want your dog to eventually use grass for bathroom duty, then you should incorporate grass or sod as part of the "paper" training surface. While cats will use a small area, dogs seem to have a harder time figuring out where the proper toilet is. Generally, you have to put the dog in a small area like the bathroom and cover the entire area with paper for a week or so, gradually removing sheets of newspaper until only a small toilet area is left.

BASIC COMMANDS

It is much easier to prevent a problem than to solve one, and that's what training is all about. You can't train your dog until you yourself know the specific behaviors that you want from him. Make a list of every reasonable thing you would like your dog to do (or not do) on command. Then set up regular training sessions, each one with a specific goal. If you have no goal, you won't know whether you've accomplished anything, other than a vague idea that it went "well" or "badly." Keep a log of your training sessions, and write down at the top of the page what your goal is for each session. Afterwards, record how the session went.

Before you begin training, have your dog or puppy checked out by a vet to make sure he is healthy. Before the training session starts, exercise your dog to take a little of the edge off. After the exercise, practice in a quiet, restricted area where neither of you will be distracted or able to run away (even though you both might feel like it).

Train often but for short periods. I recommend about 3 times a day for 15 minutes each, but with a puppy, 5 minutes at a stretch is long enough. Basic training requires only two items, a flat collar and a lead. And while not absolutely necessary, a few small treats are very helpful. I mean really small—not something that requires chewing.

Keys to Successful Training

While dogs don't understand many human words, they do understand tones. Learning to master your tone when communicating with your dog is critical to getting him to listen to you. If your tone contradicts your words, the dog will listen to the tone. Most of the time, you'll be chatting aimlessly to your dog as you wander around. But for training and bonding purposes, three tones of voice are especially useful: the command tone is a strong, clear tone used to tell your dog to sit, come, etc.; the praise tone is a happy tone used to reward a dog's good behavior; and the corrective tone is a growl-like tone used to correct bad behavior. Your tone should match your intent. You will find that most dogs associate kind words with approval and acceptance and will work for these verbal rewards.

The keys to successful training are a judicious mix of timing, firmness, and consistency.

- Timing is just as critical in obedience training as it is in housetraining. Your dog needs to be emotionally, mentally, and physically ready for each step. He must learn each command thoroughly before progressing to the next one. If you correct him, the correction must be made immediately, not five minutes later. The same is true for praise. Neither praise nor blame commands work unless they are given at the right time—which better be within half a second of the desired behavior.
- Firmness means setting boundaries for your dog. Just as you set boundaries about your properties

Physical Punishment

Never strike a dog. Physical punishment is inhumane and does not work nearly as well as gentler methods. Corrections need only be firm enough to distract the dog from the undesirable behavior.

(a fenced yard) for your dog to play in, you also need to set behavioral boundaries on him. This does not limit your dog; it helps him direct his activities into acceptable areas. No jumping, no eating from the table, or whatever limits you choose, help make your dog a well-disciplined and happier animal.

- Once you set your firm limits, you must enforce them consistently. This doesn't mean, however, that you can never let the dog onto the couch—it may mean that the dog is never allowed on the couch except when accompanied by the command "Okay, couch," or whatever phrase you choose.

Following is a list of basic commands (arranged by importance) you should work on at home with your dog. Remember when working with your dog that the specific rewards and techniques are not as important as the general principles of feedback, timing, kindness, patience, and consistency.

"Come"

This is the first and most important of all commands. If there is one command that you would like your dog to do reliably every time, this is it. Dogs who don't come on command are, at the least, annoying, and at the worst, a danger to themselves and others. If you fail with this training, your puppy may well turn the come command into a game: Your part of the game is to call him, and his part of the game is to see how long he can make you stand there looking like an idiot. I should warn you, however, that it is always possible for even the best-behaved dog not to come when called if something more interesting is moving in the opposite direction. None of us is perfect.

When you first begin teaching the command, wait until the dog is already heading in your direction, then call him. It's important to take advantage of the opportunity and wait until the dog is already headed in your direction; don't initiate the command while he's walking away from you. If he suddenly stops, call him again and use a small treat to lure him. When he gets to you, give him lots of praise and affection—and the treat, if you have one. The key is to look sharp and be prepared to call "Come" in a cheerful tone every time you see your dog doing it anyway. If your dog happens not to obey, don't chase him. Turn your back and walk in the opposite direction. He'll probably come to you. When he does, give him a treat and start walking again. The key is to make him think that coming to you and being by your side is the most rewarding activity there is.

The biggest mistake people make in training

is thinking the dog has learned the command after just a few tries. It takes repeated, long-term application to make it sink in.

"No!"

Right up there with the come command is the no command. (In fact, I would have started with that one but didn't want to seem too negative.)

"No" means: "Desist immediately!" You may combine it with a reference to what he's doing wrong: "No chew!" means "Stop eating that—it's my prom dress." Some people think that saying no is cruel and unusual punishment. Quite the contrary; it is neither cruel and is, unfortunately, far from unusual. "No" is simply a guide to correct behavior. "No" is a mysterious word to dogs unless you utter it immediately in conjunction with the forbidden behavior. You can't walk into a room five minutes after the doilies were devoured, shake one in the dog's face, and shriek, "No! No!" He will probably think, "Hmm, Mom is yelling 'No.' She'd better put that doily down." If your dog is chewing something inappropriate, say "No chew" and hand him something more acceptable. Then praise him. You won't confuse your dog or destroy his ego by saying no. You're giving him important boundaries.

Be sure you speak your "No" in a firm, clear voice that underscores your meaning. And since dogs can read faces, make sure your face mirrors your meaning, too.

"Off!"

This means "Get the heck off the couch, Arthur! How many times have I told you not to get on the couch? But you never listen to me..." and so on. You can also use "No" to make him get down, but "Off" is better because it is more specific. It tells the dog exactly what you want him to do right now, which is "Get off the danged couch!" Besides, you can use "Off" for other things, such as a command for him to jump out of the back of the van.

Submissive or small dogs can be bodily removed if they do not respond to verbal commands. More dominant dogs should be lured with a treat and praised for obedience. In fact, always reward a dominant animal for submissive behavior. In some cases, you may have to attach a leash to the dog in order to get him to come down. Some people recommend squirting some water at the recalcitrant dog, but many dogs view this as aggressive behavior on your part.

"Give It!" and "Drop It!"

These commands are not identical. A well-trained dog knows both of them. After all, you may want him to give you the stick he has so unexpectedly retrieved for you, but you'd rather he just dropped the rotten rabbit he dug up. It's good practice for you to be able to remove anything your dog has in his mouth without a protest from him.

The easiest way to make a dog drop what he has in his mouth is to offer him a tastier alternative. Luckily, puppies are likely to pick up an inedible item that isn't too interesting, like an old shoe. He will probably readily drop the item if offered something better (along with the command "Drop it!"). You'll want to practice this command with low-value items first. Practicing with tug-of-war is a good way to make him learn the command. (Contrary to what is sometimes said, there is nothing wrong with playing tug-of-war or even letting him win—the key is that you decide who wins.) Of course, if he selects a high-value, dangerous item (rotten rabbit), you may have to put on gloves and just take it. But be sure to reward him for it. Never allow the dog to have anything you don't want him to. This is one game he can't afford to win.

"Give it" is a command used for retrieving dogs. The main difference between "drop it" and "give it"

is that with the latter command, you are asking him to put it in your hand (so hold it out as a signal). Practice by handing the dog something he doesn't want to hold in his mouth all that much anyway. As you hand it to him, say "Give it" immediately and praise or treat him when he lets it drop, as he probably will. Gradually increase the value of the object (and the consequent reward). Soon he should drop whatever he has into your hand.

"Sit"

This is the easiest and most popular of all commands to teach. Say "Sit," and hold a treat slightly above his eye level; this will encourage him to sit down. Praise him lavishly when he succeeds. Be careful to praise him as he sits, not when he starts to get up. When you do want your dog to

rise, give him a "release" command such as "break." Some trainers use "okay," but since people use that word constantly in regular conversation, it's too easy for a dog to misunderstand it. You can even make up a secret release word that will amaze all your friends.

> Dogs have to have a lot of trust in you to perform the down command because lying down makes them feel vulnerable.

"Down"

This command should be taught after the sit command. While he is sitting, take a treat and hold it in front of his face, then lower it slowly to the ground. The dog should follow suit. If he doesn't, keeping him in a sitting position and very slowly pull the treat forward in front of him, close to the ground. He'll have to lie down to reach it. Praise him when he succeeds. Dogs have to have a lot of trust in you to perform this command, as lying down makes them feel vulnerable. Don't try it until you and your pooch have established a strong bond.

"Heel"

A correctly heeling dog is a pleasure to walk. The trouble involved in training him to move quietly at your side will be more than made up for later, when you are walking your dog with one hand and holding the baby/book bag/dog show trophy in the other. If you have a puppy, take heart—a puppy is much easier to teach to heel than an older dog. He naturally wants to come with you and has no bad habits to break (so far).

Use a 6-foot (2-m) nylon or leather lead for training exercises. Never use a chain leash, which is too heavy and noisy. Don't wrap the leash around your hand; it's a less effective instrument that way. Besides, you could hurt your hand if the dog lunges at something.

If your dog works well on a plain leather collar, use that. The less control you need, the more pleasurable the exercise will be for both of you. You should be able to slip two fingers comfortably under the collar. It is always best if you have accustomed your dog to walk happily at your side before attaching a leash to him. You can do this by practicing in a safe, fenced-in area, and using treats! The leash becomes, as it were, an afterthought.

It's traditional for dogs to heel at the left side of their owners, but there's no law about it. Lefties may prefer walking their dogs on the right side. However, if you're planning to show your dog in conformation or obedience, it's best to use the customary left side.

Begin by reaching out and touching your dog. He will probably look up at you expectantly, which is good. You must get him to pay attention to you and keep his eye on you. Say "Fido, heel," and begin walking. (If your dog's name happens to be something other than Fido, use that name.) Keep his chest in line with your knee, and don't allow him to lead. During a heeling exercise, stop at every curb. This is good practice for both of you. You don't want your dog to get the idea that it's all right to run across the street. When you are finished, loosen the lead completely (but still hang on to it), and say "Break." This is the signal that your dog may now sniff around and be doggish to his heart's content.

Some dogs pull at the leash, or forge. Forging begins long before you have attached the lead to the collar—it begins when your dog sees the lead. If you can't control him at this point, don't expect that the upcoming foray will be a walk in the park, even if it is a walk in the park. Have your dog sit or stand quietly while you attach the lead. Do not put the lead on while he's dancing around. Insist that he remain calm. If he starts jumping around when it's on, take off the lead. Start again calmly. He will soon learn that the only way he's getting out the door is if he remains quiet. Otherwise, you will have a struggle on your hands before the walk even begins, and the exercise becomes pointless.

"Please Leave"

I use this command to remove my dogs from the kitchen, especially when we are cooking or dining. (Actually, I say "Aroint thee, beast!" but they get the picture.) To teach "Leave," take your dog's collar and remove him to the desired room. Then praise him. When he comes back, say "Please leave," and repeat. Do this until he gets the message. You may use treats to explain it to him further.

A correctly heeling dog is a pleasure to walk.

OBEDIENCE SCHOOL

An addition to (but never as a replacement for) home schooling is more formal obedience training. While many people do an effective job of training their dog at home, others do best with the structure and companionship of a formal obedience class. If you have a puppy, a puppy kindergarten or pre-novice class will also teach him the basics of socialization, one of the most important lessons of all.

Don't select a trainer at random; get recommendations from trusted friends, veterinarians, or kennel club members. Check the trainer's credentials—many of the good ones are members of a professional organization, such as the Association of Pet Dog Trainers (APDT). And visit a few classes without your dog. Participants (both human and canine) should seem relaxed, enthusiastic, and comfortable. Look for lots of smiling. Does the trainer seem interested in listening as well as talking? That's important. And since the training is for you as much as for your dog, work with someone with whom you have a rapport. The most effective trainers use positive reinforcement rather than punishment, so pay attention to how the dogs are being asked to do what is required. And of course, the facility should be safe and clean.

Obedience classes help your dog learn the basic commands: sit, down, stay, come, and heel—commands not intended to turn your dog into a slave or robot but to help him become a functioning (and safe) member of society. You'll learn some things yourself, such as how to use your body and tone and gesture to reinforce rather than contradict a command and how and when to reward

or withhold rewards. Experience will teach you what reward works best with your pet—some must have food, others are happy with a praise and petting, and even a brief game can work. For some dogs, the best reward is a chance to be allowed to run around and play with other dogs. Each dog is different, and as an owner, you can discover a hierarchy of rewards for your own pet. Some classes also work on stopping problem behaviors, and some offer the basics in more formal obedience.

Many contemporary trainers use clicker training. The clicker first marks a genuine reward (usually a treat), and as time goes by, the clicker itself becomes the reward. Clicker training is very successful, although people like me can never remember where they put the darned thing. I have lost every one I have owned into the clicker void.

Some people do best with the structure and companionship of a formal obedience class.

THE CANINE GOOD CITIZEN®

You may not want to win an AKC obedience title with your dog, but you certainly want him to be a well-behaved companion. To achieve this end, think about having your dog pass the AKC Canine Good Citizen (CGC) test, which is open to all dogs, whether they have a pedigree or not.

To pass, a dog must successfully complete the following ten exercises:

1. Accepting a friendly stranger
2. Sitting politely for petting
3. Appearance and grooming
4. Walking on a loose leash
5. Walking through a crowd
6. Sit, down, and stay on command

> The most effective trainers use positive reinforcement rather than punishment.

7. Coming when called
8. Reacting appropriately to another dog
9. Reacting appropriately to distractions
10. Supervised separation

Dogs who pass receive a certificate documenting their achievement. Local all-breed kennel clubs conduct these tests from time to time. Contact the one nearest you for more information. For a copy of the Canine Good Citizen pamphlet, contact the AKC online at www.akc.org.

PROBLEM BEHAVIORS

According to the Journal of the American Medical Association (AMA), every year about 334,000 people in the United States are admitted to hospital emergency rooms because of dog bites. Another 466,000 report to other medical facilities. Thousands upon thousands more go unreported. Dogs kill about a dozen people, usually small children, every year. (A Yorkshire Terrier was implicated in one attack, and Dachshunds have killed three people—it isn't always Rottweilers and Pit Bulls.) This is not just a problem; it's an epidemic. And the dog most likely to bite you is your own.

9

Dogs are complex creatures and thus can develop their share of "problem behaviors," although the problems often affect us more than they do the dog. Barking, jumping, chewing, running, and biting are all natural behaviors for dogs. The problem is ours, and it is unrealistic to expect the dog to extinguish all his natural behaviors. In some cases, a dog's "problem behavior" is merely his desperate attempt to solve his own problems. For example, while we think that the "problem" is the dog tearing the living room to pieces when we're gone, for the dog the problem is loneliness, and the solution is to do something to relieve anxiety or boredom. It's largely a matter of perspective, if you stop to think about it.

It is odd that despite all our sophistication and growing knowledge about canine behavior and proper training methods, we seem to be seeing more behavior problems with dogs, not fewer. I think the reason is simple: Many people who want dogs don't really have enough time for them. Most dogs are alone most of the day. This is not how animals bred to be companions were meant to live. (Those not bred to be companions were bred to work, and most of today's dogs get precious little work, either.)

In general, most unwanted behaviors can be cured with exercise, attention, and understanding. An enormous amount of trouble occurs simply because a dog is bored and lonely. These are highly intelligent, social animals who enjoy work, company, and a purpose in life. If we relegate a dog to the corner of our life, we can expect a heck of a lot of trouble when we finally get around to noticing him. In fact, sometimes the only way a dog can get us to notice him at all is by action: barking, chewing, digging, peeing, and pooping. Not that they think (except sometimes in the case of barking), "Hey, I'm lonely, so I'll do something

to make them pay attention." No, many of these behaviors are simply responses to stress and boredom that have the additional advantage, from the dog's point of view, of getting attention. And as we all know, any kind of attention is better than no attention.

In some cases, you will need to call in a professional to help you with your "problem dog." Sometimes owners wait too long to make this important step. In fact, they can ingrain the undesirable behavior by continuing to do the same ineffective things to "cure it," even though the dog shows no improvement in the behavior. Just because a certain therapy or training technique worked for a friend of yours, or for another dog you had, or is recommended by the greatest trainer in the world does not mean it will work for your dog in your situation.

Different breeds may respond differently to different kinds of training. Small dogs may need

Consider individual temperament when deciding on an approach to training.

a different approach to training than big dogs do, and you should always consider individual temperament. Training can be a two-way street. Often enough, the owner has to change her own behavior first. The key is knowing when you need help. Think of it like home repair—you can probably change a lightbulb on your own, but you call in a pro when rewiring the house. It's the same with dogs—you can probably teach your dog to sit, but to correct a serious behavior problem (especially aggression), find an experienced, qualified expert to help you out.

Getting the right help is not always easy. Keep this in mind when looking for qualified help:

- Most good trainers belong to a recognized training organization, like the Association of Pet Dog Trainers (APDT). Their Certification Council

requires at least 300 hours of dog training experience plus an examination.

- Another top-notch bunch of specialists are veterinary behaviorists, who are board-certified specialists in animal behavior. A veterinary behaviorist not only has a degree from an accredited veterinary school but has also completed post-graduate work (internships and a residence, with a research project published in a peer-reviewed journal) and passed a certification exam. They have the additional advantage of being able to conduct physical examinations and prescribe medications if needed.

- Certified applied animal behaviorists have a Ph.D. in biological or behavioral science. Certification comes from the Animal Behavior Society (ABS). Most of the conditions listed here

Aggression is an evolutionary tool that our dogs' ancestors used to defend themselves.

can have a medical cause. Before tearing your hair out wondering what you did wrong, get your problem dog checked by a veterinarian. Behavioral problems can be caused by parasites, problems with hearing or vision, endocrine or hormonal problems, thyroid dysfunction, Cushing's disease, hypersexuality, spinal disease, hyperactivity, medications, toxins, and a host of other conditions.

AGGRESSION

Biting is natural to dogs. It's normal. It's how their ancestors caught prey and defended themselves. Aggression is an evolutionary tool, and today's dogs bite for pretty much the same reasons. While many books offer dozens of sub-varieties of aggression, we can boil them down to these two:

Prey Drive Aggression: Prey drive aggression is an interesting phenomenon. In wolves, it is an essential component of living. If wolves were not aggressive in the presence of prey, they'd starve. In many of today's dog breeds, however, prey drive has been eliminated, interrupted, or redirected.

Sheep-guarding dogs are an example—they need to have a pretty well-extinguished prey drive or they would routinely eat their charges. (Sometimes they do anyway. Things don't always work out as planned.) Their prey drive has been interrupted, so they are able to guide the sheep and not kill them. A breed with a redirected prey drive is the Greyhound, who chases mechanical lures around a racecourse.

Trouble comes about when the average dog with a lively prey drive encounters running cats, kids, joggers, and cars, which he may attack with varying degrees of success. Some dogs are stimulated by only one or two triggers, perhaps cats but not kids, or vice versa. Some breeds are genetically programmed only to stop and round up the prey, while some will go for the kill. Unfortunately, there is not a lot you can do to extinguish prey drive in an individual dog. A dog who views cats as prey can never be trusted around them, and they must be permanently separated one way or another.

Defensive (Stress) Aggression: Defensive aggression accounts for all other kinds of aggression, with the possible exception of certain neurological disorders, such as rabies. (No one is sure why rabid dogs bite, although it may be pain related.)

Some of what we term unprovoked aggression is really rather natural behavior in dogs. Mother dogs may bite if they feel that their litter is threatened. Dogs will bite if they are in physical pain. Many dogs will bite if they feel that their food,

possessions, or territory is in danger. And almost any dog will bite if he is stressed, teased, abused, or frightened enough.

So dogs feel defensive about their puppies, their food, their possessions (including their owners), and their territory (including their bodies and personal space). If they perceive themselves as threatened, they get stressed. If they get stressed enough, they will bite. Any dog with teeth is capable of biting. This does not mean that every stressed dog will bite. We all know about the fight-or-flight response, and most dogs (not all) prefer flight to fight. If for certain physical or psychological reasons they cannot flee, they will fight.

There's nothing particularly weird or strange about any of this. It doesn't take a wizard to figure it out. Yet people continue to be bitten, over and over again, because they continue to unwittingly stress their dogs. That doesn't mean biting is

Biting is a behavior that comes naturally to dogs.

excusable. It is not okay if a dog bites you because you happen to sit down next to him on the couch, kiss his face, or casually pick up a toy in front of him. However, there is a solution to the problem—reduce the stress.

The Myth of Dominance

Years ago it was assumed that the dogs most likely to bite were so-called dominant dogs. It was recommended that you show the dog who's boss by doing an "alpha roll"—rolling him on his back and holding him there until he gave in. The rationale for this absurd advice was based on some observed wolf behavior, where submissive wolves occasionally rolled before dominant wolves. The fact that the dominant wolves were not the ones instigating the roll did not seem to occur to those doling out this suspect advice. Dominant wolves do not force submissive wolves into a roll. Your own dog will occasionally roll over submissively in hopes of a tummy rub, thus showing you he thinks you're the boss. That doesn't mean he won't bite you, however. Many, many dog bites come from submissive dogs who roll over all the time. They don't bite because they feel dominant; they bite because they're stressed or scared.

Attack biting has nothing to do with dominance. It's all about fear and stress. The dog most likely to bite you is not the most high-ranking dog—it is, as my friend and trick-dog trainer Laura Hussey calls him, the "middle management dog." A truly high-ranking dog is relaxed and self-confident. He doesn't go around biting people he loves. (This does not mean, by the way, that the dog feels dominant to you. It is uncertain how dogs regard the humans in their families, perhaps as quasi-dogs but probably as another order of being who dispenses food, walks, and affection.)

A truly submissive dog has such a strong flight

rather than fight impulse that it would take extreme provocation, like intense physical pain, to get a bite reaction. Middle management dogs, on the other hand, like middle managers in the human world, tend to be insecure about their position in regard to you, more stressed in general, and more likely to bite when stressed. These are the dogs most likely to become aggressive.

It is true that a dominant dog can bite his owner—if he feels dominant to his owner and also feels threatened by the owner. The simple truth, however, is that firmly, kindly, and quickly establishing your dominance role by being a trusted leader can avert nearly all situations in which your dog is likely to bite you. That doesn't mean he won't go after the kid next door, who he regards as a threat. Certain breeds of dog are much more likely to take this attitude than others.

Aggression is largely a matter of genetic makeup.

It's in the Genes

Aggression is largely a matter of genetic makeup. One of the biggest myths about aggression in dogdom is this one: "It's not the dog, it's the training." Unfortunately, training (or lack of it) does not mold a dog's temperament. The major factor influencing a dog's behavior is his genetic inheritance. Correct training can help manage a dog, but it cannot change his basic behavioral makeup. This does not mean aggression per se is written into the genetic code. There is no "bite gene." But there are genes responsible for making dogs respond differently to stress, and biting is one response to stress. So we can say that aggression is genetically based.

Three kinds of dogs in particular exhibit overactive aggression (usually directed at strangers): guard and fighting breeds, terriers,

and toy dogs. How surprising can this be? Breeds who were designed for protection and guard duty (Akitas, Rottweilers, German Shepherd Dogs, and the like) need an inherent fierceness of disposition. A cheerful tail wagger just doesn't do a very good job protecting the valuables. These are powerful dogs with a low bite threshold and the desire to run things their way. They need strong, dog-savvy owners. Guard dogs who are also easily stressed make the most dangerous animals of all, and since the tendency to become stressed can be genetic, we have a very dangerous situation on our hands. Fighting dogs were formerly bred to be aggressive only towards other dogs and not people; however, the boundaries seem to have grown increasingly fuzzy over the years. Dogs many generations removed from their fighting ancestors are usually safe enough; those still bred (illegally, of course) for this purpose by ignorant and criminal breeders are often very dangerous indeed.

Terriers, while they were (as a rule) bred for protection, were also meant to hunt rats and other nasty vermin; this takes a relentless, driving character whose roots lie in unremitting fierceness against whatever it designates as prey, often small children.

And what about those tempting toy dogs? Well, their charm is your doom. Because these dogs are so small, many breeders pay no attention to temperament at all! After all, it's only a tiny little thing…how much harm can it do? Temperament is left to run rampant in these breeds, and as a result, most toy breeds have even worse temperaments than guard dogs—only they are too small to be effective, unless you happen to be a small child. In addition, tiny dogs are likely to feel more easily threatened than large ones.

Of course, not every terrier, toy dog, or guard dog exhibits this kind of aggression, and most never do towards their owners, since they were

bred to love, protect, and attach themselves to them. Such owners are the beneficiaries of limitless loyalty.

One apparent exception to stress/aggression link are the dogs who Dr. Karen Overall calls "masters of the universe" in her book *Clinical Behavioral Medicine for Small Animals*. James O'Heare, author of *The Canine Aggression Workbook*, calls them "control complex aggression" dogs, and they can be of any breed. These overconfident, manipulative animals have little bite inhibition and simply snarl, nip, or bite to force their owners to do their bidding. This kind of aggression usually shows up very early, often before the animal is four months old. Usually these highly independent puppies show much more interest in exploring their surroundings than in interacting with people. They also seem fairly insensitive to pain. When they do play, they enjoy tugging, fighting, and jumping games. These dogs can be controlled, usually by working hard to make them very dependent

> Unstable temperaments are becoming more common, both because of puppy mills and breeders who are more interested in creating a show dog than a reliable family pet.

on their owners and rewarding engagement and submissive behavior.

Unfortunately, unstable temperaments are becoming more common, both because of puppy mills and some breeders who are more interested in creating a show dog than a reliable family pet. The common practice of line breeding intensifies undesirable traits as well as good ones, and until pet temperament becomes a priority, we'll continue to see nice-looking dogs with foul tempers.

Managing the Aggressive Dog

If you can reduce the stress your dog feels, you can reduce the chance that he will bite you or anyone else. Some of the conditions that lead to stress aggression may already have been set into play before you ever got your dog. If he was reared in an unsocialized, isolated, or (by contrast) overcrowded environment, if he was kicked, neglected, starved, or abused, the aggressive side of his nature is awake. Again, how your dog responds to stress is primarily influenced by genetics. A basically submissive animal tends to become a shy or terrified one; a basically dominant dog will become aggressive or even vicious. Guard and protection dogs were bred for dominance, so these breeds are more likely to become aggressive with poor treatment.

It is true that dominant dogs may also become bossy if paired with a weak or wishy-washy owner. Animals prefer hierarchy, and if you don't want to be the boss, these dogs will be happy to take over. This doesn't mean that these animals will bite their owners; they may instead become control freaks who push, nudge, and stubbornly insist on their way at all times. If they feel that the family hierarchy (which they really need) is not clear, they may feel compelled to make a try for leadership themselves. They are actually being pushed into this situation by the stress they feel in a leaderless society.

Whether you have a naturally submissive or a naturally dominant dog, it is up to you to take control of the situation. Again, there's little or nothing you can do to change your dog's basic temperament. Let management be your goal.

Leadership: Your first job is to be a wise, firm, consistent leader. Dogs appreciate good leadership, and they are preternaturally astute at spotting weakness or indecision. If you feel weak or indecisive, you will betray it to your dog by your body language, tone of voice, and other behaviors. A complicating factor can be your family. It frequently happens that while one person in the family has control of the dog, the others, particularly children, do not. A naturally dominant

dog will repeatedly test his place against every member of the family. And while some guard dogs will decide that a child is an item to be protected rather than prey to be attacked or a lesser pack member to be dominated, you are running a risk with this kind of dog unless you supervise him very carefully.

The first thing to do is not allow your dog to display dominant behaviors towards you, such as growling over a food dish, guarding a toy, or the like. This does not mean punishing him; it means convincing him that he has nothing to fear. This isn't as easy as it sounds, and it doesn't mean continuing to approach him, murmuring, "Good boy, good boy" while the dog continues to growl. In fact, the first step in reducing stress is to lower your level of contact with the dog, especially when he seems excited or agitated.

Never assume that a dog "doesn't mean it" when he growls at you. A growl is just a bite that hasn't happened yet; it is part of the bite sequence. It may never happen, but it is a warning sign. It does not mean the dog hates you, but ignore it at your peril. Nor should you attempt to eliminate the growl without eliminating the stress that it represents. Refusing to allow a dog to growl (as some recommend) takes away an important element in his system of notifying you that

No Genetic Base

While it is well recognized that aggressive behavior has a genetic base, no single gene has ever been identified that "causes" aggression. Aggression is the result of other genetically determined behavior patterns, not a genetically coded behavior in itself.

something is wrong. If you get rid of the growl, you may end up with the bite. The key is to reduce the number of situations likely to elicit a growl.

People who claim their dog suddenly just went bonkers and bit them are probably mistaken. Unless the dog has a physical problem, such as a brain tumor (it's possible), he's been giving you signs for weeks or months about a possible aggressive move. You just didn't notice until it was too late. Dogs are much more attuned to our body language than we are to theirs.

Warning Signs

Learn the body language of a dog who may be thinking about attacking. He stands tall, a posture dog behaviorists call "on the muscle." His tail is high and possibly wagging slowly and rather stiffly. Do not mistake this for an invitation to play! His ears are pitched forward (at least in the case of dogs who have mobile ears). His hackles are raised, and he looks you straight in the eye. This is a natural sign of aggression in dogs and is so ancient that all domestic dogs have to learn over and over again from their loving owners that when we stare at them, we are not being menacing! A dog who's thinking of attacking may also growl or snarl; that's when you know you're in trouble.

Other kinds of dominant body language from dogs include mounting behavior, nudging with the nose, or placing a paw on your shoulder when you are sitting peaceably in your chair. Dominant dogs don't ask for attention—they demand it. They guard their food, toys, chews, or sleeping areas. They push kids out of their way without so much as a by-your-leave. They charge out doors ahead of you. They refuse to obey commands like "down" that place them in a vulnerable, submissive position. Males may mark. (Most dominant dogs are unneutered males, and most, for what it's worth, are purebred.)

The one good thing you can say about a purely dominant/aggressive dog is that his signs of aggression are easy to read and unmistakable. Things get trickier with a dog who bites from fear (called "sharp-shy dogs"), an animal whose aggression is even more strongly related to fear. This dog may present submissive behavior, such as crouching or flattening the ears. He won't look at you at all and may roll over and display his belly. But these are not happy animals. They often dislike grooming, especially having their feet touched. In fact, they don't like to be touched at all but are often so fearful that the bite comes when the person has stopped touching them and is walking away. They may also bite if they feel cornered. Because these dogs give so many mixed signals (to humans, anyway), it is usually said that they are "crazy" or aberrant. In reality, they are behaving with a logical consistency—to them.

Puppy Selection: Aggression is much easier to prevent than to cure, and it starts with selecting the right breed. Unless you are a strong and experienced owner, stay away from breeds (and breeding lines) that encourage or permit aggression. This includes Akitas, most Bull Terrier-type dogs, Rottweilers, and the like. Choose a breed for whom you can provide adequate exercise as well; an ordinarily exuberant dog may become stressed and aggressive if not provided a chance to run and play. Choose a breeder who stresses good temperament in her breeding program and who socializes and temperament tests the puppies in the litter.

When you bring your new pet home, make sure everyone in the family handles, feeds, and helps to train the dog. One person should, of course, be the coordinator of these activities, but if the entire family participates in the care of the dog, which should include formal socialization and obedience classes, your chances of raising a nonaggressive, happy, well-socialized dog are vastly improved.

If your puppy acts inappropriately, do not punish him—simply redirect his behavior into a more acceptable mode. For example, if the puppy is chewing your hand, distract him with treats or toys. The key is not to try to take your hand away, because the dog's instinct will make him grab harder; instead, you want the dog to remove his mouth. Then praise him. This illustrates a basic rule—never allow your potentially dominant dog to get away with anything. You must win every time. (You can "lose" with a submissive pet but not with a dominant one.) If he wins, he will advance to the next step, and you won't like it.

Teach your children to stand still, speak low, and act firmly when the puppy exhibits dominant behavior. Ask them to fold their arms, look off into the distance, and walk away. Soon the puppy will understand that aggressive actions result in

no playtime. Don't let the kids scream at the dog; it can trigger aggression. Never leave any dog alone with a baby or toddler, and allow older children unsupervised play with the family dog only after both parties have proved themselves responsible.

> If your dog behaves inappropriately, simply redirect his behavior into a more acceptable mode.

Take the puppy for many walks, and allow him to meet new people and animal friends in a positive way. The earlier you start, the better! Dogs have inherited from their wolf ancestors the ability to make immediate and bonding friendships, but if this process has not begun by the time the puppy is three months old, it becomes progressively more difficult.

To assert your leadership, always have the dog sit before his leash is attached, sit for meals, sit for treats, sit for any reward. If any particular person in the family is having trouble controlling or exercising dominance over him, that is the very person who needs to feed and walk him, making sure that the dog exhibits proper submissive behavior before engaging in any of these activities. The dog should be rewarded for all submissive behavior. Again, this does not apply to a dog who has bitten someone! Professional help is required in such cases.

What to Avoid: To avoid triggering aggression, don't permit a dangerous situation to develop. When it is safe (i.e., the dog isn't present), remove any possessions that cause a stress reaction in him. If he is food aggressive, get rid of the food bowl and hand-feed him until he figures out that you are the provider of food. If he is possession aggressive, take away his toys. If he is protective of the couch, don't let him sleep on it. Keep a leash attached to him, but don't reach over him to grab his collar. Don't kiss your dog or get your head anywhere near his head. (That is an aggressive action to a dog.) In other words, observe the kinds of behaviors that set him off (the so-called triggers) and omit them if you can. And never punish an aggressive behavior; that will only make it worse. Instead, reward non-aggressive behavior with a bit of delicious food.

If your dog tends towards dominance, don't go around petting and praising him all day simply for existing; such behavior tends to give the dominant dog a rather exalted notion of his own importance and may encourage him to take a stab at a

leadership position. In fact, a standard treatment for a dominant dog is for the entire family to totally ignore him (except for basic care) until the dominant behavior ceases. Submissive dogs, on the other hand, need to have their weak egos boosted by praise, and lots of attention tends to improve their self-confidence. The basic rule is, the more confident the dog, the less petting and praise should be handed out. This is why gentler, less dominant dogs are best for nearly everyone—because petting dogs is fun!

None of this is meant to punish the dog, and it is imperative that you stay calm and relaxed yourself. The point is to remove the stress trigger. Use treats to reward nonaggressive behavior instead. It is a long, drawn-out, difficult job, and one that will need the help of a trained dog behaviorist. Don't overestimate your own ability to handle the situation.

Be aware that no matter how successfully you retrain your aggressive dog, he will remain a dominant or sharp-shy animal and can be never be completely trusted, especially around children or strangers. Once a dog has bitten, his bite inhibition may be lowered forever.

If you do have an aggressive dog, you'll need to find a trained behaviorist to work with you. Get in touch with an experienced behaviorist who is qualified to work with an aggressive dog.

BARKING (NUISANCE BARKING)

Between 13 and 35 percent of behavior complaints by dog owners concern what is termed "nuisance barking." The problem is exacerbated if you live in an apartment or condominium with thin walls.

"Overbarking" is something that is defined by human levels of tolerance, though some breeds in particular are barky—Beagles, Shetland Sheepdogs, German Shepherd Dogs, Yorkshire Terriers, and Dachshunds top the list.

Barking is one of dogs' most annoying and difficult-to-break habits, particularly since barking in itself is a normal canine activity. It is also one of the dog's most effective ways to communicate with you. And while you don't want to reward annoying barking, it is also not reasonable to ignore a dog who is so clearly trying to say something important.

What You Can Do

The first step in solving the problem is to identify the cause. While some experts suggest that nuisance barkers bark for "no particular reason," I submit that that view is nonsense. Just because you do not know the reason does not mean there is no reason.

Medical Causes: In a few cases, especially if the dog doesn't have a history of barking, the problem could be medical. The barking might signal pain, so it's worth a trip to the vet for a complete physical.

Loneliness or Boredom: In some cases, barking may be a sign of loneliness or separation anxiety, a condition that is treated later in this chapter. In most cases, a dog barks to draw your attention to something—perhaps it's to himself. Attention-seeking behavior is one of the most common causes of barking. He may be saying "I'm bored and lonely out here! Bring me in or come outside with me!" Or he may be trying to draw your attention to a robber, wildlife, a kid on a bike, the mail person, or strange visitors from outer space only he can see.

> The first step in solving problem barking is to identify the cause.

Internal Conversation: More rarely, the dog is talking to himself. I've known several individuals from hunting backgrounds (mostly Beagles) who found enormous joy in walking about, staring at the ground, and barking. One was named Topper. I could almost hear him saying "Whoa, I see a mouse ran by here and over there, hmm—a squirrel—and, er—the Cocker next door must have peed on this rock and hmm—wow! What's this, a meadow vole? Hmm...."

Alert: While most people enjoy having a dog alert them to visitors, many dogs alert to any visitor, including squirrels, birds, and falling leaves. I had a Gordon Setter who barked at the air-conditioning unit.

Recreational Barking: Some dogs just seem to bark for fun, whether you are with them or not.

Demand Barking: Some dogs bark for a treat, a ride, or a walk. In most cases, the dog senses that the treat or ride or walk is in the offing and responds to these signals with a joyful bark. Smarter dogs may take the lead and think that the treat or ride or walk was in response to their barking, so they decide to urge you along a bit.

In any case, incessant barking is annoying, not just to you but also to your neighbors. So one thing you cannot do about barking is just let it continue. For one thing, dogs don't get tired of barking very easily. You'd think they would, but they don't. Some dogs in my neighborhood are ignored by their owners 24 hours a day, and they bark constantly. Dogs under a year old who are left outside tend to turn into the most stubborn barkers.

While some sources tell you to avoid all interaction with the attention-seeking dog, including eye contact, by the time the dog figures out that he is being ignored and stops barking, your eviction notice may be in the mail. While you might be able to outlast your dog and ignore him until he stops barking, you can be sure your neighbors aren't going to be so patient. However, if you live in a fairly soundproofed area, you can try ignoring his ruckus. When doing this, supervise him carefully and give him a treat and your company for being quiet. This works best if the dog is an in-house barker. When he barks for attention, just get up and leave the room quietly. Soon he will learn that barking for attention doesn't lead to the desired result. Unfortunately, most dogs bark outside the house, not inside. First of all, there is more to bark at out there, and second,

> Between 13 and 35 percent of behavior complaints by dog owners concern what is termed "nuisance barking."

half the time they are barking because they want to come in.

If your dog is outside and barking (assuming this annoys you or the neighbors), bring him in. If you bring your dog in every time he barks, he will learn to stop barking. If he is barking because he wants to come in, you will satisfy his needs and spare the neighbors. Do not allow him to go on barking and barking endlessly. Another option is to go out and play with the dog, but be forewarned—you're teaching him that barking gets extra playtime with you, something you may not want him to learn.

If your dog is outside barking for the glory of barking, make him come in immediately—he may get the idea that the only way to stay out and have fun is to be quiet. (Then again, he may not.) And then there are situations in which you cannot be at home with your dog and he barks while you are gone, upsetting the neighbors. In this case, the dog may be suffering from separation anxiety, which is a particular problem when you live in an apartment! With a problem dog, you need to be the kind of owner who can provide the consistent training your dog really needs.

A demand-barking dog will continue to bark whenever he wants something. In this case, he is training you; you have to untrain the dog. When you get out the treat box and he barks, put it back. Do the same with the leash for walking—only when the dog sits quietly without barking do you reward him with the treat or leash.

For indoor barkers, it sometimes works to muffle stimuli by closing curtains and generally masking the environment. In other cases, it may help to give the dog more stimuli to occupy his mind. It depends on whether the dog is barking in response to stimuli or out of sheer boredom.

The first thing to do if you're not getting results is consult a professional trainer who can work with you and your dog. See Chapter 8 for advice and information on finding the right trainer for you.

If all else fails, you may have to resort to an anti-bark collar. There are two major types: electric (which I do not recommend) and citronella.

The electric collar is largely considered inhumane. It works by delivering an adjustable jolt of electricity whenever the dog barks.

The electric collar delivers an adjustable jolt of juice when a vibration sensor in the collar detects barking. Electric collars are illegal in most of Europe, being considered too inhumane for use on pets. I think the Europeans are quite right. Using a device that relies on pain to get results will too often actually make the problem worse and can even unleash aggressive behavior.

The only humane anti-bark collar is the citronella collar, and it should be used along with behavior modification. It releases a spray of citronella fragrance (which most dogs hate, although you might find it rather nice and possibly preferable to the way your dog smells normally) under the chin when a microphone in the collar registers barking. These collars were first marketed in the United States in 1995, although they've been used in Europe for years. It is not only more humane than the electronic shock collar, it is actually more effective, according to a test conducted by the Animal Behavior Clinic at Cornell's College of Veterinary Medicine. Dog owners preferred it as well, according to a report in *Journal of the American Animal Hospital Association*. (Having said this, I should mention Topper, the Beagle/Basset cross, who positively enjoyed his citronella collar and delighted in setting it off.) You also have to be careful in adjusting this collar because a maladjusted citronella collar can pick up the sounds of other dogs' barking and release a puff of the hated citronella into your own dog's face, and that definitely would not be fair. Citronella can also stain furniture, so be forewarned. These collars are meant as supplements to, not replacements for, behavioral modification.

The most radical solution is "debarking," a surgical procedure that reduces the bark to a hoarse, ragged, whispery sound. It sounds inhumane, but some experts make a strong case for the fact that in the dog's mind, it probably doesn't matter what kind of sound he is making. Still, the American Animal Hospital Association (AAHA) recommends that canine devocalization only be performed by a licensed veterinarian and only as a final option, when all behavioral modification avenues to correct the excessive barking have been explored and have failed. This should be a last resort, but it is certainly better than euthanasia. New Jersey has passed legislation that makes it illegal to debark a dog unless a veterinarian can substantiate that there is a medical need for it.

Again, barking is a behavior that can only be managed, not "cured." Barking is a natural, genetic, ingrained behavior that is natural for most dogs and a way of life for some.

CHASING

Chase behavior is an integral part of the dog's prey drive. When things run, most dogs chase them. The prey drive can be activated by sight, smell, or sound. This is not a behavior that can be easily cured—only managed. If small animals or cars activate your dog, you will simply have to keep him leashed when these objects are likely to make an appearance. I would not trust a dog with a powerful prey drive to answer to "Come!" if a rabbit is running in the other direction. This same drive makes certain individual dogs unsafe around cats.

What You Can Do

You cannot train a dog with a strong prey drive not to chase or even kill the family cat. The dog may bide his time, but eventually disaster will strike. You must keep such dogs separated from the cat or at least under supervision.

CHEWING

Chewing is certainly a normal behavior, especially for puppies. It is a puppy's way to find out things about the world, after all. Dog chewing goes through distinct phases as the dog ages, and each stage can become more destructive. A chewing puppy is not as destructive as a chewing adult. At the age of three to four months, the adult teeth are beginning to form under the gums; most puppy chewing at this stage is done to learn about the world. The teeth begin to erupt from four to six months, and chewing actually helps ease the teething pain. When the adult teeth fully come in (6-12 months) and the dog is still chewing everything in sight, it can be disaster time. Most adult chewers come from shelters or pounds, and their behavior is a way of relieving stress, just like people chewing their fingernails. (If only dogs would chew their toenails, we wouldn't have to clip them.)

However, when the dog starts chewing on the furniture, bedding, and kids, it becomes a problem. Dogs do need to chew, so make sure there is an appropriate outlet for his chewing, such as a variety of chew toys on hand. Some dogs chew gently and happily on a toy for months or even years without destroying it. Others belong to the kill, rip, and tear school of thought. These dogs run through a toy in five minutes, so you have to be creative. You can make disposable chewable toys by knotting up dishtowels.

What You Can Do

Provide your dog with interesting toys—but not a boxful of them. Too many distractions make the dog even more distractible; soon he'll start looking for something else to chew. The more things your dog has to chew, the wider the chewable universe seems to him. My training mentor Laura Hussey solved the problem with her "hedgehog solution." All her dogs' toys look like hedgehogs. The rule is, "If it looks like a hedgehog, it's chewable; if it doesn't, it's not." Find some toy that your dog really enjoys, and make that his chewing outlet.

You can make or buy a toy box, which can be placed in the living room or kitchen. Make the toy box easily accessible. Soon your dog will learn where his toys are and get them out when he wants to play with them. I'm afraid he probably won't put them back, though. If your dog ignores his toys, you can show him how much fun they really are by playing with them yourself.

If your dog is chewing out of boredom, try giving him more vigorous outdoor exercise, perhaps borrowing another dog to play with. A tired dog is a good dog, as they say.

Simple good management can avert a lot of inappropriate chewing. Keep your shoes in the closet, and keep the closet closed. Put away the not-to-be-chewed throw rugs and other movable objects. And certainly remove possibly poisonous plants. (For a list of poisonous plants, see Chapter 4.) Tape down electrical wires close to the floor or wall. If your dog chews furniture, there are a variety of bitter-tasting commercial sprays available that won't hurt the furniture or upholstery but will keep your puppy from chewing them. They work, so use them liberally and frequently. But remember, your young dog has to chew something—so make that something fun and easily available.

One special subdivision of chewing is mouthing, or puppy biting. It is easy to teach your puppy not to chew on you by crying "Ouch!" in a high hurt voice. If he doesn't take his mouth away immediately, gently take his nose and remove his mouth from your hand or whatever body part he happens to be chewing on. Do not try to pull your hand away—that encourages a clamping-down reflex and may make the problem worse.

The first step is to get control of the situation. You can do that by cutting down on the amount of liberty the dog has—in fact, you might have to actually tether the dog to you for starters, or at least keep him in the same room with you.

COPROPHAGIA (STOOL EATING)

As disgusting as eating feces is to human beings (at least to most of us), it's quite normal and natural in dogs. Mother dogs eat the stools of their young to keep the puppies clean. Coprophagia comes in several interesting varieties: There are dogs who eat their own feces (autocoprophagia), dogs who eat the feces of other dogs (intraspecific coprophagia), and dogs who eat the feces of other animals (interspecific coprophagia). They all seem equally annoying.

Usually, this habit causes no serious problems for the afflicted dog, although there are some important exceptions to this. The most critical is the possibility of ingesting internal parasites. Also, certain diseases like hepatitis and canine parvovirus can be transmitted in this way. The most dangerous is *Toxoplasma gondii*, which can be transmitted in some cat feces. This organism causes many problems of the central nervous system and also a variety of other issues, including muscle damage. Unfortunately, most dogs can't resist cat poop. If you have a cat, you'll have to keep the litter box in a place inaccessible to the dog. (Some people put a cat door in the bathroom door and keep it shut.)

In a few cases, coprophagia may be due to medical problems like exocrine pancreatic insufficiency, pancreatitis, intestinal infections, malabsorptive syndromes, and overeating on a high-fat diet. But in nearly all these cases, the dog will have other symptoms to alert you that something is wrong.

In some cases, the dog is exhibiting attention-seeking behavior. (He gets yelled at, and that is attention.) In other cases, dogs may be imitating their owners as best they can—after all, good owners pick up dog poop. Or they could be copying other dogs. In a few cases, submissive dogs have been noted consuming the feces of more dominant dogs, perhaps trying to imbibe some of that dominance themselves. Or they may be hungry, especially if they are fed only once a day. Or perhaps they just enjoy the taste. Whatever your dog is eating that he shouldn't (a medical condition we call pica), never punish the dog. It won't work and will weaken the bond between the two of you. And in the rare case where the dog is eating something he shouldn't in order to gain your attention, it worked. Even punishment is attention.

What You Can Do

Many treatments have been offered to break dogs from this habit, including adding meat tenderizer to the diet. The theory is it adds important enzymes that help break down nutrients, so the dog gets better nutrition and doesn't need the feces, or else finds them less nutritious.

Forbid is a powdered supplement that supposedly makes feces taste bad, even to dogs. It is available by veterinary prescription only. Deter is an over-the-counter pill that does the same thing. Some people even recommend putting hot sauce on the feces in order to (eventually) create a permanent deterrent. I think in all cases it is better and healthier just to pick up the poop. In serious cases, you might consider a basket muzzle when the dog is outside. A study conducted at the Canine Behaviour Institute, Queen's University, Belfast, showed that citronella spray collars were also effective.

One solution, especially if the activity is due to boredom, is to give your dog plenty of exercise. Supervise him as much as possible as well. Holistic practitioners suggest that perhaps the dog isn't making enough digestive enzymes. In that case, supplementation is possible; they can be sprinkled on the dog's food. In some cases, it helps to increase the amount of dietary fiber your dog is eating.

Counter surfing is a difficult habit to break because it is natural for a dog to scavenge food.

COUNTER SURFING AND SIMILAR THIEVISH ACTIVITIES

Some dogs are inveterate counter surfers. Turn your back on them for a second and they are gobbling up the lasagna. This is an extremely difficult behavior to break because it is so natural.

What You Can Do

The best way to handle the problem is to change your own habits. Just put the food away and don't leave it where the dog can get at it. That's healthier for him, too.

You can also try a few simple tricks to discourage him. They're so simple they don't always work, but you can try. The most famous method is the booby trap. This involves stacking several soda cans precariously on the counter and attaching them to the target item with a couple of feet (m) of string and duct tape. Of course, you need to set out "bait"—some safe but appealing food like barbecue or liver. The idea is that while the dog will get the treat, he will learn that the attached cans that rattle scarily make it not worth

the struggle. This may work—and then again, it may not. Some dogs enjoy rattling soda cans around the house, and many will only learn not to eat anything that has a string and soda cans attached.

One surefire method not to solve the problem is to allow the dog the run of the house. What generally happens is that you see the dog snatch something, catch him running through the house with the stolen object, and then scream or start chasing him. This generally results in the dog swallowing whatever he had in his mouth.

DIGGING

Dogs have a reason for turning your yard into a minefield, even though the reason may not be apparent to you.

- Your dog may be hot. Digging down into the cool soil is both soft and refreshing. This kind of behavior is very often seen with heavily coated dogs.
- He may be bored. Dogs left alone outside for long periods of time need to do something to while away the empty hours.
- He may be giving way to predatory instincts. There are a lot of moles and other underground prey scampering just below the surface.
- He may be trying to escape. This can be a combination of wanderlust, boredom, loneliness, and predatory instinct—all the good game is outside the fence.
- She may be pregnant. You're looking at normal nesting behavior.
- He may be having fun. Lots of dogs enjoy digging, especially in soft earth, just for the fun of it, the way kids will play in a sandbox.

What You Can Do

The solution partly depends on the cause. If your dog is bored and lonely, entertain him, exercise

him, and give him more of your company. Most people seriously underexercise their dogs. If he is trying to escape, make sure he can't. In some cases, this requires installing some cement below the fence line. If she is pregnant, find her a suitable whelping box. If he's hot, bring him inside (where I hope it's air conditioned). And if he is digging for the pure pleasure of it, install a sandbox full of fresh soft earth in an appropriate place in your yard and encourage him to dig there by loading it up with hidden bits of food and special toys. Play there yourself until he gets the idea, and spray forbidden areas with a dog repellent. (There are plenty of them on the market.) By the way, if you are fertilizing your yard with bone or blood meal, the scent could be teasing your dog into believing there's something really good buried in your yard.

JUMPING UP

Dogs jump up in happy greetings. This is because they want to get face to face with you and have no way of knowing this is not what you want. Flailing your arms or yelling "Stop it!" usually has no effect. In fact, lots of loud noises and arm motions convince your dog that an interesting game is afoot. The problem is compounded because (admit it) sometimes you permit jumping and sometimes you don't. How is the dog supposed to know when it is okay to jump and when it's not when you haven't made up your mind yourself? And certainly your dog can't be expected to know that your visiting friends love it when he jumps up but your Great Aunt Ida does not. He can't tell the difference between grubby clothes and dress-up duds, either.

What You Can Do

You can solve the problem by teaching your dog a jump command and allowing him to jump only when you give it. An alternative way of teaching

Bone Burying

Everyone knows that dogs bury bones, but not everyone knows why. The reason lies deep within the canine collective memory. When dogs were wolves, no one could be sure of getting a meal every day. The smartest thing to do then was to hide, or cache, leftovers from other members of the pack. Bones are filled with nutritious marrow and work well to tide one over during hungry times. So even though your pet dog is well fed, his genetic heritage may compel him to hide bits of his dinner in the yard, under the sofa, or even behind the pillows.

him not to jump is to grab the dog's paws when he leaps up and hold them past the time when he wants to get down. A few episodes of being held up will usually convince him that four feet on the floor is a better model of behavior. But you must be consistent with whatever discouraging behavior you want to use.

You can also teach your dog not to jump by steadfastly crossing your arms and looking away when he does it. You have to be consistent and do it every time. Or you can give him an alternate method of greeting, like sitting; only be sure you reward him by bending down close to him when he is quiet. You'll also need to practice; try going in and out the door several times, over and over. If you only do it once or twice a day, he may not learn the lesson. If you start training him when his excitement level is low, he'll remember better when you come home after having been gone a really long time—like an hour. Keep working at it to get the results you want.

NUDGING

Dogs tend to nose people, and if they are tall enough, they nudge them in the genital or anal area. While this is perfectly good manners for dogs, most people find it offensive. Dogs also tend to nudge at mealtimes. Our first instinct is to push off the nudging dog, but unfortunately, this has the effect of convincing him we are joining in play behavior.

What You Can Do

If possible, the best response is to turn away or otherwise ignore the nudging. You may wish to give an alternate command such as sit or stay. Or firmly remove him from the room.

REFUSING THE RECALL (NOT COMING WHEN CALLED)

This is probably the most common, aggravating, and dangerous misbehavior. It is more common in naturally adventurous, independent breeds such as hounds and least apt to occur in retrievers. If you don't start working with a naturally independent dog to come when called very early, you are fighting an uphill battle.

What You Can Do

To make your task easier, keep in mind some essential dos and don'ts:

- Don't call your dog to punish him, medicate him, bathe him, or provide further training.
- Don't chase him. (That's a game.)
- Do encourage him to come by kneeling and opening your arms or by moving away from him so that he can use his natural inclination to chase.
- Don't scream. Use an encouraging, friendly voice.
- Do offer high-value treats for resisters, like pieces of beef or chicken.

- Do praise him, do something fun, and then let him do something else.

No matter how perfect your dog gets at recall, you can never be 100 percent sure he will come to you (or even stay with you) under any given situation. A sudden item of great interest may flash across his field of vision or smell, and he will be gone. For a Beagle, for example, nothing in the world can compete with a rabbit racing across his path. That's why they make leashes.

PSYCHOLOGICAL PROBLEMS

Sometimes the balance tips from a normal (albeit annoying) behavior to a real psychological problem. I define the difference this way: problem behavior is normal for a dog, although it may be driving you crazy. A psychological problem is a problem for the dog as well. Like human beings, domestic dogs are subject to many psychological problems, including obsessive-compulsive disorders, separation anxiety, phobias, and panic disorders. Perhaps it is the price we all pay for living in such a civilized society. (It has been estimated that 1 out of every 50 dogs suffers from a compulsive disorder.)

Obsessions and phobias are primarily medical problems, even if they have a behavioral origin. The source is usually some sort of conflict or stress. Before treating the condition, you need to address the source of conflict or stress. One way to do this is to give the animal as much control over his environment as possible. Animals who feel trapped, bored, or stressed are even more likely to become or remain obsessive. Overattendance to the obsessive dog is also a no-no. As with

Getting Help

Aggression and many obsessions are beyond the capacity of the average dog owner to deal with. If you have a problem dog (or more likely, a dog with problems), it is only smart to find the best professional help you can for the problem. To find a qualified consultant, check with your veterinarian, kennel club, or trusted trainer. When you have your recommendation, contact the consultant. Be prepared both to ask questions and to give information.

When giving information, it is essential to be absolutely honest. Underplaying or exaggerating the dog's misbehavior will not serve anyone. Be as complete as possible in describing the problem, noting especially when and where it began and under what circumstances.

Don't be afraid to ask a few questions yourself. First, discover what the therapist's basic principles of therapy are; avoid those who work with punishing equipment. How long and often will the therapy sessions be? Good therapists will work with you, not for you. Therapy for behavior problems is always a joint effort. Is the consultant permitted to prescribe medications? Find out exactly what happens at the sessions and what equipment will be needed. And of course, you will need to know the cost.

Nearly every canine problem behavior has a solution. The solution may be expensive and time consuming, and it may require a radical repositioning in your relationship with your dog. On the other hand, it may be nothing more than a simple, easy-to-manage change in your own attitude.

a stressed aggressive dog, the best therapy is sometimes to step back and allow the dog to cool down. If the strange behavior does not cease, your veterinary behaviorist may resort to such medications as fluoxetine (Prozac), paroxetine (Paxil), fluvoxamine (Luvox), or other anti-obsessional drug therapy.

The great secret to having a sane dog is to make an emotional, heartfelt commitment to it. Dogs know very well when you are feeling ambivalent or when you are not sure if you want to keep him—particularly dogs who have come from a shelter. These dogs have already had one bad experience with abandonment, so to protect themselves they are prepared for another. Another way to help keep your dog sane is to provide a safe (but interesting), consistent environment.

Here are a few of the more common psychological problems exhibited by domestic dogs. In all cases, early intervention, exercise, and veterinary consultation are critical. If possible, distract the dog from the destructive behavior and provide him with a healthy, acceptable alternative. Punishment is never effective or kind.

Cage Rage

Also called barrier anxiety, this problem most commonly occurs in shelter dogs, puppy mill dogs, or in animals who have been neglected. (Many of them have previously spent months in solitary confinement in a cage.) This results in many cage-raised dogs who consider the cage their own (and only) territory, their only "safe place," and they will defend it with vigor. To make things worse, a caged dog has no "flight" option, and all he can do is attack. Other animals may respond to their enforced confinement with hyperactivity.

What You Can Do

With a dog like this, the first thing you have to do is remove the hated crate. Once the animal feels calm and safe in his new environment, you can reintroduce it and encourage him to use it by leaving it open while you feed him there. It will probably be a long time before he's willing to stay there quietly if the door is shut. Be patient. By the time he's secure, he may not need a crate. I never crate any of my dogs until they are ill or traveling, and they are just fine.

House Soiling

When a previously housetrained dog seems to forget his housetraining, there may be a medical problem, such as colitis, inflammatory bowel disease, diabetes mellitus, a bladder stone, a urinary tract infection, inflammation of the prostate gland, hormone responsive incontinence, Cushing's disease, or kidney or liver disease. An older dog with arthritis might be too stiff to get to the door quickly enough! And many older dogs are victims of canine cognitive dysfunction (CCD), one of the signs of which is incontinence.

What You Can Do

Unless you have good reason to suspect the

problem is stress related or psychological, have these conditions checked out first.

If it's not a physiological problem, go back to the beginning and refresh your dog's housetraining lessons. (See Chapter 8.)

Paw Licking

A number of bored, stressed dogs develop an annoying and possibly harmful habit of licking or chewing their paws. If allowed to continue, your dog can develop a case of lick granuloma, a permanently sore and swollen paw.

What You Can Do

Take care of the problem early by attempting to distract the dog from his chewing.

If that doesn't work, take a topical arthritis product and place a little on the fur. It tastes so bad that most dogs won't lick their paws again. If worse comes to worst, you may need to put your dog on an antidepressant.

Separation Anxiety

It has been estimated that up to 20 percent of American dogs suffer from separation anxiety. It has a high incidence in rescued animals. Unfortunately, many owners unwittingly support their dog's problem by overstimulating him when they are at home, loading him up on kisses, pats, and affection. The inevitable withdrawal that occurs when the owner leaves for work produces severe stress in vulnerable dogs.

Signs of separation anxiety include pre-departure anxiety, loss of appetite, heavy salivation or drooling, whining or yelping, loss of housetraining, pacing and licking of the coat, destruction of property, and desperate escape measures (including going through windows). To be classed as true separation anxiety, this behavior only occurs when the owner is absent. When the owner returns, she may notice exaggerated greetings and Velcro-like behavior on the part of the dog, who will follow the owner from room to room, never leaving her side.

Remember that although your dog may not be the center of your world, you are the center of his. Perhaps you may consider curing separation anxiety the natural way—take him to doggy day care and let him get the companionship and exercise he needs.

There is a high incidence of separation anxiety in rescue dogs.

Give a dog with separation anxiety the companionship and exercise he needs.

What You Can Do

Many people try to treat separation anxiety by crating the dog. Unfortunately, unless the dog is already used to and enjoys his crate, it has the opposite of the desired effect. Dogs with separation anxiety who are caged often develop barrier or enclosure anxiety. Never punish a dog with separation anxiety; it will only make his condition worse, since any kind of stress on your part contributes to stress in your dog.

Make leave-takings and arrivals casual. If you are relaxed, maybe your dog will be also. To this end, you might want to change your "departure cues." Dogs associate alarm clocks, rattling keys, and even lipstick application with imminent departure. While you can't do much about the alarm clock except to get rid of it, you can change the order of many of your other leave-taking rituals. The point is not to give the dog enough time to get stressed out. While working to desensitize your dog, start with very brief absences (10 or 15 seconds). Gradually extend the absences. The

biggest mistake people make is not giving their dog enough time to get used to things. Even smart dogs take a lot of time to develop patience. If you want your dog to learn patience, you'll have to be patient yourself. Treat your dog to a Nylabone or other safe chewable treat. (This should be a special treat that he doesn't get at any other time.) It will not only keep him busy but also teach him to associate your leaving with at least one good thing.

Some dogs take alone time best if they are kept in a quiet room without a lot of outside distractions. Others thrive on at least being able to look through the window. Decide what works best for your pet by trying both.

Therapy may include more exercise, counter-conditioning, lifestyle change, and medication containing clomipramine hydrochloride, such as Clomicalm. Clomicalm is a tricyclic antidepressant that works on the neurotransmitter system in the brain. It blocks the uptake of serotonin and norepinephrine in the brain, leaving these substances free to work their magic of reducing stress. Pheromone therapy, a plug-in system that delivers soothing, dog-appeasing hormones through the air to comfort your dog, also works. You may want to switch the dog's food to one lower in protein. In mild cases, distracting the dog by hiding food or interesting items around the house sometimes works. Sometimes, but not always, getting a second dog as a companion for the dog suffering separation anxiety will help relieve the condition.

Shyness

Shyness is mostly inherited. In fact, shy people— and presumably, dogs—have a different structure of the amygdala (a part of the brain) than do extroverts. A congenitally shy dog will never become a roaring extrovert. However, most owners of shy dogs make the problem worse by overprotecting their dog and reinforcing his fear. Consoling a fearful dog convinces him that something must indeed be terribly wrong, or perhaps he perceives the attention as praise. At any rate, it doesn't work.

What You Can Do

To combat shyness, expose your shy dog to positive, fun experiences. You can take him for lots of walks, rides, or even enroll him in a socialization class. Every experience should be one of enjoyment, praise, and treats. Some people suggest yawning at your dog. In the dog world, yawning is a calming signal, and it is hypothesized that repeated yawning will help calm the animal. Playing with your dog is another great way to build confidence. If you play tug-of-war, let the dog win. If your dog fears the veterinarian, try taking him for several brief visits just for treats handed out by the white-coated staff. Punishment, of course, only serves to strengthen shyness.

Tail Chasing

Tail chasing is a part of normal play behavior in dogs; however, it sometimes becomes so excessive that the dog can actually hurt himself. When the behavior becomes so obsessive or ritualistic that the dog cannot be distracted from it, there's a real problem. (Oddly, Bull Terriers seem to have more of a propensity towards obsessive tail chasing than do other breeds.)

Obsessive tail chasing may start when a dog becomes bored, underexercised, or anxious. Or it may begin as a way to attract the owner's attention, which it certainly does! The owner may laugh or even say "Stop it, Fido!" but in either case, the dog has received what he wants— attention.

To combat shyness, expose your dog to positive, fun experiences.

Thunderphobia

Fear of thunder is a problem noted especially in herding and hunting breeds, dogs who historically worked outdoors and for whom thunderstorms were a very real danger.

What You Can Do

Anti-anxiety drugs (like Xanax or others prescribed by your veterinarian) work if the problem is crippling. There is also a mechanical aid in the form of an anxiety wrap, a wrapping that maintains light pressure to help reduce stress. More information can be found at www.anxietywrap.com. One of the newest therapies is Comfort Zone, a plug-in product that releases dog-appeasing pheromones. (The same substance is used for separation anxiety.) Some people have also had luck with melatonin or plain old Valium. In many cases, a combination of tactics works best.

What You Can Do

As with other obsessive-compulsive behaviors, tail chasing may require a combination of drug therapy and behavior modification.

Some neurological conditions may also cause this behavior. If you notice the behavior in your dog, take notes about when and how often it occurs, and try to think back to when it started and what your response to it was. If there is no neurological cause (determined by your veterinarian), then a good first step is to totally ignore the behavior, no matter what. At first, the dog may try harder to attract your attention, and the behavior may get worse. Any kind of attention (even negative attention) will just compound the problem. In some cases, drugs have proved helpful.

PART THREE

CARING FOR YOUR DOG'S

HEALTH AND WELLNESS

10

PESTS

Fleas and ticks didn't get where they are today by being stupid. They are creatures of opportunity, and owners who relax their vigilance even briefly may wake up to a flea-bitten dog. Let's take a look at a few of these unwelcome guests.

FLEAS

Fleas are brown, bloodsucking, wingless insects, and there are more than 2,000 species of them worldwide. Apparently they don't need wings, since with their three pairs of legs, they can jump pretty high (about 7 feet [2 m]). Once a flea lands on your dog, it can start sucking blood within eight minutes. Fleas have specialized mouthparts to pierce skin and siphon blood. As the flea sucks, it injects saliva to keep the blood flowing. Dogs who are allergic to the protein in the saliva can develop flea allergy dermatitis—the most common skin disease in dogs. Fleas also carry tapeworm eggs, which they share with your dog.

Two days after taking a blood meal, the female flea is ready to reproduce. She can lay hundreds of eggs directly on the dog, but most fall off onto the ground, floor, or whatever the dog is lying on. The eggs hatch into larvae that live in rugs, bedding, or any dark corner. Each larva ingests any organic matter—dandruff, specks of blood—it can find. Larvae develop into pupae that hatch into adults. The adult flea then emerges from the pupa and leaps onto its host—your dog (or you, if your dog isn't around). The whole process takes about three weeks under favorable (warm and humid) conditions, but the pupae can lie dormant for months.

Most of a flea's adult life is lived right on your dog, although eggs and immature fleas can be found all over your house. Tiny as they are, enough fleas can cause anemia in a small puppy or kitten. Dogs who are not allergic to fleas may not scratch, thus fooling their owners into thinking they are not infested with

Inspect your dog for fleas after he's been playing outside.

them. The truth is, your puppy could be loaded with the bloodsucking monsters.

To check for fleas, look for flea dirt—black pepper-like specks in the fur. Flea dirt is actually dried blood from your pet excreted by the flea. Even if you don't actually see any live fleas, if there is flea dirt, there are fleas.

What You Can Do

Luckily, fleas are easy to treat, and there is a plethora of products on the market to help your war against them, including the old standbys: flea shampoos, sprays, rinses, and collars. But you're no longer limited to these short-lived and bothersome remedies.

Newer flea treatments (both oral and topical) focus on prevention, which is always preferable to treatment. Nowadays you can choose a "flea birth control," which is available in monthly oral tablets or a topical adulticide applied to the dog's coat, between the shoulders, once a month. The medication is absorbed into the skin and spreads throughout the body. If a dog is heavily infested, your vet may start out with a fast-acting flea-killing tablet that contains nitenpryam (like Capstar) that kills biting fleas in 30 minutes. Capstar has no known side effects, although it only works for 24 hours. With all of these options, no dog in the modern world has to have fleas.

Common Fleas

This may be adding insult to injury, but the most common type of flea to afflict your dog is the cat flea, *Ctenocephalides felis.*

Flea Populations

Fleas are tougher than previously thought, remaining active even during cold weather. However, the highest flea infestations are in still in the South. Fleas are least numerous in February.

Look for these ingredients in other anti-flea products:

- Selamectin, used in a monthly topical prescription (like Revolution) that kills fleas, heartworm, and one species of tick, the American Dog Tick.
- Fipronil, used in a monthly topical prescription (like Frontline) that kills adult fleas and ticks.
- Imidacloprid and permethrin, used in a product like K-9 Advantix, which controls fleas, ticks, and repels mosquitoes.

Many of these products are dangerous for cats, so do not use them on the family feline.

It helps to clean your dog's toys every week in warm soapy water—especially stuffed toys that could harbor fleas. The same goes for his bedding and collar. If your whole house is infested, however, you'll still have to go to environmental control—vacuuming (stick flea killer or a chopped up flea collar in the bag and dispose of the bag afterwards), spraying, and using carpet powder. If the fleas are outside (they like shady, moist, debris-filled areas), rake the lawn and prune your trees. Sunlight is a major enemy of fleas.

FUNGAL INFECTIONS
Blastomycosis

Blastomycosis is a deadly yeast or fungus found in moist soil, usually emerging in the fall in certain regions of the US. It releases spores into the air that both people and dogs can inhale. It infects

up the infection from other dogs, different kinds of animals, or even from the soil. It is contagious to people, though animals and people with weak immune systems are the most likely victims. Your vet may be able to diagnose ringworm with a tool called Wood's Light, under which the most common ringworm culprit (microsporum canis) will glow green. Your vet may also want to look at some hairs to check for spores or even do a biopsy. Treatment includes disinfecting the environment with bleach, vacuuming, and steam cleaning.

What You Can Do

Oral medications include griseofulvin (to be given with a fatty meal) and itraconazole (which can cause nausea in many animals). Treatment must continue for a couple of months to be safe. Topical treatments or twice-weekly lime sulfur dips can also be used. It also appears that certain flea medications may help treat or prevent ringworm. Although ringworm will probably go away (in about four months) on its own, it's much better to treat it right away so that the whole family doesn't come down with it.

FLIES

While flies aren't usually noted for causing a specific dog disease, there is a new exception: leishmaniasis (visceral canine leishmaniasis), an exotic disease prevalent in southern Europe but now seen in many states. The disease is actually a protozoal infection that is primarily carried by sand flies, at least in Europe. No one really knows how it got to the US and how it is transmitted here. Leishmaniasis can be transmitted to human beings and can be fatal to dogs. Signs of the disease include debilitation and kidney failure.

What You Can Do

There is no cure, although remission does occur.

the lungs, bones, joints, lymph nodes, kidneys, and brain. Symptoms include fever, lack of appetite, weight loss, and coughing, among others.

Newer flea products focus on prevention, which is always preferable to treatment.

What You Can Do

The disease can be treated with newer generation anti-fungal medications, but the therapy is expensive. Without treatment, the disease is fatal; with treatment, survival rate is about 85 percent.

Ringworm

Ringworm is not a worm but a skin infection caused by fungi (dermatophytes) that feed on the dead cells of the skin and hair, sometimes leaving a dry, gray, scaly patch. Dogs can pick

GIARDIA

Giardia is a one-celled parasite found in ponds, streams, springs, and contaminated tap water. It is a common intestinal parasite that is hard to diagnose. Giardia affects both human beings and dogs, causing vomiting, diarrhea, and fever, although some dogs remain asymptomatic. Dogs who spend a lot of time outdoors are most at risk. Because infected dogs shed the critter in their feces, another dog can pick it up that way because the organism can survive for months in the environment. Veterinarians use the ELISA (enzyme-linked immunosorbent assay) test to diagnose the disease.

What You Can Do

A vaccine exists to prevent giardia, but it's

> Giardia is a one-celled parasite found in ponds, streams, springs, and contaminated tap water.

recommended only for high-risk dogs. It does not prevent infection but does reduce or prevent cyst shedding. The infection is treated with fenbendazole.

MANGE MITES

Dog owners also have to deal with mange mites. Mites are not insects, by the way, but are almost microscopic creatures related to spiders.

Sarcoptic Mange

Sarcoptic mange, or scabies, is actually the name of a skin disease caused by the mite *Sarcoptic scabei*. The adults live on the skin, with the female burrowing into the skin and laying her eggs. The eggs hatch in a few days, producing young that move around on top of the skin until they mature. They are usually found on less hairy areas such as the earflaps and the abdomen, which contributes to the extreme itchiness. Dogs usually develop an allergy to the mites, which makes the skin even itchier! Mite-infected dogs have red itchy skin that closely resembles an inhalant allergy (atopy) or a food allergy. Many dogs also get crusty-edged ears as the disease develops. Mites are usually spread by direct contact from host to host.

What You Can Do

Testing for mites usually includes a skin scraping. Mites are treated by dipping your dog in parmite, mitaban, or a lime sulfur dip, often in combination with milbemycin oxime. If one dog in a household has been diagnosed with scabies, it is best to treat all household pets at once. Luckily, mites can survive off their host for only about 36 hours, so it usually is not necessary to decontaminate the entire household, although dog bedding and collars should be washed or replaced. Mites cannot complete their life cycle on humans, and usually go away on their own.

Cheyletiella Mange

Cheyletiella mange, or walking dandruff, is a mite that mostly affects puppies. It is not very serious.

What You Can Do

Cheyletiellosis is easily cured with the proper diagnosis and treatment.

MOSQUITOES

Mosquitoes carry heartworm and a host of other diseases. Most recently, they have been charged with the spread of West Nile virus. While the

Dogs can usually expect a full recovery if infected with West Nile virus.

disease is serious for horses and people, dogs can usually expect a full recovery if infected. There is no vaccine or cure, and treatment is merely supportive, just as with most viral infections. If your dog does come down with this disease, you shouldn't worry about your family. There is no evidence of dog-to-person transmission of West Nile. Even more heartening, the evidence suggests that dogs do not develop enough of the virus in their bloodstream to infect more mosquitoes. However, if your dog gets West Nile, it means there are infected mosquitoes in your area, and you should be careful. Veterinarians should take normal infection control precautions when caring for any animal (including birds) suspected to have this or any viral infection. Signs of infection include incoordination, decreased appetite, tremors, circling, and abnormal head posture. Convulsions are also possible.

What You Can Do

With all the problems that mosquitoes pose, you might want to use an insect repellent on your pet. Look for a natural repellent, and try to keep your dog indoors when mosquitoes are worst—usually around sunset.

TICKS

The ticks you see on your dog are the females, who need a blood meal before they can reproduce.

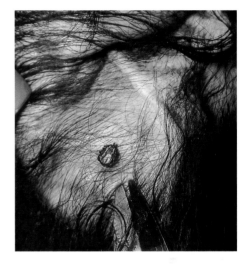

One of the most disgusting things about ticks is the way they look (much worse than

If you see a tick on your dog, remove it with tweezers.

fleas, which are, all things considered, rather handsome). The term used to describe a tick swollen with blood is engorged. Ticks can swell up to 100 times their body weight! They are usually found on the ears, the head, or the feet, attaching themselves with their horrid little mouthparts. Ticks lurk in grassy, woodland areas, where they wait on the tips of twigs and grasses until your hapless dog trots by. They prefer high humidity.

Tick bites can transmit the following serious diseases:

- Lyme disease, the most common of tick-borne illnesses. The responsible agent, the bacterium *Borrelia burdorferi*, is carried by the deer tick and the western black-legged tick and possibly other varieties as well. Signs of the disease include fever, lethargy, enlargement of the lymph nodes, and arthritis. Antibiotics are effective against the disease.

Blood Testing

Happily, there is an in-clinic blood test that tests for Lyme disease, heartworm, and *Ehrlichia canis* using only one blood sample.

- Babeiosis, a serious disease caused by *Babesia canis*, which destroys red blood cells.
- Ehrlichiosis, a disease caused by five different pathogens, causes lameness, depression, and stiffness. Eventually it can destroy blood cells and platelets. It has historically been hard to diagnose, although a new test is now available. Treatment is with antibiotics.
- Rocky Mountain Spotted Fever, caused by *Rickettsia rickttsii*. It is a disease with deceptively mild symptoms, which if left untreated can cause coma and death. Signs may include fever and stiffness. When caught early, antibiotics are effective.
- Tick paralysis, which occurs when a toxin injected by the tick causes a temporary paralysis of the hind legs. When the tick is removed, the paralysis ceases.
- Other possible tick-borne diseases include tularemia, hepazoonosis, relapsing fever, and anemia due to blood loss.

If you see a tick on your dog, remove it with tweezers. Never touch a tick with your bare hands. Grasp the tick by the body and pull it straight out. Don't worry about the head getting stuck in the skin; it won't. It's possible that the mouthpart might get left behind, but that's okay—it will fall out naturally later. Contrary to what some people believe, ticks don't burrow beneath the skin. They are always visible. It's true, however, that the deer tick, which carries Lyme disease, is very small, even when engorged.

What You Can Do

As with every parasite, prevention is the ticket. Protect your dog with a tick collar or topical anti-tick medication, and check him over every day during tick season. Tick season is any time the temperature goes above 40°F (4.4°C). Transmission of disease does not usually start until the tick has been on the dog for 36 to 48 hours. When using any tick preventive, follow instructions carefully. If you have any questions, consult your veterinarian. Do not combine different flea and tick products without permission—it can be dangerous. Some products are not recommended for puppies or for pregnant or nursing dogs.

WORMS
Heartworms

Heartworms (*Dirofilaria immitis*) are transmitted to dogs via mosquitoes. (Immature heartworms can't complete their life cycle without the help of the friendly little mosquito.) The infective larvae are deposited under the skin and develop in several stages, but when completely developed, they enter the bloodstream, moving to the heart and its blood vessels. Dogs of all ages are vulnerable.

Heartworms live inside the pulmonary arteries and begin to damage them within days. The arteries dilate and begin to turn, resulting in aneurysm and blood clots. Blood must be shunted to other, worm-free arteries, while fluid accumulates in the lungs around the wormy arteries. Blood that does reach the lungs does not pick up enough oxygen. The dog starts to cough and becomes unable to participate in strenuous physical activity. You may even see nosebleeds or signs of pneumonia. Another heart problem caused by heartworm is caval syndrome, in which the entire right side of the heart becomes filled with worms that then begin to back into the large veins feeding that side of the heart. Collapse, shock, and sudden death may result.

What You Can Do

Luckily, heartworms can be prevented. In the late 1980s, a once-a-month (as opposed to daily) heartworm preventive therapy was developed. It works by using an extremely low dose of

ivermectin. In addition to killing the larval worms (microfilariae), ivermectin also suppresses reproduction of the adult female worms. By itself, ivermectin as a heartworm preventive is not strong enough to kill common intestinal parasites, but it is available combined with pyrantel pamoate to control hookworms and roundworms. Some Collie-related breeds have difficulties with ivermectin, although not at the low doses used in heartworm prevention.

Other heartworm control products include topically applied selamectin (a cousin of ivermectin), which protects dogs from ear mites, mange mites, fleas, and some internal parasites as well. Milbemycin oxime is another option; it controls roundworms, hookworms, and whipworms without the addition of a second parasiticide. It is also available combined with Lufenuron for the control of fleas. There are no breed-related sensitivities for milbemycin, and it is also used effectively to treat demodectic mange. It should

Protect your dog with a tick collar or topical anti-tick medication, and check him over every day during tick season.

be noted, however, that while ivermectin seems to control heartworm even if the owners forget to give the medication for a prolonged period, milbemycin doesn't seem to work as well in this regard. Still other products are available—check with your vet for what's right for your dog.

Roundworms

Dogs can harbor two kinds of roundworm: *Toxocara canis* and *Toxascaris leonina*. Both are treated with the same medication, so it's not necessary to determine which species is present. Dogs can become infected with roundworms by ingesting worm eggs from soil, nursing from an infected mother dog, eating an animal affected

feces. However, in pregnant dogs, the larvae move to the dog's uterus instead of the lungs. Thus, they infect the new puppies. Unfortunately, regular de-worming does not affected encysted worms, just the adults.

Roundworms cause vomiting and diarrhea. They can grow very large (up to 7 inches [18 cm]) and in some cases actually can obstruct the intestine or cause pneumonia.

What You Can Do

All puppies and adult dogs should be tested for roundworms and de-wormed. Many heartworm and flea control medications provide a monthly de-worming, which is very helpful as well. Most medications work by anesthetizing the worm so that it loses its grip on the intestine and just passes out into the environment, where it dies. Roundworm medications include febantel, pyrantel pamoate, piperazine, fenbendazole, and milbemycin oxime. However, none of these products kill the larvae in migration. This is why de-worming must be repeated two or three times.

And if you need another reason to keep your dog worm-free, I'll give you one you won't be able to resist. British scientists report that people can become infected with *Toxocara canis* simply by stroking the coats of dogs who carry the parasite. The eggs are very sticky and could easily be picked up. The finding, reported by *New Scientist*, challenges a previous assumption that the worms only spread to people who come into contact with dog feces. In the US, about 10,000 people a year—mainly children under 12—become infected with the worm. In infected people, the worms can grow in the back of the eye, causing lesions that can interfere with vision or be mistaken for tumors. Occasionally they cause blindness.

Research by Ian Wright and co-investigator Alan Wolfe, whose study is reported in *The Veterinary*

with the worms, and most frequently during embryonic development. (Most puppies are infected this way.) *Toxocara canis* has an

One of the ways in which dogs can become infected with roundworms is by ingesting worm eggs.

incredibly complex and successful life cycle. The worms develop in feces but actually take about a month before they can become infective. So fresh feces are not infective, but once the eggs do become infective, they remain that way for months or even years.

Roundworm larvae have two stages. When the larva develops into what is called the second stage by a passing host, it hatches in that animal's intestinal tract, encysting itself in other body tissues, usually the liver in dogs. If the host turns out not to be a dog, the clever worm waits until it can actually get into a dog's system. Once there, it can stay encysted for years. When it does get out of ex-cyst, it usually moves to the lungs and develops into third-stage larvae. (The dog starts to cough, as you may imagine.) The dog then swallows the worms, which head for the intestinal tract, where the larvae mature, mate, and lay new eggs, which are passed out of the body with the

Record, suggests feces might be only one route of infection. Of 60 dogs examined, 25 percent had worm eggs in their hair. Three of the 71 eggs they recovered contained mature worm embryos, which can infect humans. Wright says the findings show that dog owners should regularly wash and worm their pets, especially puppies, who are more likely to have worms. And wash your hands after petting unknown puppies!

Tapeworms

Tapeworms (*Dipylidium caninum*) are flat, segmented creatures that attach themselves by the head to the small intestine and reach a length of 20 inches (51 cm). Each segment is almost independent, with its own reproductive organs, and new segments form constantly in the neck region of the worm as old ones are cast off (and found in the feces), where they can be consumed by flea larvae. The segments look like grains of raw rice. Tapeworms are carried in fleas, so when dogs lick off fleas, they ingest the tapeworm. Interestingly, tapeworms themselves have no digestive system—they absorb nutrients directly through the skin.

Luckily, tapeworms seldom do serious damage to dogs, although obviously they are not good for them. However, heavy infestation can cause discomfort and nervousness in the dog, and in extreme cases, the dog may vomit or even have convulsions.

What You Can Do

The most common treatment is Praziquantel (Droncit) by pill or injection. Since the tapeworm goes through an intermediate stage in fleas, flea control is an essential part of the ultimate solution. Nearly all cases of canine tapeworm come from fleabites. Many vets will recommend two treatments three weeks apart.

Whipworms

One of the nastiest worms is the whipworm (*Trichuris vulpis*), an intestinal parasite that can invade the large intestine (cecum) of dogs of any age. Dogs acquire them by eating whipworm eggs from a contaminated environment. The adults deposit eggs, which are then passed in the dog's feces. Annoyingly, the eggs can survive in the soil for years. Whipworms cause bloody diarrhea and serious debilitation.

What You Can Do

Your vet can diagnose whipworms through a fecal examination, although the eggs themselves usually cannot be detected in the dog's stool until three months after whipworm infection. Whipworms can be treated successfully with medications like Panacur that are available from your veterinarian, although re-treatment may be necessary after one or two months.

11

FIRST AID

Accidents happen. You can't predict them, so the best thing to do is to be prepared. Your first job is to get together a first-aid kit.

YOUR CANINE FIRST-AID KIT

Although you can buy a basic commercial kit, it's cheaper and more fun to make one yourself. First you need a box—a fishing tackle or other shoebox-sized container is perfect. It should be strong, waterproof, and unlocked. Try to get one with a handle. Label it "First Aid" with a felt-tip pen on all sides. Keep it in plain view. Under the lid, tape an index card with the name, number, and hours of your vet and of poison control. (ASPCA National Animal Poison Control is 800-548-2423.) Also write down the name, description, and weight of each of your animals. In case you are not home when disaster strikes, your pet sitter will thank you. Put an emergency blanket under the first-aid kit, and keep one in the car as well. It helps prevent shock by preserving the animal's heat.

Your first-aid kit should include:

Items to Help Handle Your Dog

- Gloves: Two pairs—one set of thin plastic gloves to avoid contamination and heavy gloves if you're afraid of being bitten.
- Muzzle: If you don't have one, you can make one from nylons, pantyhose, or a strip of fabric.

First-Aid Training

The American Red Cross offers a four-hour pet first-aid training course at many of their chapters across the country. You can get more information at www.redcross.org/services/disaster/beprepared/firstaid.html.

Implements

- Blunt-nosed scissors: To cut tape and clip hair. Keep these scissors with the kit, and don't take them out to use for anything else. You won't put them back, and when you need them, you'll wonder where they are.
- Canine rectal thermometer: Normal canine rectal temperature is 102°F (38.9°C).
- Electric clippers, #40 blade: For clipping hair around wounds.
- Eyedropper or dosage syringe: To apply medication.
- Nail clippers: In case of accident to the nail bed.
- Magnifying glass: To locate tiny objects.
- Styptic pencil: To stop minor bleeding.
- Tweezers or hemostat: To pull out splinters and other foreign objects.

Items for Bandaging Wounds

- Cotton balls and swabs: Various uses.
- Nonstick adhesive tape: For taping bandages.
- Nonstinging antiseptic spray or swabs: For cleaning wounds.
- Stretch bandage or Vet Wrap: For wounds.
- Two rolls of 3-inch (7.6-cm) gauze bandages: For wrapping wounds.

Miscellaneous Products

- Activated charcoal: For poisonings (1 gram per pound [.45 kg] mixed with water).
- Antihistamine tablets: For insect stings and allergic reactions.
- Betadine or Nolvasan: For cleaning open wounds.
- Cortisone ointment: Topical anti-inflammatory.
- Eyewash: To irrigate eyes.
- First-aid cream: To soothe and protect wounds.
- Hydrogen peroxide 3%: Various cleaning and disinfecting uses.
- Ipecac: To induce vomiting (1 teaspoon per 20

pounds [9 kg]).

- Kaolin and pectin: To help diarrhea (1 teaspoon per 10 pounds [4.5 kg]).

Your vet can handle emergency situations that may arise.

- Otomax: For ear infections.
- Stomach coater: Over-the-counter stomach coater (like Pepto Bismol or Maalox) for minor intestinal upset. Warning! Kaopectate has come out in a new formulation that should not be given to dogs who take aspirin, steroids, or another nonsteroidal anti-inflammatory drugs (NSAIDs).
- Petroleum jelly: To accompany the rectal thermometer, also for constipation (1/2 teaspoon per 10 pounds [4.5 kg]).

- Saline solution: Various uses, such as irrigating wounds.
- Vegetable oil: For mild constipation (1 teaspoon per 5 pounds [2 kg], mixed in food).

RECOGNIZING AN EMERGENCY

An emergency is a situation in which you need to get your dog to the vet as quickly as possible. Of course, not every ailment needs professional treatment, and even professional treatment can sometimes be scheduled somewhat at your leisure. But these symptoms require immediate action:

- Spurting blood (arterial bleeding)
- Bleeding from the nose or mouth
- Choking
- Seizures or disorientation
- Problems with breathing or swallowing
- Broken bones
- Repeated vomiting
- Diarrhea lasting more than 18 hours
- Refusal to eat for 48 hours
- Muscle tremors
- Unusual swellings, especially sudden, hard, or fast-growing ones

EMERGENGY SITUATIONS
Airway Obstruction and Choking

If you suspect a foreign object in the throat or back of the mouth, try to retrieve it unless it is an item like tinsel or string; in that case, let the vet take it out. There's no time to lose. Keep the dog as calm as possible, because the more excited he gets, the more air he needs. You must clear an airway for your dog; try a doggy Heimlich maneuver (discussed below), though clapping the dog hard on both sides of the chest may be enough. Try to clear the obstruction by laying the dog on his side, then extending the head and neck by tilting the head back carefully. If possible, open the mouth with a flat object like a tongue depressor.

Pull the tongue out gently between the front teeth so that the throat is not blocked. Then remove any foreign objects or vomitus from the mouth by swiping sideways. If the dog is not breathing, use mouth-to-nose breathing. If the dog is biting and snapping, just wait. Lack of air will make him lose consciousness—you'll have time to do the checking then. If you see nothing, the object may be located in the esophagus, and you should perform the Heimlich maneuver to dislodge it.

Heimlich Maneuver

The Heimlich maneuver is used to dislodge obstructions in the throat. If the dog is small, lay him on his side, with the head lower than the hindquarters. Put one hand below the breastbone and the other against the back. Press in and up sharply. If the dog is large, kneel down facing the dog's stomach and put both hands against the center of the upper abdomen, right below the rib cage. Push in and up repeatedly until the dog coughs up the obstruction. If that doesn't work, rush your dog to the vet, who may be able to remove the blockage with the help of an endoscope or other equipment.

Allergic Reaction

A swollen face and difficulty in breathing signal an allergic reaction. Give Benadryl, an over-the-counter antihistamine, and take the dog to

CPR

CPR is a handy skill that can save your dog's life. It's worth your time and trouble to take a class in CPR. It could save more lives than your dog's. Here are the basics:

- Check for breathing by watching for chest movement or breath inhalations. You may rest your hand lightly on the dog's side.
- If the dog isn't breathing, you need to clear the airway. If the dog is unconscious, pull out his tongue and check for obstructions. Pull the head and extend the neck gently.
- If no blockage is visible, close the dog's mouth gently, and cover his nose with your mouth, making an airtight seal. Keep the neck straight. Breathe gently into your dog's lungs at a rate of 10 or 12 breaths a minute. You must hold the corners of the mouth tightly closed while you breathe the air into the dog. Force the air into the chest until you see it expand. Continue until the dog breathes on his own. Continue while you transport him to a rescue facility.
- Feel for a heartbeat behind the dog's left front elbow. If there's no heartbeat, lay the dog down so that his back is against you. Place your hands, one on top of the other, over the heart area, and firmly press both hands down and forward towards the head, which has the most critical need for blood. You may need to use very strong pressure. It is even possible to break a rib during this procedure, but nothing is more important than getting the heart started. Repeat five or six times at a rate of one compression per second.
- Alternate the cardiac massage with the artificial respiration. Do not give up while there is even a faint heartbeat.

the vet immediately. (While antihistamines like Benadryl are fairly safe, you want to make sure you are giving your dog an antihistamine with only diphenhydramine in it. Some brands add other active ingredients (like caffeine) that can have adverse effects for dogs with glaucoma or cardiovascular disease.) The usual dosage is 1-2 mg of drug per pound (.45 kg) of dog three times a day.

Bee Stings

If you can see the stinger, scrape it out with a credit card. (Just pulling it out can release more venom into the wound.) Apply cool compresses as well as a paste mixture of baking soda and water. You may want to give an over-the-counter antihistamine, 1-2 mg per pound (.45 kg) of dog three times a day. If your dog seems to be having a serious allergic reaction or is having trouble breathing, take him to the vet immediately.

Bleeding

With severe bleeding, the main rule is: Stop the bleeding. A loss of as little as two teaspoons per pound (.45 kg) of body weight can cause shock.

Bright red, spurting blood may signal an arterial cut and is especially dangerous. Use a clean absorbent cloth or towel to apply pressure until the bleeding stops or you can get the dog to the vet. If you don't have a clean cloth, use a dirty cloth. If you don't have a dirty cloth, use your hands, but stop the bleeding. If the cloth soaks through, add another one—don't remove the first, since you might be pulling off a clot. Pulling the bandage off to see if the bleeding has stopped is counterproductive.

For minor bleeding or tearing, apply a moist dressing to prevent the tissues

You can't predict accidents, so the best thing to do is to be prepared.

from drying out and dying. Petroleum jelly or even water will help.

For a nosebleed, observe whether the blood is coming from one or both nostrils. Keep the dog lying down and calm, and place a cold compress on the nose. If the bleeding continues for more than ten minutes, call a vet.

Blood in the stool may be a cause for concern. If the blood is dark, it probably originates in the stomach or small intestine. (It's dark because it's partly digested.) Bright red blood probably comes from the large intestine or rectum. See your vet as soon as possible.

Bloat or Gastric Torsion

Bloat is a life-threatening emergency in which the stomach fills with air and then twists on itself. Signs include unproductive retching or vomiting, salivation, pacing, and most telling, a round, drum-

like belly. Unless you get your dog to a veterinary hospital for surgery immediately, he will die. No condition is more serious. Don't attempt to treat this yourself—only professional help can save a dog with this condition. For more on this deadly disease, see Chapter 13.

Burns

Superficial burns can be treated with ice packs or cold water compresses; don't use butter, ointments, or oil. Change the pack frequently, and continue treatment for at least 30 minutes. Don't attempt to remove any burned skin or hair yourself.

Deep burns require veterinary attention. If your dog chews through electrical wire, the superficial burns around the mouth are much less serious than the damage to his internal organs and nervous system. Make sure you turn off the electricity before touching the dog. If you can't, use a nonconductive material like wood to detach the dog from the wire. Check for breathing and pulse rate. If the dog is breathing, apply a cool compress to the burn, and cover the animal with a blanket to prevent heat loss. Treat him for shock and get him to the vet, even if he seems quite normal afterwards.

Acids or alkalis can cause chemical burns. If you don't know the cause, wash the area with flowing water for at least 15 minutes. Make sure the water is flowing; putting the animal in a pool of water could activate the chemical. If it's an alkali burn, such as might result from drain cleaner, use vinegar and water; if it's an acid burn, use a paste of baking soda and water. Get him to the vet.

Car Accident

Check for oncoming traffic before dashing out into the road. If your dog gets struck by a car, he may begin bleeding internally, even if he seems all right. If your dog can't walk, he may have a back injury.

Put a muzzle on him, since dogs in pain can inflict a terrible bite. Cover the dog and take him to the vet immediately.

Dehydration

Skin that is inelastic, that doesn't spring back when pulled, may mean your dog is dehydrated, a condition that may be a result of diarrhea. Serious cases of dehydration must be corrected by intravenous fluids. Simply pouring water down the animal's throat won't work; in fact, the water may pass through the system and make the condition worse.

Diarrhea

Diarrhea is an extremely common problem in dogs. It is not a disease but a sign of something wrong in the system. If your dog does get diarrhea, your job as a dog owner is to pay attention to it, distasteful

Do your best to prevent emergency situations by supervising your dog and making sure that he doesn't get into trouble.

as it may be. Note its color and consistency as well as when it started. Your vet needs to know if it is bloody, black, or mucus filled. Diarrhea is more serious in puppies than in adult dogs. If your dog is an adult and there are no symptoms other than moderate or mild diarrhea, try withholding all food for 12 to 24 hours. You can actually make a guess as to the source of the problem by looking at the diarrhea. A large volume of watery stool and a sick-acting dog indicate a problem in the small intestine. Mucus or bloody stools with a smaller volume of feces indicate the problem is in the colon. So many illnesses exhibit these symptoms that it could be anything. Do not attempt to feed your dog. Get to the vet.

Eye Injuries

Apply a sterile solution to the eye to prevent further damage, and take the dog to the vet. Your dog's sight is nothing to fool around with. If the eye has actually been detached from the socket or something has happened so that the lids cannot close over the eye, keep the eyeball moist with water or contact lens wetting solution. Lubricating jelly or honey also work. If the eye has been invaded by a foreign object, flush it with running water for 15 minutes. You can also use saline—dissolve 2 teaspoons of salt into a quart (1 l) of water.

Fainting

Place your pet so that his hindquarters are higher than his head. Cover the dog with a blanket to preserve body heat. Take him to the vet.

Fractures

If the bone is protruding, cover it loosely with a clean cloth and tape it carefully. Splint the limb in the position you find it. Do not attempt to straighten it out—you can make things worse. Use a rolled magazine, stick, or something else rigid on both sides of the limb and tape in place, though not too tightly. If this scares you, don't worry. Just place the animal in a box and carry him to the car for a ride to the vet's office.

Hyperthermia (Overheating)

Dogs suffer from heat stress, and a hyperthermic dog is in serious danger. Remember that we humans are tropical beasts, and what's fun exercise for us, at a balmy 80°F (26.7°C), can be life threatening for a dog. Black-coated and short-snouted dogs are most at risk.

Signs of heatstroke include fast breathing or panting, a bright red tongue, and bright red mucous membranes. Your dog may also vomit. This is a true medical emergency. Use cool (not icy) water to cool off the dog. If you plunge a hyperthermic dog into icy water, it can shut down

A sick dog may not behave as he normally does.

the surface blood vessels that help transfer the heat away from the body. As a result, the dog's internal temperature can actually increase.

Hypothermia (Freezing)

If your dog becomes hypothermic, get him dry as soon as possible. The dog will not get warm until he is dry. Use a hair dryer on low, plus vigorous towel drying. Warm the towels if possible. Frostbitten skin is red or gray; it may peel. If a dog has actual frostbite, don't rub the skin; you'll make it worse. Apply warm, moist towels to thaw the affected areas, or slowly submerge the dog in lukewarm (101°F [38.3°C]) bathwater until the skin looks flushed.

Intestinal Obstruction

A hunched-up dog may be suffering from an intestinal obstruction. Get him to the vet; there's nothing you can do at home. The same is true of an intussusception, a condition that occurs

when the bowel folds over onto itself. Surgery is necessary to correct this problem.

Poisoning

Call your vet or the poison control center (800-548-2423). In most cases, make the dog vomit by using a couple of tablespoons of hydrogen peroxide every 10 or 20 minutes.

Seizures

If your dog has a seizure, the best thing you can do is calmly monitor the situation until it passes. Take careful note of the length and severity of the seizure, but otherwise do not interfere. If you have other dogs, keep them out of the way. Notify your veterinarian. For information on epilepsy, a major cause of seizures, see Chapter 14.

Shock

Shock is a common word with a specific medical meaning. In shock, the entire cardiovascular system collapses, the blood doesn't circulate properly, and all the body organs are in danger of oxygen deprivation and death. Any serious injury or medical emergency can produce shock. Signs include weakness, shivering, collapse, rapid pulse and heartbeat, and pale gums. The whiter the gums, the more serious the situation. Dogs in shock should be kept warm and taken to the vet immediately for care and intravenous fluids. Untreated dogs are in danger of death.

Dogs in Cars

Everyone knows by now not to leave a dog in a car when it's warm. Warm means any time the temperature is over 65°F (18.3°C) in the shade. Cracking the windows is not enough. If you must leave the dog in the car, put on the air conditioning.

Snakebite

See Chapter 4 for what to do if your dog is bitten by a snake.

Spinal Injuries

Do not attempt to move a dog with a suspected spinal injury unless you absolutely must. Construct a makeshift stretcher and carefully support the dog's whole body. Keep the dog as quiet as possible.

Swallowing Sharp Items

If your dog swallows sharp items such as hooks, pins, or staples, pop a few cotton balls down his throat; the foreign objects will embed themselves in the cotton and pass safely through the digestive system. Soft bread may also work to gather up the sharp objects.

Vomiting

Remove all food for at least 12 hours, after which you may start him with a bland diet. Since vomiting may be a sign of a serious illness, check with your vet.

Wounds

These happen most often to younger, more athletic animals, but of course, any dog can be injured. You can usually judge the seriousness of

an injury yourself. Some injuries, like broken legs, obviously require immediate care, while others, such as a torn cruciate ligament (an amazingly common injury in athletic dogs), can wait for a day or so if necessary. The problem, of course, is that unless you've had firsthand experience, you'll need the vet to tell you what exactly has gone wrong. Bite wounds are usually infected with bacteria from the biting animal's mouth. Without prompt antibiotic treatment, they may abscess. An abscess is a localized accumulation of pus, usually accompanied by a painful swell. If the abscess has ruptured, clean it gently with mild soap and water several times a day. If there is swelling under the open abscess, apply warm, wet compresses a couple of times a day. You may want to take the dog to the vet as well. If the abscess has not opened, don't try to do it yourself. Take the dog to the vet.

With a minor wound, the first step is to clean it to remove debris like dirt and dried blood. Use mild soap and lots of water. Clip away hair that gets in the way of the wound. Dry the area and place a sterile, absorbent, stickless soft pad on the wound. You can smear some antibiotic cream on the pad if you like. If possible, wrap the area in a gauze bandage, then apply a self-adhering bandage. Change the bandages frequently.

12

PREVENTIVE CARE

Nothing is more important to conscientious dog owners than the health and well-being of their pets. While some things, such as the dog's genetic heritage, may be out of our hands, we do have control over our dogs' diet and exercise—huge factors that go into good health. We can also vaccinate, use flea, tick, and internal parasite protection, and get regular checkups for our dogs. However, responsible dog owners also familiarize themselves with major disease threats and keep a watchful eye on their dog's behavior for signs of illness or trauma.

THE ROLE OF GENETICS

Good health may not be carved in stone, but it is largely written in blood. The brutal truth is that while good nutrition, exercise, and veterinary care can vastly improve the health of our dogs, the foundation for good health depends on genetics.

Dogs have 39 pairs of chromosomes and perhaps as many as 100,000 genes, far more than people. No one has yet figured out why some animals have more chromosomes (or genes) than others, since they don't relate very well to size, intelligence, or specialization. But these tiny little markers control a lot of what dogs (and people) think and feel, including how they feel physically. A properly fed dog will probably grow larger than a malnourished one, but no amount of good feeding will turn a Chihuahua into the size of a Great Dane. And no amount of care can prevent progressive retinal atrophy (PRA), a genetically controlled form of blindness. It was coded (or not) into your dog before he was born. Your dog will either develop it or he won't.

The number of genetically controlled diseases is frightening. Here's just a sampling of inherited diseases that affect the cardiovascular system alone: aortic stenosis, atrial septal defect, cardiomyopathy, mitral valve insufficiency, patent ductus arteriosis, vascular ring anomaly, portosystemic shunt, pulmonic stenosis, sick sinus syndrome, tetralogy of fallot, tricuspid valve dysplasia, and ventricular septal defect. There are a like number of heritable conditions for the other systems: blood, endocrine, eye, skin, nervous system, gastrointestinal system, immune system, respiratory system, urinary-reproductive system, musculoskeletal system. Sometimes it seems a cause for wonderment that your dog is walking around at all!

The foundation for good health depends on genetics.

You can't do anything about your dog's genotype—that was arranged before you got him. Think of it like a game of poker. You can't do anything about the hand you drew (unless you stack the deck by choosing a breed with fewer than average inherited diseases and find an extremely conscientious breeder who puts health first). But how you play it is up to you. The right care will maximize your dog's chance to win the game.

The first step on the road to good health for your dog is a healthy relationship between you and your veterinarian. People who visit their vets only when their dog is ill have usually waited too long. Your dog should have a thorough going over when you first acquire him and a physical examination every year (at least) until he has reached senior dog status, when he should be checked every six months.

FINDING A GOOD VET

If this is you and your dog's first trip to the vet, be sure to check the place out—don't be afraid to ask for a tour. Consider the following questions:

- Is the staff relaxed, friendly, and compassionate? Or do they have a "this is just a business" aura? A harried, stressed staff will probably produce the same effect on your dog.
- What services do they provide? Boarding? Grooming? Home visits?
- Are any of the staff specialists in orthopedics, holistic treatments, behavior, or cardiology?
- What hours is the clinic open? Evenings? Weekends? Who answers the calls when the office is closed? (If you work days, you should choose a clinic with evening hours.)
- Does the clinic accept pet insurance?
- Is the clinic a member of a spay/neuter program?

- How many of your breed of dog does the clinic handle? How familiar is the staff with the breed's special health concerns?
- How close is the vet to your home? A difference of five minutes can mean life or death to your pet.

Adding up the answers to all these questions may make it easier to decide on the right vet for your dog.

ALTERNATIVE AND COMPLEMENTARY VETERINARY PRACTICES
Acupuncture

While there is no replacement for modern Western veterinary care, we can also take advantage of other modalities of care, including Chinese and Western herbal medicine and acupuncture. Acupuncture actually began as a veterinary practice in China thousands of years ago. According to Chinese thought, a system of life energy, or Qi (pronounced chee and sometimes spelled "chi"), circulates through the body along meridians, special pathways through the body. Acupuncture points lie along these meridians, and when the points are stimulated, the acupuncturist can manipulate energy flows.

Hereditary Diseases

Not all hereditary diseases are purely hereditary. For example, cataracts are hereditary in several breeds, but they can also develop as a result of trauma, toxins, or another disease like diabetes (which in itself may be hereditary). Your veterinarian may be able to tell you if the defect or disease in your dog's particular case is hereditary.

A trained acupuncturist knows what meridians pass through a certain area and stimulates the appropriate points on the meridian. Different conditions require different kinds of stimulation. Contemporary acupuncturists even use laser beams, which are completely painless. Electro-acupuncture can also be used. Acupuncture has been shown to improve hip dysplasia, arthritis, certain gastrointestinal ailments, skin problems, hormone imbalances, and some cancers and diseases of the nervous system.

To find a veterinary acupuncturist (and there are more than 1,000 of them), search the website of the International Veterinary Acupuncture Society (IVAS) at www.ivas.org or the American Academy of Veterinary Acupuncturists (AAVA) at www.aava.org.

Chiropractic

Another alternative therapy is chiropractic care, the purpose of which is to get the neuro-muscular-skeletal system aligned by using gentle manipulations. It also helps to keep the joints flexible. Not all veterinarians approve of chiropractic procedures, but many people have had great success with them, especially for chronic pain in the joints or back. Chiropractic procedures can be used effectively for dogs with disc problems, hip dysplasia, and arthritis. You should expect to see improvement after a few treatments.

Chiropractic aligns the neuro-muscular-skeletal system by using gentle manipulations.

For a list of certified veterinary chiropractors near you, contact the American Veterinary Chiropractic Association (AVCA) at www.animalchiropractic.org or the American Holistic Veterinary Medical Association (AHVMA) at www.ahvma.org. There are currently more than 350 veterinarians and chiropractors certified to treat animals.

Massage

This is a great technique that can be used on most dogs. Best of all, you can learn to do it yourself. Massage can speed healing, improve circulation, relax tight muscles, promote healthy skin, remove toxins, relax your dog, and help you bond with him. It can be done with a variety of strokes and touch techniques, including effleurage, compression, joint rotation, and tapping, using slow, deliberate movements. Choose a time for massage when you're both quiet and relaxed. Work slowly, moving your hands towards the heart. Watch your dog carefully, noting any signs of pain or distress. To learn more about massage, visit www.petmassage.com.

Reiki

Reiki (pronounced ray-KEE and meaning "spiritually led life energy") is a Japanese technique. It is a touch-healing system that works by opening the energy centers, or chakras, of the body. It is a complementary therapy that is not meant to replace traditional healing. If you are interested in learning more about reiki, visit www.reiki.7gen.com.

TTouch

TTouch therapy is another massage-like technique. Developed by Linda Tellington-Jones about 40 years ago as a horse therapy, it is now used on dogs as well. In TTouch, the practitioner makes gentle clockwise circles for one and a quarter revolutions on the animal, using slightly curved fingers. Therapists use pressure degrees from 1 (the lightest) to 9 (the heaviest). Sessions last from 10 to 30 minutes. The most common massage site is the ear, which helps soothe dogs and fight stress. To learn more about TTouch, go to www.lindatellington-jones.com or www.ttouch.com.

VACCINATIONS
Your Frontline Defense Against Deadly Diseases

No responsible dog owner ignores vaccinating her pet. Before the development of vaccines, dogs regularly died from rabies and distemper. When

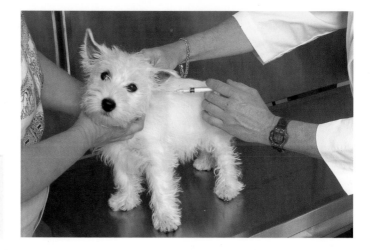

If your dog is sensitive to vaccines, it is probably best to avoid giving him several vaccinations at once.

canine parvovirus first appeared in the late 1970s, it took a devastating toll on canine life. Nowadays, distemper is quite rare because of the widespread use of vaccines, and parvovirus appears only when people fail to vaccinate their dogs or vaccinate them too late. While there has recently been sentiment against vaccinating dogs from certain practitioners, in my opinion, the benefits far outweigh any potential hazards. Vaccinations are lifesaving—unvaccinated dogs exposed to dogs with distemper or parvo will probably get distemper or parvo. Dogs who are vaccinated against these diseases almost certainly will not.

As we learn more about the immune system, there have been advances in veterinary practice regarding vaccination. Nowadays, organizations like the American Veterinary Medical Association (AVMA), the American Animal Hospital Association (AAHA), and others are recommending reduced frequency of most vaccinations and increased vaccinations of others. Discuss a good vaccination protocol with your vet.

Some animals do experience problems with vaccinations—most commonly muscle soreness, some lethargy, or a mild fever. In a few rare cases,

a dog may develop an allergic reaction, which is an inflammatory response against specific proteins entering the body from the vaccine. Typical allergic reactions may include hives or facial swelling, usually occurring within 48 hours of the shot. In very rare cases, a dog can go into shock.

If your dog is sensitive to vaccines, it is probably best to avoid giving him several vaccinations at once (or a combination vaccine) and to avoid others (like the leptospirosis vaccination) altogether. Make sure to discuss the problem fully with your vet. Keep in mind, vaccinations have saved the lives of millions of dogs!

Currently, vaccinations are divided into two sorts: core and non-core vaccines. Core vaccines are those that every dog should receive. They are designed to protect against very dangerous, highly transmittable diseases. These include vaccines against rabies (required by law), canine distemper, canine parvovirus, and adenovirus. Most vets administer vaccinations at 8, 12, and 16 weeks, with the rabies vaccine given at 16 weeks. For some vaccines, a booster shot may be recommended at one year. After that, these vaccines are good for three years, according to the latest protocols. However, it is still very important to get your dog to the vet for his annual checkup whether he needs shots or not.

Core Vaccines

Distemper: Distemper is the main killer of dogs worldwide. It is caused by an airborne, measles-like virus that destroys the nervous system and attacks every tissue in the body. The incubation period is 7 to 21 days, and initial symptoms include lethargy, fever, runny nose, and yellow discharge from the eyes. The dog will also have labored breathing and will lose his appetite. Later symptoms include a nervous twitch and thickening of the nose and pads of the feet, which is why the disease was once known as "hardpad." Dogs who progress to this stage are unlikely to make a complete recovery.

Hepatitis: Hepatitis is a serious disease caused by an adenovirus and is most dangerous to puppies. It is spread by contact with an infected dog or with his urine or feces. The white blood cell count drops, and some dogs experience clotting problems. It also affects the kidneys and liver. Symptoms include high fever, red mucous membranes, depression, and loss of appetite. Small blood spots may appear on the gums, and the eyes may look bluish. Even dogs who recover often experience chronic illnesses—they may also continue to spread the virus for months, infecting others. Luckily, this disease is seldom seen nowadays, largely because of the effective vaccines against it.

Parvovirus: Parvovirus is a highly contagious, deadly virus that first appeared in 1978. Dogs are usually infected through contact with the feces of infected dogs. It attacks the white blood cells, intestinal tract, and even the heart. The incubation period is from two to seven days, and symptoms include depression, appetite loss, vomiting, severe diarrhea, and bleeding. Even with excellent veterinary care, most puppies who contract this disease die; older dogs are better able to handle the disease. Parvo is a cold-hardy virus that can survive in infected feces at temperatures as low as 20°F (-6.7°C).

Regular vet checkups will help keep your dog healthy.

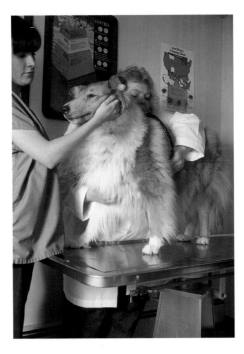

conditions require frequent vaccinations (every six months) to be effective. Your vet will talk to you about your dog's lifestyle to see which, if any, non-core vaccines might be required.

Kennel Cough: Your dog should be vaccinated against kennel cough if he is boarded, shown, or goes out often amongst other dogs. Kennel cough is similar to bronchitis, in which the dog coughs in a very distinctive, gagging manner. He may spit up foamy slime, too. Most of the time, kennel cough is not serious and will resolve on its own.

The disease is infectious and can be brought on by certain infectious agents or stressful conditions like shipping, crowding, or exposure to smoke and dust. It is more likely to occur in cold places with poor ventilation. The main bacterial agent is *Bordetella bronchiseptica*, which can bind to and immobilize protective cilia (hair-like cells) in the respiratory system and secrete nasty substances that disable the immune cells. However, bordetella seldom acts alone, which is why this disease can be hard to vaccinate against. Bordetella doesn't just pick on dogs, either—it can infect kittens, rabbits, guinea pigs, and swine. People cannot get kennel cough, although we get its cousin—the whooping cough.

The incubation period for kennel cough is 12 to 14 days. Many vets will prescribe an antibiotic for kennel cough, along with a cough suppressant designed for humans. Very young puppies and older dogs need special care so that they do not develop pneumonia. Vaccinations are available but are not very effective due to the many other agents other than *Bordetella bronchiseptica* that can cause the disease. In fact, the vaccination is useless if the dog has already been exposed. It is also a

Rabies: The rabies vaccine is one of the most important, since the disease is invariably fatal to both humans and dogs. Rabies is caused by a virus present in the saliva and is usually transmitted through a bite wound. The virus attaches itself to the muscle wall for a day or so and then penetrates the nerve cells, at which point the virus is protected from the host's immune system. Dogs usually become infected through contact with infected skunks, raccoons, foxes, and bats.

Non-Core Vaccinations

Non-core vaccinations are not required for every dog but are recommended in certain geographical areas or for dogs exposed to a large number of other dogs. These include vaccines against parainfluenza/bordetella (kennel cough), Lyme disease, leptospirosis, and so on. Many of these short-lived vaccine that needs to be repeated every six months in dogs who are boarded frequently or who visit other dogs.

Leptospirosis: Leptospirosis is a severe, contagious infection that can be caused by several species of the *Leptospira* spirochetes. They thrive in wet, moderate temperatures and prefer to live in mildly alkaline soils. There are more than 200 strains of the disease around the world, and unfortunately, leptospirosis vaccines don't provide protection against most of them (although new vaccines include protection against more strains). Formerly in the US, the disease was primarily caused by *L. canicola* and *L. icterohaemorrhaiae*. Current cases, however, are most commonly caused by *L. Pomona*, *L. gripptotyphosa*, *L. bratislava*, and *L. autumnalis*. Dogs are usually infected when they are exposed to contaminated urine; other sources may include bite wounds or eating infected carcasses. The bacteria penetrate the mucous membranes of the skin; then the disease usually attacks the kidney, pancreas, and liver.

Signs appear within 4 to 14 days of infection and include fever, muscle pain, loss of appetite, excessive thirst and urination, and swelling of the legs. Leptospirosis can be passed to human beings and other animals. Therapy consists of supportive fluids and antibiotics. This is a very serious disease.

If you live in an area where leptospirosis is prevalent, consider vaccinating your dog against it. However, you should be aware that some dogs who are sensitive to vaccines may have a reaction to this one in particular. Although the newest generation of vaccines seems to be safer, make sure you discuss the issue with your vet. You can try to prevent this disease by using a 1:10 solution of bleach or an antibacterial cleaning solution to water when cleaning up urine. When done, always wash your hands thoroughly. Of course, never let your dog urinate near pools, ponds, or streams.

KEEPING YOUR DOG SINGLE: THE VALUE OF NEUTERING

Neutering your dog is the good dogkeeper's only responsible option. More than 12 million former pets are put to death every year because they are no longer wanted. Rather than producing more puppies, try adopting one of these needy animals instead.

Neutering not only cuts down on the number of puppies born but will also protect your dog from several reproductive-related health problems, including pyometra (a deadly infection of the uterus), mammary and ovarian cancers in female dogs, and prostate and testicular cancers in male dogs. In fact, unspayed females are at an extremely high risk for mammary tumors—about 50 percent of which will be malignant.

Breeding correctly is also very expensive, requiring genetic testing and frequent examinations of both mother and puppies. Can you afford to spend several hundred dollars up front in the hope of making a profit later? And if the genetic tests turn out unfavorably, will you forgo breeding? Dogs with a history of diabetes, allergies, hip dysplasia, cancer, and the like should not be bred.

TESTING, TESTING! COMMON MEDICAL TESTS AND WHAT THEY TELL YOUR VET

Contemporary dogs get the same basic blood and urine tests that we do. They provide your vet all kinds of information about your dog's health. Since you will get a copy of your dog's lab work, it's a good idea to know a little bit about what it means.

Urinalysis

Owners can often tell something is wrong by the quality (color, cloudiness, and so on) of a dog's urine. Ordinary urine is yellow or amber. Red urine suggests blood, while dark yellow probably results from excess bilirubin and suggests liver disease. Cloudy urine may be caused by crystals, blood, mucus, casts, or bacteria. Urinalysis is needed to give a real diagnosis. Sometimes you will be asked to collect dog urine yourself—attach a clean plastic cup to a dismantled wire hanger and carefully maneuver it under the dog while he's in action. You don't need a lot, which is a good thing.

The official urinalysis will include the following values:

Bacteria: Bacteria are not normally found in urine. They may indicate a urinary tract infection.

Blood: Blood is not found in normal urine. If it is present, there may be infection, kidney stones, trauma, or a tumor.

Casts: Casts are clumps of blood or kidney cells and usually form in the presence of protein and an acid pH.

Crystals: Crystals in urine can result from diet, drugs, or a variety of disease conditions.

Glucose: Normal urine does not contain glucose (the principal sugar found in the blood). When present, glucose may indicate diabetes or kidney

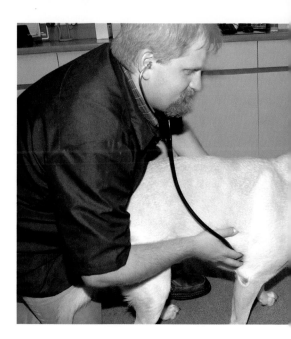

disease. It might also show up if your dog has just eaten.

Ketones: Ketones are not present in normal urine. They may indicate diabetes or malnutrition.

pH: The pH measures the acidity of the urine and must be measured from a fresh sample. A pH outside the normal range may indicate kidney trouble. Normal pH is 6.2 to 6.5—somewhat on the acidic side. Like many tests, however, this one can be thrown off by diet and drugs.

Protein: Normal urine has no protein. If protein is present, there may be kidney disease or infection.

Specific Gravity: The specific gravity test measures the particulate concentration in urine. If the test comes back high, it means the urine is highly concentrated; if low, it means the urine is diluted. Results off normal may mean kidney disease, diabetes, or an adrenal problem, but drugs and water intake may also affect it.

Urine Color and Clarity: Normal urine is clear

The best way to prevent your dog healthy is to keep him from getting sick or hurt in the first place.

Platelets: Platelets help blood clot. A high numbers may occur with cancer, bone cancer, or blood vessel injury. A low number suggests bone marrow depression, autoimmune hemolytic anemia, lupus, or hemorrhage.

MCHC: MCHC (mean corpuscular hemoglobin concentration) measures how much hemoglobin is in the red blood cells. A high number suggests too much iron in the blood, while a low number suggests anemia.

MCV: MCV (mean cell volume) is a measure of the red blood cell size. A high number reveals vitamin (usually folic acid) deficiency. A low number suggests iron deficiency.

Red blood cell count (Hematocrit [HCT] or Packed Cell Volume [PCV]): Red blood cells, which carry oxygen, are produced in the marrow. A high count may reveal dehydration. A low count suggests anemia, parasites, bone marrow disease, B-12 deficiency, hemorrhage, or a chronic disease.

Reticulocytes: These are immature red blood cells. A high count suggests chronic hemorrhage

and pale yellow. Cloudy urine suggests infection, but drugs, the presence of blood, and even vitamins can alter the color.

White Blood Cells: White blood cells are absent from normal urine. If present, your dog may have an infection or inflammation of the urinary tract.

Blood Test (Hemogram or Complete Blood Count [CBC])

There are three kinds of blood cells: red blood cells, white blood cells, and platelets. Blood tests analyze the blood cells that circulate through the bloodstream. Results may include:

Hemoglobin (Hb): Hemoglobin is the part of the blood that carries oxygen. A high hemoglobin count is associated with a high red blood cell count and suggests dehydration or B-12 deficiency. A low number suggests anemia, iron deficiency, or hemorrhage.

How to Prevent Illness

The best way to keep your dog healthy is to keep him from getting sick or hurt in the first place! You can do this by:

- Feeding him a healthy diet. Many dogs eat too much and get fat and sick.
- Keeping him safely in your yard or on a leash.
- Making sure he gets regular vaccinations and veterinary checkups.
- Giving him plenty of exercise, love, and attention.
- Training him.

or hemolytic anemia. A low count is also associated with anemia.

Blood tests analyze the blood cells that circulate through the bloodstream.

White blood cell count: These cells are produced in the marrow or lymph nodes and are the body's main way to fight infections. A high count reveals infections, stress, or various blood disorders. A low count may reveal an out of control infection or poisoning. Special white blood cells such as segmented neutrophils, lymphocytes, monocytes, and eosinophils are also measured. The first three are infection fighters, so a high number of the first three may indicate infection; a high number of eosinophils suggests parasites or allergies. The last kind fights against allergic reactions and parasites.

Chemistry Panel

The chemistry panel checks the chemistry of the blood and primarily evaluates organ function. Kidney and liver problems are especially likely to show up on this battery of tests. It gives results for the following values (among others):

Alanine Amino-Transferase (ALT): High levels of this liver enzyme suggest liver/kidney disease.

Low levels may mean stress or fatigue.

Albumin (ALB): High levels of albumin (a small liver protein) indicate dehydration and protein loss. Low levels mean chronic liver or kidney problems, intestinal disease, or heart failure.

Aspartate Amino-Transferase (AST): High levels suggest heart, liver, kidney, pancreas, or muscle damage. Low levels suggest a vitamin B deficiency.

Alkaline Phosphate: High levels of this substance, which originates from many tissues in the body, indicate Cushing's disease, injury, or liver problems. Low levels indicate anemia or malnutrition.

Amylase (AMYL): High levels of this pancreatic and intestinal enzyme indicate pancreatic/liver/kidney problems. Low levels may suggest malnutrition.

Bilirubin: High levels of bilirubin, a waste product produced by the liver and usually eliminated in the urine and feces, may indicate a liver or gall bladder problem.

BUN (Blood Urea Nitrogen): A high BUN, which measures the waste products circulating in the blood, indicates kidney disease; a low BUN may mean liver disease or low protein.

Calcium: High values may suggest cancer (often bone cancer) or problems with the parathyroid gland or kidney. Low levels (less common) indicate pancreatitis or stress.

Chloride: High chloride suggests acidosis or kidney disease. Low values may also indicate kidney failure.

Cholesterol: High levels of cholesterol can indicate hypothyroidism or liver and kidney disease. Decreased levels may mean an overactive thyroid.

Creatinine (CREA): Creatinine is a by-product of muscle metabolism. High creatinine indicates renal problems or diabetes. Low creatinine can also indicate kidney or liver damage.

Electrolyte levels: The electrolytes are sodium, potassium, and chloride. An imbalance in the levels may indicate Addison's disease, kidney failure, or bladder problems.

Gamma Glutamyl Transpeptidase: High levels suggest liver disease or pancreatitis. Low levels may mean hypothyroidism or malfunction of the hypothalamus.

Globulin: High globulin suggests infections or inflammations, liver disease, heart disease, or cancer. Low levels may mean immunodeficiency or infection disease. The ratio between globulin and albumin may also indicate certain problems.

Glucose: High blood sugar can mean diabetes, an overactive adrenal gland, Cushing's disease, or stress. Low glucose suggests liver or pancreas problems. Low blood sugar is more of a problem with toy breeds.

Phosphorus: High phosphorus may mean kidney or liver disease. Low values can indicate cancer, parathyroid problems, or liver disease.

Potassium: High levels suggest renal problems or diabetes. Low levels suggest renal problems or malnutrition.

Sodium: High sodium suggests anemia, kidney or liver disease, or just a poor diet. Low sodium can indicate Addison's disease or poor nerve function. Both conditions may suggest a poor diet.

Total protein: High levels indicate dehydration or bone or bone marrow cancer. Low levels may indicate liver or kidney disease, malnutrition, or hemorrhage.

Triglycerides: High levels can be related to seizures and behavior problems. Low levels suggest malnutrition.

T3 (Triiodothyronine) and T4 (Thyroxine): These tests are performed to evaluate thyroid function.

Fecal Exam

The vet may use a fecal test to check for parasites and help diagnose parvo, certain malassimilation syndromes, ulcers, inflammatory bowel disease, and some tumors. You may have to collect the fecal sample yourself. Use a clean plastic bag, scoop up some of the stool, and put it in a disposable plastic container. Take it to the vet as soon as you can. It is possible to refrigerate the stuff—but who wants to?

Imaging

Various imaging techniques, including radiograph, electrocardiogram, CT scans, ultrasound, and MRI, are all extremely useful in diagnosing abnormalities of organs.

13

THE HOME HEALTH CHECK

To be a full partner to your vet, learn to do a frequent health check on your dog. To help you do this, we'll go over the body systems, explain how they work, and show you how you can alert your vet for any signs of abnormality. Your veterinarian is responsible for the systems health of your dog. However, it is helpful for you to know what's going on as well, so without further ado, here is what your dog is made of.

THE MUSCULOSKELETAL SYSTEM

The musculoskeletal system (in both dogs and people) consists of bones, cartilage, muscles, ligaments, and tendons. Its main function is to support your dog's body, help him move, and protect his vital organs. In addition, the bones store calcium and phosphorus and contain essential components of the blood-making system.

Diseases of the musculoskeletal system often involve motion problems. Skeletal and joint disorders are the most common; however, primary muscular diseases, nerve weakness, toxins, endocrine aberrations, metabolic disorders, infectious diseases, blood and vascular disorders, nutritional imbalances, and congenital (hereditary) defects may also play a part.

Bone diseases can be congenital, nutritional, or traumatic. Bone defects due to poor nutrition are caused primarily by imbalances or deficiencies in minerals. Other nutritional disorders are caused by excessive protein intake by growing animals. Either deficiency or excess intake of certain vitamins, particularly vitamins A and D, may influence growth and development of bone. Incorrect amounts of zinc or copper also cause trouble. Traumatic causes of bone disorders include fractures as well as a host of other problems.

Common diseases of the musculoskeletal system include arthritis, hip dysplasia, ligament rupture, and various cancers.

Cranial Ligament Rupture

Cranial (or anterior cruciate) ligament rupture is the most common orthopedic condition to affect large and mid-sized dogs. The cruciate ligaments are part of the knee joint. When the problem occurs in people, it's usually because of an injury. With dogs, it can be due to degeneration or basic wear and tear of the system. While at one time the disease was limited to older dogs, nowadays we are seeing

To be a full partner to your vet, learn to do a frequent health check on your dog.

University of Bern in Switzerland have discovered that nitric oxide in a young dog's urine may be an early indicator of osteoarthritis and hip dysplasia.

Good treatment begins with medical management (glucosamine/chondroitin and nonsteroidal anti-inflammatory drugs like adequen, Rimadyl, and cosequin)—especially for older dogs who develop the condition later in life—range-of-motion stretching exercises, acupuncture, and diet control. Surgery can also be an option. Many types of surgery are available, depending on the severity of the condition, the age and weight of the dog, and the owner's choices. They have exotic names like triple pelvic osteotomy (TPO), a sort of preventive treatment performed on young dogs, femoral head excision, in which the ball part of the hip is removed, and total hip replacement using a steel alloy and high-density plastic.

younger and younger dogs develop the problem. A sign of the disease includes limping on the rear leg. In some cases, the inflicted dog seems better able to run than to walk or trot. The condition usually needs to be corrected with surgery.

Hip Dysplasia

Hip dysplasia is a widespread, polygenetic (caused by many genes) disease that can be worsened by environmental influence. The normal hip is a ball and socket arrangement in which the ball (femoral head) of the thighbone fits into the socket (acetabulum) of the pelvis. Muscles and ligaments hold it all together. In hip dysplasia, the femoral head or acetabulum can be deformed or dislocated, or the muscles or ligaments may be in poor condition, or the bones may be growing at the wrong or an uneven rate. The disease is painful and hinders movement. Dogs with hip dysplasia often have trouble getting up, lying down, and climbing stairs. The disease is diagnosed by X-ray. Large breeds are most at risk, although the disease can strike any breed. Researchers at the

Legg-Calve-Perthes Disease

This condition, which is a loss of blood supply to the cap of the femur bone in the hip, affects mostly smaller dogs and causes painful rear-leg lameness. It is diagnosed by X-ray and treated by a surgical removal of the diseased joint cartilage.

Patellar Luxation

Patellar luxation (slipping stifles, loose knee) is a hind leg lameness that occurs in many small breeds. A dog with this condition has a kneecap that slips out of joint, then tends to rest on the inside of the knee. Dogs with patellar luxation are intermittently lame, moving with the bad leg held off the ground. The disease is hereditary, although several different genes are involved in its transmission.

Veterinarians rank the seriousness of patellar luxation from grades 1 to 4. Grade 1 cases may be so slight as to be unnoticeable, while grade 4 cases produce permanent lameness, with the kneecaps not in position. Serious cases require an operation followed by several weeks of forced rest. The results are usually excellent, and the surgery is not particularly difficult.

Spinal or Disc Disease

One of the most commonly affected areas in certain breeds (like Dachshunds) are the intervertebral discs that sit between the vertebrae in the spine. The discs are like little shock absorbers that help dissipate pressure on the spine. They have two portions, an outside fibrous covering (the annulus fibrosis) and an inside, more gelatinous portion (the nucleus pulposis). If the discs become damaged, it is usually called intervertebral disc disease (IDD), or slipped disc, although in reality nothing has slipped. It can occur in any part of the spinal cord, usually because too much force was placed on the spine. The sooner medical treatment (which often means surgery) is sought, the better the chances for a complete recovery.

What You Can Do to Help Your Dog's Bones

To keep your dog's bones strong, keep him active. Weight-bearing exercise and water exercise will maintain your dog's bone health. Too much jumping and twisting can have the opposite effect. (Dogs weren't born to catch Frisbees.) And while calcium supplementation may be valuable for people, it can be dangerous for growing dogs. Check with your vet before supplementing minerals. Neutraceuticals are another matter— aging, arthritic dogs do well with the addition of glucosamine/chondroitin to their diet.

THE RESPIRATORY SYSTEM

The canine respiratory system is remarkably similar to ours. It is made up of the nostrils, nose, sinuses, pharynx, larynx, windpipe, bronchi (branches of the windpipe that go into the lungs), and the lungs themselves.

Like us, dogs have two lungs, each of which is divided into lobes. The lungs are filled with air pockets (alveoli) where the blood connects with individual cells in the lungs and oxygen and carbon dioxide are exchanged. The respiratory system also acts to cool the body. Dogs don't have sweat glands (except a few on the pads), so they can't perspire like people and horses. To cool off, they need to pant, exchanging old hot air for fresh cool air and evaporating water off the tongue. It is not very efficient, but dogs do what they can.

The most common problem affecting the respiratory system is kennel cough. Smaller breed dogs can also suffer from collapsed trachea.

What You Can Do to Help Your Dog's Respiratory System

Many respiratory problems come from easily preventable conditions like bordetella or heartworm. If you vaccinate your dog properly, you'll avoid them. Take the same care of your dog's environment as you would a child's. Don't smoke around him, and keep him away from pollution as much as possible. Pure air means healthy lungs.

THE CARDIOVASCULAR SYSTEM

The heart is only about one percent of your dog's body weight, but without it, life would be impossible. The heart consists of four chambers: two atria that take in blood and two ventricles that expel blood, along with four one-way valves. The atria and ventricles work in harmony; as the atria contract, the ventricles relax, and vice versa.

There are many diseases of the cardiovascular system, including pulmonic stenosis (common mostly in terriers, Chihuahuas, Beagles, and Bulldogs), heart murmurs, congestive heart failure, patent ductus arteriosus (for small breeds, Collies, Irish Setters, and German Shepherd Dogs), as well as cardiomyopathies (a group of heart muscle disorders). In fact, almost all heart disease problems found in humans are also found in dogs. Mitral valve disease is extremely common in older dogs—more than one-third of them are affected. Modern veterinary science is working wonders for heart disease with the development of balloons, coils, pacemakers, and other devices to correct congenital defects. If it is your choice (and within your financial means) to correct such problems, the earlier it is done, the better.

Doggy Blood Types

Everyone knows that humans have blood types, but do dogs have them, too? Well, yes. Current classification systems (there are more than one) give between 8 and 12 blood types for dogs, all categorized under the Dog Erythrocyte System Antigen (DESA) system. The good thing is that dogs don't seem to have naturally occurring antibodies to different blood types the way humans beings (and cats) do. This means that transfusions are not generally a problem, as an allergic reaction is very unlikely. (Of course, it is best if the types match, and canine blood banks do exist.) There are also synthetic blood replacers that are lifesavers for many dogs.

What You Can Do to Help Your Dog's Heart

Holistic veterinarians believe that supplementing your dog's food with the amino acids carnitine (essential for the transport of fatty acids) and taurine (important in normal heart function) will help regulate heart function. Coenzyme Q10 (ubiquinone) aids cell metabolism and probably helps the heart use energy. Fish oil aids congestive heart failure patients by helping to stop muscle wasting. If there is any salt in your dog's diet, get rid of it. This will help lower blood volume. Consider a pacemaker. Manufacturers donate excess pacemakers that have reached the end of their shelf life for human use but are still fine for dogs.

To learn more about the cardiovascular system or to find a cardiologist certified by the American

College of Veterinary Internal Medicine (ACVIM), go to www.acvim.org.

THE INTEGUMENTARY SYSTEM

The integumentary system consists of the skin and coat. The skin helps regulate body temperature and blood pressure, stores vitamins, proteins, and electrolytes, makes vitamin D, and serves as a primary sense organ. (It also, as you may have noticed, produces hair and claws.) The most common scare dog owners have in dealing with skin health is the appearance of a sudden lump or bump. There's a chance it could be nothing, or it could be cancer. In most cases, the only way to be sure is to have a veterinary pathologist make a microscopic examination of the cells inside the lump. Noncancerous bumps include lipomas, warts, cysts, infected hair follicles, and blood blisters. Some can be uncomfortable for the dog, but they are generally nothing to worry about. Cancerous lumps include mammary gland tumors, mast cell tumors, cutaneous lymphosarcoma, malignant melanoma, and fibrosarcoma. Mast cell tumor is the most common skin malignancy to occur in dogs. It is a strange cancer that does not seem to behave predictably, although new approaches, including kinase-inhibitor therapy, are being developed to treat it.

Most lumps are lipomas or sebaceous cysts. A lipoma is a soft, fatty, noncancerous tumor just below the skin. Most do not have to be removed unless they grow very large. In a very few cases, a lipoma can turn malignant. A sebaceous cyst is a plugged gland in the skin. Sometimes they erupt and disappear, and sometimes they become chronically infected, in which case they need to be removed. Certain breeds, such as Basset Hounds and Cocker Spaniels, are very prone to these cysts. In some cases, a sebaceous cyst can develop into a tumor called sebaceous adenoma.

These usually cause no trouble after they are removed.

Dandruff

In case you're wondering, dogs can get dandruff. Labrador Retrievers seem especially susceptible. If your dog is a victim of doggy dandruff (and many more serious conditions can mimic it), a good coal tar shampoo followed by a moisturizer will usually clear it up.

Hotspots

Hotspots are common summertime lesions. The most common cause is a fleabite, but allergies can also be responsible. Sometimes dogs seem to develop them for no reason at all. Labradors, Golden Retrievers, Saint Bernards, German Shepherd Dogs, and Collies seem especially vulnerable. It starts with a tiny red spot but can spread alarmingly quickly. In most cases, a hotspot can be treated through gentle cleaning and the use of a drying agent.

Cancerous and Noncancerous Lumps

While you cannot tell a cancerous from noncancerous lump just by looking, there are a few guidelines. In general, benign bumps have defined borders and are the same color as the surrounding skin. They start small and stay small. Cancerous bumps have indistinct borders and are often a different color from the surrounding skin. They have rapid growth and may or may not ooze. Inflamed or infected bumps are usually very red and may contain pus. You should always check any suspicious lumps with your vet.

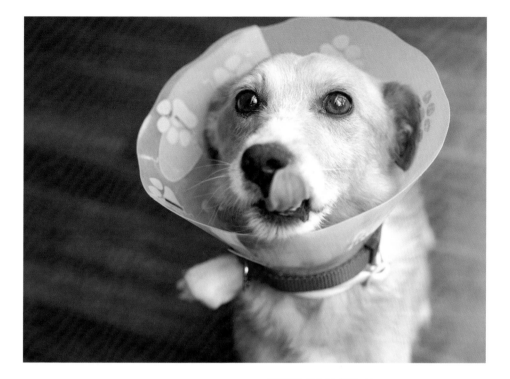

Lick Granuloma

Lick granuloma, also called acral lick granuloma or acral lick dermatitis, is also a very common ailment. Affected animals continually lick one area of the body (usually a paw or area on the lower leg) until this area becomes raw, scarred, weepy, red, or inflamed. Most times, the cause appears to be hereditary, possibly due to a neurological problem. Other precipitating causes may include allergies, boredom, overlicking a wound or sore place, and so on. The affected animal is usually an older male, with the following working and sporting breeds having a particularly high incidence: Dobermans, Pointers, German Short-Haired Pointers, Golden and Labrador Retrievers, Great Danes, and Irish Setters.

The physical treatment of the lesion can include

The vet may have your dog wear an Elizabethan collar to keep him from worrying at a skin problem.

surgical removal, or in some cases, the lesion can be bandaged. But in order to treat lick granuloma, the cause of it must be determined. After treating the cause, further therapy can include increasing the amount of interaction with the dog or distracting him from the behavior, which usually works only in the earlier stages. Often medical treatment is required, especially antidepressants used in the treatment of obsessive-compulsive disorders in humans. Other drugs can include tranquilizers or sedatives, endorphin blockers, corticosteroids, endorphin blockers, and pentoxifylline. Lick granuloma is a tough disease to handle once it becomes a habit.

Seborrhea

Seborrhea is a clinical syndrome rather than a specific disease and is usually secondary to some other problems like allergies, fungal infections, dietary problems, or hormone imbalances. Sometimes, however, it appears alone (primary seborrhea). It can appear as flaky, dry skin or conversely as rank, greasy, scaly skin. Sometimes it appears as both at once, and symptoms are usually most noticeable in the folds of the skin. The dog may have ear problems as well.

Treatment includes trying to discover and treat the underlying cause, if possible. Primary seborrhea has no cure, although it can sometimes be helped with vitamin A derivatives or oral cyclosporine. Anti-seborrheic shampoos are also important, although they can be hard to use, since they must stay on your pet for several minutes. It is very important to get the shampoo into all affected areas, including the feet.

Skin Problems Due to Allergies

Skin problems due to allergies are perhaps the most common ailment in dogs. While humans react to allergies by sneezing, dogs react with skin problems. If your dog is scratching constantly, allergies may be the culprit, so be sure to talk to your vet. Many treatment options are available, including treating the symptoms, immunotherapy, corticosteroids, antihistamines, adding fatty acids to the diet, or environmental control.

What You Can Do to Help Your Dog's Skin

Here's one place you can really shine! Keep your dog clean and well groomed. Bathe him frequently. Once a month, feel him carefully all over. If you find a lump that was not there before, don't panic. It is probably a lipoma or a sebaceous cyst. Both of these conditions are usually harmless, although they may have to be removed if, as sometimes

happens with a lipoma, they grow large enough to interfere with movement, or if they erupt, which sometimes happens with a cyst. Anything that is reddened and nasty-looking warrants a trip to the vet. Most lumps can be tested by a simple needle biopsy that does not require anesthesia or surgery.

Approach each case individually. If your dog has a history of harmless lumps, the new lump is probably of the same sort, but the only way you can be sure is to have it examined by a veterinarian. For more information about the skin and its problems, or to find a veterinary dermatologist, go to www.acvd.org.

THE DIGESTIVE SYSTEM

The dog's digestive system always arouses interest, especially for the dog. A dog's digestive system basically works the same way our digestive system works. There are several digestive disorders that can afflict your dog.

Bloat

Bloat (gastric dilatation volvulus or gastric torsion) is probably the greatest digestive emergency that can strike your dog. In bloat, the stomach swells with trapped air or gas. It may then twist (that's the torsion) on its long axis, which closes off the esophagus. Normal blood flow is cut off from the liver and spleen. The blood return to the heart decreases, and the heart may go into arrhythmia. Toxins build up in the stomach, and shock from low blood pressure develops. There is nothing at all trivial about this disease.

Factors leading to bloat include:
- Breed disposition. Large-breed dogs, especially Great Danes, Newfoundlands, Saint Bernards, Bloodhounds, Basset Hounds, Greyhounds, Weimaraners, and setters are at increased risk.
- Family history. Close relatives of bloat victims have a 63 percent greater risk of developing

bloat than those without such relatives.

- Weight. Underweight dogs are three times more likely to suffer bloat. They don't have the fat that can "cushion" the stomach and prevent it from moving around.
- Age. The risk increases with age. For large breeds, the risk of developing bloat goes up 20 percent each year after the age of five. Giant breeds are even more at risk.
- Dogs of a nervous, fearful, or aggressive temperament. Calm, happy dogs are at a reduced risk.
- An all-kibble diet. During the past 30 years, there has been a 1,500 percent increase in bloat. This corresponds to the increase in feeding dry food. If you feed your dog kibble, add canned food or table scraps to every meal.
- Kibble with citric acid as a preservative.
- Feeding conditions. Raised food bowls increase the risk of bloat by 110 percent, just the opposite of what was believed for years. Dogs who eat too quickly and gulp air with their food have a 15 percent greater risk of developing bloat. Try scattering the food over a large tray to slow down fast eaters.

- Once a day feeding. Divide daily rations into two or more meals.

Signs of bloat include a visibly enlarged, tight abdomen (like a drum), belching, repeated, unsuccessful attempts to vomit, restlessness, salivation, and panting. The dog may lie in what is commonly called a "praying position," with the front legs drawn fully forward. At the first sign of bloat, call your vet. This is a life-threatening emergency that cannot wait. Approximately one-third of all dogs who get bloat die. A few minutes can make the difference between life and death.

The dog must be stabilized, usually with IV fluids and corticosteroids. Often the vet will try to pass a lubricated stomach tube to vent the stomach gases and fluids. If this doesn't work, a large-bore needle may be passed directly into the stomach. Then a surgical procedure is performed to reposition the stomach. This is risky surgery, but there is no other option.

Most veterinarians now also recommend a gastropexy for at-risk dogs, which tacks the stomach to the abdominal wall and almost always prevents further episodes of torsion, although the stomach can still bloat. This procedure can also be done prophylactically during a spay. At many clinics, this kind of surgery can be performed laparoscopically for at-risk dogs. The procedure requires only two small incisions.

Hemorrhagic Gastroenteritis

Hemorrhagic gastroenteritis (HGE) primarily affects small dogs. It is non-contagious, but no one knows what causes it. Symptoms include bloody diarrhea and perhaps vomiting. An untreated dog can quickly go into shock and collapse, so it's essential to get the affected animal to the vet immediately for treatment with intravenous fluids.

What You Can Do to Help Your Dog's Digestive System

Many digestive disorders (including simple gas) are due to a lack of digestive enzymes in the dog's system; you may want to add them to your dog's diet. You can buy them in any health food store. In addition, monitor your dog's diet —don't overload it with fat, sugar, and dairy products. Feed your dog smaller, more frequent meals, and avoid all-kibble diets. Don't let your kids play the "Let's see what the dog will eat" game, either.

LIVER PROBLEMS

The liver is also part of the digestive system. Many liver disorders plague the contemporary dog, including cancer, infections, certain drug-induced toxicities (high doses of anti-inflammatory corticosteroids, ketoconazole, carprofen, phenobarbital, and Tylenol can all have adverse effects), hepatitis, and congenital liver shunts. A new urine test, urine bile acids (UBA), can help detect liver disease. Signs of liver disease include intermittent gastrointestinal upset, loss of appetite, weight loss, vomiting, pale feces, orange urine, and yellowing gums.

What You Can Do to Help a Dog with Liver Problems

Recently, veterinarians have found that supplementing S-adenosylmethionine (SAMe), a substance naturally produced by the body from the amino acid methionine, is very helpful for liver patients. If the liver is damaged, the body produces less of the critical antioxidant glutathione. With less glutathione available, even more liver cells become damaged, and a vicious cycle is started. SAMe is available as an oral dietary supplement that boosts glutathione production. A stabilized form of SAMe called Denosyl SD4 is made by Nutramax Laboratories, Inc., for veterinary use. Use a dosage

recommended by your vet, and give the medication only when the dog has an empty stomach. (You

To help your dog's digestive system, feed him smaller, more frequent meals.

can put it in a very small treat if necessary.) Make sure the dog swallows the pill quickly; otherwise, it can cause irritation to the stomach.

DENTAL PROBLEMS

Digestion begins in the oral cavity, and so tooth and gum problems can be serious. Signs of dental problems include bad breath, bleeding gums, loss of appetite, depression, and irritability when touched or petted on the head. Some dogs rub at their mouths as well. All breeds, especially small ones (who tend to have crowded mouths) are at risk, and the risk increases with age. Regular, thorough brushing can help prevent dental problems, but once they set in, the dog will probably require veterinary dental cleaning and perhaps extraction. Dental disease often starts with plaque, a sticky but invisible substance full of bacteria that coats the teeth, even below the gum line. Long-standing plaque develops into tartar, a hard yellow substance starting at the base of the tooth. As the bacteria population grows, the gum begins to pull away from the tooth, and a "periodontal pocket" is formed. More dangerous bacteria fill this pocket and begin to destroy the periodontal ligament and perhaps even the jawbone. Soon the tooth can abscess or fall out. We know now that the danger doesn't restrict itself to the oral cavity. The bacteria can invade the bloodstream and attack the liver, heart, lungs, and kidneys.

What You Can Do to Protect Your Dog's Dental Health

Brush, brush, brush. Every day, if possible. While your dog may resent brushing at first, he will get used to it and live a happier life with his clean strong teeth. Eating will be a joy rather than a challenge, and he will play happily with his toys. Remember to use toothpaste designed for canines. (They come in beef and chicken flavors.) When brushing, don't overrestrain your dog; that will serve to make him more fearful. Start with a short session, lots of praise, and a treat afterward. If your dog won't accept a toothbrush, use your finger with a thin dental gauze over it. (They can be purchased at a pet supply store, and while not as good as brushing, they're better than nothing.) There are also some new products you can add to your dog's water that contain zinc chloride, which fights bacteria buildup.

Also check the inside of your dog's mouth frequently. If the teeth are clean and white and the gums are a healthy pink, everything is probably well. On the other hand, if you see that the place where the teeth meet the gums is red and inflamed, your dog needs work. Don't forget to

All breeds, especially small ones, are at risk of dental disease, and the risk increases with age.

smell his breath! A sweet breath signals a healthy mouth. Your dog should have a dental cleaning every year, more frequently if he is elderly or has a history of gum disease. While hard chews and certain toys may help to some extent to keep the mouth clean, they don't replace brushing because they can't get below the gumline.

To learn more about dental problems or to find a veterinary dentist, go to: www.avds-online.org or www.vetdentistry.com/membership.

URINARY SYSTEM

The urinary or renal system filters wastes from the blood and makes and stores urine. The four parts of the renal system are the kidneys, bladder, ureters, and urethra.

The most important part of the renal system is the kidneys, two bean-shaped organs located outside of the peritoneum—the membrane enclosing the organs of the abdominal cavity. The ureters are muscular tubes that transport urine from the kidneys to the bladder. The bladder is a sac that stores the urine temporarily. Finally, the urine leaves the bladder through the urethra, a tube running from bladder to the outside of the body. It is much shorter in the female than in the male, disposing the female to more frequent infections. The male's urethra is also used for reproductive purposes, as in people. In both sexes, of course, the animal has voluntary control over the external urethral sphincter. (Without this function, dogs would make really bad pets.)

Kidneys

Kidneys work to keep the body's chemical reactions in balance; these reactions include blood pressure, acid-base balance, and mineral levels. And most familiarly, they help eliminate waste. Kidneys can be damaged by bacterial infection, inherited problems like renal dysplasia (found most commonly in Shih Tzu and Lhasa Apsos), toxins (like antifreeze), and amyloidosis (an often fatal condition in which immune proteins are deposited in kidney tissues). Kidney failure, a general name for a condition in which the kidneys fail to remove waste products, is one of the most common diseases in older dogs. Signs of kidney failure include loss of appetite, vomiting and diarrhea, lethargy, depression, and excessive thirst. (Unfortunately, these are also the signs of many other diseases.)

One of the curses of kidney disease is that it is often not discovered until it is quite advanced. This is because the kidneys continue to function well enough even while they are being destroyed. However, a new test is able to detect very small levels of protein in the urine, which often signals the start of kidney disease.

Dogs with kidney failure can also benefit from dialysis, which involves the use of semi-permeable

If your dog seems unusually lethargic, take him to the vet.

membranes that filter toxins from the body and regulate water levels. There are two types: peritoneal (in which fluid is placed into the body cavity) and hemodialysis, a more effective (and much more expensive) method that uses the dog's circulatory system. A few places perform dog kidney transplants but without much success.

What You Can Do to Help Your Dog's Kidney Health

To help your dog's kidneys get a good workout, make sure he has plenty of opportunity to eliminate. Dogs who are compelled to "hold it" for hours and hours can develop bladder and kidney trouble. Observe the frequency and amount of your dog's urine, and report anything unusual to the vet. Get his urine tested yearly, and have a blood chemistry panel done at the same time. Prevention is the cure here.

BLADDER STONES

One of the most common problems affecting the renal system is bladder stones. Signs often include bloody urine and recurrent bladder infections. Other dogs may just give indications of discomfort; still others may show no signs at all. (Sometimes a stone can be passed in the urine, but even then, the stone should be taken to the veterinarian for analysis—there may be more of them.) Bladder stones come in different mineral compositions, the most common being struvite and oxalate. It is important to know what kind your dog has, since they require different dietary treatments after removal. Removal is generally done by surgery, although if this is not possible for some reason, other methods can be tried, including a special diet. One new noninvasive method is extracorporeal shock wave lithotripsy, which is usually used on calcium oxalate stones that can't be dissolved medically. In this treatment, shock waves are focused to break down the stone so that the smaller particles can be voided in the urine. It is available only at a few places and is very expensive. To learn more about it, go to Healthtronics at www.healthtronics.com or Focus-It at www.shockwavetherapy.com.

NERVOUS SYSTEM

The nervous system controls the signals that are sent from one part of the body to another using a complex system of interconnected, electrically active nerve cells. These nerves, often called neurons, are bundled together like strands of rope. Their special shape allows them to communicate with each other. The places where the nerves communicate are called the synapses. Your dog's brain has billions of them (not as many as you do, but still a handy number). Unfortunately, if these nerves die, they cannot be replaced.

Cognitive Dysfunction Syndrome (CDS)

The most common ailment that affects the nervous system is cognitive dysfunction syndrome, also called canine cognitive dysfunction (CCD). It is signaled by a decline in learning, memory, and perception. Dogs with this disease tend to wander aimlessly, bark for no reason, forget housetraining, and become distant from their families. It has been successfully treated with L-deprenyl (seleigiline hydrochloride or Anipryl), an enzyme inhibitor; the drug is also used to treat Parkinson's disease. The addition of vitamins C and E, L-carnitine, lipoic acid, and fish oils may also help. There are even diets specifically designed to help dogs with cognitive dysfunction syndrome.

What You Can Do to Help Your Dog's Nervous System

Believe it or not, exercise can help keep your dog's nervous system in gear. Nerves work along with muscles, so a simple dash through the park or hike in the woods can be immensely helpful.

IMMUNE SYSTEM

Two different cellular systems work together to create the immune system. One cellular system provides what is called B-cell immunity, which includes circulating antibodies (immunoglobins). The other kind of immunity is the T-cell (cell-mediated) immunity that involves the lymph nodes, thymus, spleen, intestines, and tonsils. (Tell the truth, did you know dogs had tonsils?) Dogs can develop autoimmune disease, which is literally immunity against the self, a problem caused by poor genes, hormones, infections, or stress.

Autoimmune Hemolytic Anemia (AIHA)

One of the more serious problems of the immune system is autoimmune hemolytic anemia, a life-threatening disease where the body attacks its own red blood cells. It is considered a "primary" immune disease because no underlying cause of the immune destruction has been found. (A "secondary" disease is immune-mediated hemolytic anemia [IMHA], which includes all anemias that occur when the immune system destroys its own blood cells secondary to an immune attack directed against an underlying condition, such as cancer or heartworm.) The clinical signs of AIHA are related to low oxygen in the blood and include weakness, lethargy, loss of appetite, and an increase in heart rate and respiration. While the disease cannot be cured, it can be managed with cortisone and other drugs.

What You Can Do to Help Your Dog's Immune System

Keeping your dog's immune system up to strength requires a balance of protection and challenge. Challenge his immune system by feeding him a variety of food from puppyhood, having him meet other dogs, and exposing him to new environments. Don't overrely on antibiotics, but if they are needed, be sure you give the entire amount prescribed. Protect your dog by vaccinating him properly, and if possible, keeping him away from known allergens like fleas.

LYMPHATIC SYSTEM

The primary organs of the lymphatic system are the thymus gland (located above the heart and below the trachea) and bone marrow (as soft material in the center of bone). Secondary organs include the lymphatic vessels, lymph nodes, spleen, and aggregated lymphoid tissue. The lymphatic system has three important jobs to do: First, it helps maintain the fluid balance between the blood vessels and the tissues. Second, it plays a part in immunity. Third, it absorbs digested fats from the small intestine.

Spleen

The spleen is an oblong organ located right below the stomach. Your dog doesn't actually need it to live, but it does perform some useful functions. The "red pulp" of the spleen is a sort of blood storage area that can come in handy if the dog loses a lot of blood during trauma. It also helps remove old blood cells from the system and traps some parasites so they cannot continue to circulate through the bloodstream. The "white pulp" of the spleen is more directly connected with the lymphatic system and serves many of the same functions, although it is connected through the circulatory system.

Occasionally spleens develop masses. These can be benign hemangiomas or malignant hemangiosarcomas. Both of these tumors come from the blood vessels of the red pulp; they look like wildly growing abnormal blood vessels. Eventually they can cause the spleen to rupture, which can be life threatening. The dog becomes weak and cold, and his gums look pale. The spleen must be removed; otherwise, the dog is in real danger of bleeding to death. Unfortunately, if the tumor is malignant (and keep in mind it may not be), the dog is not likely to recover. Your vet may be able to detect a splenic mass through physical examination, blood panel testing, or X-ray.

What You Can Do to Help Your Dog's Lymphatic System

The complex lymphatic system responds to the same basic preventive care as the rest of the body: exercise, good diet, and monitoring.

ENDOCRINE SYSTEM

The endocrine system is a complicated system of glands that produces hormones and secretes them directly into the blood. Diseases of the endocrine

Keeping your dog's immune system up to strength requires a balance of protection and challenge.

system include diabetes mellitus, hypothyroidism, Cushing's disease, and Addison's disease. See Chapter 14 for more information on these diseases.

EARS

Ears are largely an extension of the skin but are usually so troublesome in dogs that they need to be treated separately. The most common problem dogs have with their ears is bacterial or fungal infection. This is because the ear canal has both a horizontal and a vertical compartment. The ear canal in dogs is much longer than it is in people. Infections cannot work themselves straight out but must also go upward. The problem is compounded in dogs with heavy, floppy ears (like Cocker Spaniels, setters, and Bassets), as well as with breeds like Schnauzers and Poodles who have hair

growing in the ear canal itself. Dogs with upright ears are much less likely to get ear infections. In addition, dogs with excessively narrow ear canals are likely victims. Systemic diseases, allergies, tumors, and polyps can also cause ear problems.

Ear Infections

Signs of infection include scratching, rubbing the ears on the floor, or head shaking. If the infection is in the middle ear, you may also see head tilting and lack of balance. You have an additional problem once the dog starts shaking his head—it could result in an aural hematoma, in which a blood vessel in the earflap ruptures. If you even suspect an ear infection, get your dog to the vet. Left untreated, infections can result in deafness. While most ear infections begin in the outer ear, they can quickly migrate to the middle or even the inner ear through a ruptured eardrum (much more common in dogs than in people). Obviously, this development complicates matters.

Treatment begins with a thorough, professional cleaning (often done under sedation), examination with an otoscope, and medication. This usually clears things up, but some dogs may have chronic infections, in which case the ear discharge needs to be cultured to identify the exact organism responsible. In many cases, recurrent ear infections are caused by an allergy, which may also need to be treated. In very severe cases, your veterinarian may need to surgically open the vertical canal to remove debris, and as a last resort—when absolutely no other relief is to be found—the entire ear canal is removed. Many cases of ear infection can be resolved in a week or ten days with the right medications. However, certain bacteria infecting the ear, such as

Signs of an ear infection include scratching, rubbing the ears on the floor, or head shaking.

Pseudomonas aeroinosa, are resistant to almost every antibiotic (although very high doses of Baytril can be effective).

Vestibular Disease

Vestibular disease is another common ear problem. The word vestibular refers to the special equipment responsible for perceiving position and orientation to the earth. (It helps you know whether you are right side up or not.) The receptor for all this lies within the ear. Tiny hair cells project out into fluid-filled canals. When the body moves, the fluid moves, and the hair cells move along with the fluid, reporting back to the cerebellum (part of the brain) to let it know what's happening.

In vestibular disease, you no longer know which way you're oriented. A person or dog can become dizzy, nauseated, and uncoordinated. A dog may circle and carry his head to one side. The cause may be in the brain, or it may be an infection of the ear itself. This is particularly likely if the dog has a history of ear infections. A more sinister variety can be caused by a brain tumor, although in some cases, these can be operated on. One common variety of the disease is canine idiopathic vestibular disease, sometimes known as "old dog vestibular disease." This strange condition shows up suddenly and usually resolves itself within 72 hours.

What You Can Do to Protect Your Dog's Ears

Clean your dog's ears thoroughly and regularly. Don't overdo this if your dog's ears are already in good condition or tend to dryness—too much cleaning can make them red, irritated, and flaky. If you live in a humid climate or if your dog goes swimming regularly, try to dry the ears thoroughly. Place cotton balls in the dog's ears during baths. With heavy-eared breeds, try leaving the earflap open for a period each day by lifting the flap on the visible side when the dog is asleep. Some people recommend taping up the ears, but dogs hate that. If you need to medicate the ears, be sure you clean them first.

EYES

The eye is a complicated organ with a single critical function: to provide vision. Unfortunately, something can go wrong almost anywhere in the system.

Besides the main structures of the eye, dogs also have eyelids, eyelashes, tear glands, and a nictitating membrane (a clear "third eyelid") that help keep the eye clean, moist, and free of debris. Dogs also have a reflective layer in the choroids (the middle layers of the eye) called the tapetum lucidum, which causes the eye to shine in the dark.

Unfortunately, canine vision problems can be hard to diagnose, so you need to be doubly careful in noting the onset of symptoms. Even an apparently mild sign could mean a true emergency.

Most serious of all eye diseases, of course, are the ones that cause blindness, such as glaucoma and progressive retinal atrophy (PRA).

Do Dogs See in Color?

We now know that dogs do see in color, although a little differently than people do. They can't tell the difference between red, orange, yellow, and green. (Colorblind humans are often in the same fix.) However, they do see various shades of blue and can distinguish between closely related hues of gray better than people. On the other hand, people are better at depth perception, as well as at picking out details of an object. Dogs have the edge in dim light vision, movement detection, and peripheral vision.

Cataracts

Cataracts are opacities of the lens that typically look gray or white. They are categorized by age of onset, physical appearance, and cause. There is no way to prevent or slow the progression of the disease; surgery is the only treatment and may provide a return of vision. It can be performed on an outpatient basis.

Cherry Eye

Cherry eye, or prolapse of the nictitating membrane, is a rather common problem in young dogs. In an acute case, a red, swelling mass appears in the corner of the eye, along with a discharge. Treatment involves putting the lacrimal (tear) gland back where it belongs and anchoring it with sutures. (The gland should not be removed. It is needed to produce tears, a mixture of oil, mucus, and water.)

Conjunctivitis

Conjunctivitis is a reddening of the portion of the eye called the conjunctiva (the membrane lining the eyelids), which may act as a general measure of your dog's health. Conjunctivitis can have many causes, some serious, such as a corneal ulcer. Don't delay in getting your dog to the vet, preferably to a veterinary ophthalmologist. You can find a veterinary ophthalmologist at www.acvo.com.

Dacryocystitis

Dacryocystitis, or inflammation of the lacrimal sac, is caused by debris or foreign bodies and results in tearing, conjunctivitis, and sometimes a draining opening (like a sore) in the lower eyelid. Treatment depends upon the cause but usually involves removing the debris and using topical antibiotics.

At his annual checkup, the vet will examine your dog's eyes.

Epiphora (Tearing)

Epiphora is a watery, teary discharge. Over time, the tears create red-brown stains on the face, and worse, can cause irritation, infection, and odor. It's caused by irritation to the eye (ingrown eyelashes, for example) or by abnormal tear drainage, usually from abnormal ducts. Poodles, Bichon Frises, and brachyocephalic (short-nosed) breeds are most at risk. Chronic cases of epiphora are extremely difficult to control. In some cases, surgery is required. Some holistic practitioners suggest that adding a little parsley to the diet is helpful for tearstaining, but as far as I know, there's no scientific evidence to support this. While some people use low doses of certain antibiotics to control the staining, this practice is generally not encouraged.

Glaucoma

Glaucoma is an elevation of pressure within the eye. (The technical name is intraocular pressure.) Left untreated, this extremely painful disease almost always results in blindness; glaucoma patients frequently also need to have the entire eye removed for comfort. In addition, most owners delay treatment for so long that there is no hope of saving the dog's sight. To be most effective, your dog needs to see a vet within 24 hours after symptoms develop—after 48 hours, it's usually too late. The signs of glaucoma are obvious: swelling, redness in the white part of the eye, dilated pupils, cloudiness, sensitivity to light, squinting, pawing at the eye, eye discharge, and so on.

There are two basic categories: primary glaucoma, which accounts for the majority of cases, occurs without any other cause, while secondary glaucoma occurs as a result of some other condition. Primary glaucoma is further divided into open angle glaucoma (Beagles

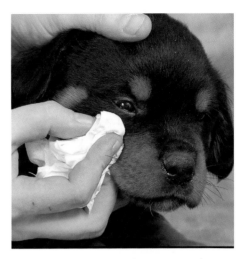

and Norwegians Elkhounds are especially prone) and narrow angle glaucoma. (Cocker Spaniels are

> Because vision problems can be hard to diagnose, be careful in noting the onset of symptoms.

prone.) A further kind of primary glaucoma is a developmental abnormality of the drainage angle called goniodysgenesis, which occurs in Bassets, Cockers, Samoyeds, and Chow Chows.

Keratoconjunctivitis Sicca (Dry Eye)

Keratoconjunctivitis sicca (KCS, or dry eye) results from a tear deficiency. Tears are critical to eye health: They provide lubrication and even contain anti-bacterial proteins, salts, and sugars to help nourish the eye. They also work mechanically to flush away irritants. To diagnose dry eye, your vet will perform a Schirmer Tear Test.

There are many possible causes of dry eye, but treatment usually consists of artificial tears and sometimes antibiotic-corticosteroid combinations. (If the cornea is scarred, corticosteroids cannot be used.) Cyclosporine topical therapy helps control the immune-mediated gland destruction and can stimulate the tear glands. In some chronic cases, parotid (salivary) duct transplantation can be performed by an ophthalmologic veterinary specialist. Certain breeds like the American Cocker Spaniel, Miniature Schnauzer, and West Highland White Terrier seem predisposed to this condition.

Progressive Retinal Atrophy (PRA)

Progressive retinal atrophy is a gradual deterioration of the retina. The first signs appear as night blindness and gradually progress to total (but painless) blindness. The disease has several forms, but unfortunately, there is no treatment for any of them. Breeds most commonly affected include Cocker Spaniels (both kinds), Australian Cattle Dogs, Briards, Mastiffs, Bullmastiffs, Cardigan Welsh Corgis, Chesapeake Bay Retrievers, Irish Setters, Labrador Retrievers, Miniature Schnauzers, Poodles, Nova Scotia Duck Tolling Retrievers, Portuguese Water Dogs, Samoyeds, and Siberian Huskies.

SARDS

Sudden Acquired Retinal Degeneration Syndrome (SARDS) is an acute vision loss associated with

changes in thirst and appetite. The cause is unknown, and there is no treatment.

What You Can Do to Protect Your Dog's Eyes

Examine your dog's eyes by cupping his head with your hands, using one thumb to open the upper eyelid and one to open the lower. The white part of the eye, the sclera, is covered by the transparent conjunctiva. The sclera should be about the same color as healthy gums. If it is very red, pale, yellow, or bruised, there may be problems. The iris should be free of black spots, blood spots, or growths. The pupils should be perfectly round and of equal size. When you pull down the lower lid, you may see the third eyelid, or nictitating membrane. It should be pale pink or white. Any squinting, clouding, tearing, swelling, or redness in the eye can signal trouble.

When bathing your dog, make sure to protect his eye from irritating soaps. You may want to first coat the eye with mineral oil or sterile veterinary ophthalmic ointment.

THE NOSE

The nose, of course, is the entryway to the respiratory system, but it is also so much more. Dogs have great noses. In fact, the scent organ inside is about four times bigger than ours, and their sense of smell is hundreds or thousands of times better. (They can find people buried under a collapsed building or an avalanche, which is no easy trick. They even have a special organ called the vomeronasal organ that allows them to smell underwater!)

Breeds with big noses are the best smellers, and some breeds, like Beagles, Bassets, and Bloodhounds, are called "scenthounds" because that's the way they find game. It is usually claimed that these breeds are better smellers than other breeds, but studies have not confirmed this. They are, however, more naturally attuned to following

CERF

CERF, or the Canine Eye Registration Foundation, established in 1974, is working hard to eliminate heritable diseases in purebred dogs. It works in cooperation with the American College of Veterinary Ophthalmologists (ACVO) to maintain a registry of dogs found to be unaffected by major heritable eye diseases. You can find them online at www.vmdb.org/cerf.html.

smells. Bloodhounds seem more adept at following quite old scents, but this seems to say more about their perseverance than their actual smelling powers.

MEDICATING YOUR DOG

Medications can save your dog's life, but they must be administered appropriately. And while most drugs are safe as prescribed, all of them can have side effects. Some side effects are mild and common; others might be severe enough to require you to stop medicating the dog. Before giving medication to your dog, ask the vet what the possible side effects might be. The dose is the amount of medicine your dog will get at one time. How much the dose is depends on your dog's size, age, physical condition, and other medications the dog may be on. Don't try to adjust dosages yourself, like figuring that a 20-pound (9-kg) dog gets half the medicine of a 40 pounder (18 kg); it doesn't always work that way. In the same way, don't assume that if 50 milligrams works, 100

milligrams will work faster (or better). Most drugs are measured in milligrams—that's because only a tiny bit is necessary to treat the condition. (There are about 464,000 milligrams in a pound [2.5 kg], if that's any use.)

Always follow directions. Some meds go on an empty stomach, some after a meal. Don't skip or double dose. If you skip accidentally, call your vet for advice.

Giving Antibiotics

The worst and most common error we make administering antibiotics is not giving them long enough. The average household has several bottles of various antibiotics, held on to by the family in the vague hope that some of them will

Medications can save your dog's life, but they must be administered appropriately.

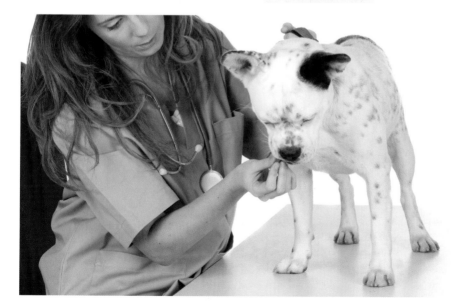

come in handy "later on." (The truth is that their effectiveness wanes over time.)

Even worse, however, is how we are depriving our pets the full benefit of the drug. We decide the dog seems well and discontinue the medication. However, that usually indicates only that the infection is under control, not that it has disappeared! If we stop antibiotic treatment before we actually killed off all the organisms, it can recur with a vengeance, only this time it will be more deep-seated and even more difficult to conquer.

There's a larger issue as well. When we don't give enough antibiotics, we are actually helping bacteria grow into super-resistant strains. We've seen it happen; as more bacteria become resistant, there are fewer and fewer antibiotics that are effective against them. We have to keep using higher doses and developing new medicines just to keep up. All because we've been too lazy or cheap to finish a course of treatment.

Giving Liquid Medications

If you're lucky (and with your vet's permission), the easiest way to give liquid meds is to sneak them in the food and make sure the dog eats it all. If this is not possible or if you're afraid that the dog won't get it all, then you have to devise another plan.

Have everything ready before you need to administer the medicine—it's awful to stagger around the kitchen clutching a reluctant dog's collar in one hand while trying to find the medication. When you're ready to medicate, go find the dog. Don't call him to you unless you know the dog will enjoy the experience. Don't try to trick him, either, or he won't come when you really need him to, like when he's escaped into the road. Arrange your dog so that his hind end is squashed up against something solid; you don't want him backing away at a crucial moment! If it is a small dog, put him on top of the dryer. (The slipperiness

of the surface will take his mind off anything you are doing!) In this case, it is best to have a helper. If you feel nervous, practice using water or chicken broth, which your dog will like.

Most liquid medicines are given by eyedropper. Place the eyedropper into the pocket between the cheek and molars. Administer the medicine slowly, certainly no faster than your dog can swallow. If you try to shove it all down there at once, you risk choking your pet. Gently close his jaws and tip his head up slightly. Rub your dog's nose to stimulate a swallow. Wipe off any medication, and clean the eyedropper for next time. You're all done! Give yourself and your dog a treat.

Pilling Your Pooch

The easiest way to pill a dog is simply to put the pill in a piece of soft cheese and let him swallow. There are a few medications that should not be given with food, however. (Check with your vet.) In that case, or if you're out of cheese and feeling

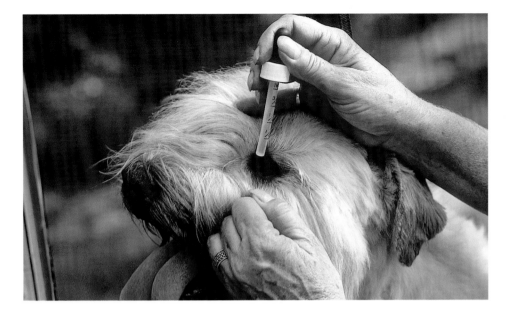

brave, simply tilt the dog's chin upward and insert the pill as far down the throat as you can. Then hold his mouth shut and stroke his throat until he swallows. Most dogs are easy to pill, which is more than can be said for cats.

Medicating Your Dog's Eyes

Put a small dog on a table. (In some cases, you may need to encourage the dog to lie on his side.) If he is a big dog, straddle him from the rear and tilt his muzzle upward. Rest the heel of the hand holding the medication on the dog's forehead so that the container doesn't touch the eye. If you are using more than one kind of medication, separate treatments by ten minutes unless directed otherwise. If you are using both drops and ointments, apply the drops first.

Before giving medication to your dog, ask your vet what the possible side effects might be.

Be Cheap: Go Generic

When you need medication for your dog, ask your vet or pharmacist about using the generic equivalent. These drugs have the same active ingredients and potency, and are often available in the same form (tablet, liquid, or injectable). They are as safe and effective as the original product. There may be a difference in fillers and dyes, but these inactive ingredients do not affect the efficacy of the drug. Also, since 1984, no generic drug has been approved in the US unless it has been shown to have the same rate and amount of active drug absorbed as the brand name.

14

DOGS WITH DISABILITIES

Sometimes dogs suffer from ailments that are not readily curable. In some cases, there is no known cure; in other cases, a real cure is so expensive that it is beyond our financial means. This doesn't mean, however, that we have to abandon our dogs. In fact, many incurable diseases and permanent disabilities can be managed with proper care. In this chapter, we'll take a take a look at some common disabilities (presented in alphabetical order) and how they can be controlled.

ADDISON'S DISEASE

Addison's disease (hypoadrenocorticism) is a major disease of the endocrine system that affects the adrenal glands, which are found next to the kidneys. The center (cortex) of the gland produces a group of special hormones called corticosteroids, including mineralcorticoids such as aldosterone. These handy hormones help mammals adapt to stress. In fact, one subcategory of them, the glucocorticoids (e.g., prednisone) are responsible for producing that all-important fight-or-flight response. Other kinds of hormones produced by the adrenal glands help balance electrolytes (sodium, potassium, and chloride) in the system. So when something goes awry with this system, your pet is in big trouble.

The typical Addison's patient is a four- to five-year-old female, although any dog of any age may be affected. While any breed can be affected, Standard Poodles, Great Danes, Portuguese Water Dogs, West Highland White Terriers, Soft Coated Wheaten Terriers, Labrador Retrievers, Basset Hounds, and Rottweilers seem most at risk. Signs may include lethargy, lack of appetite, vomiting, or diarrhea, but the symptoms are usually vague, intermittent, and various. This is one reason that Addison's is called "the great imitator." Your vet needs to perform an ACTH stimulation test to determine if your dog has the disease. If left unnoticed or untreated, your dog will experience an "Addisonian crisis" in which his blood sugar drops dangerously low and the imbalance of electrolytes disrupts the heart rhythm. Untreated dogs usually die.

Care of Your Addison's Dog

While there's no cure for Addison's, the disease can be managed with medications. Treatment includes replacing the missing mineralcorticoid hormones. Your vet will be able to prescribe the right medication for your particular dog, which he will remain on for the rest of his life. Low-dose prednisone (to replace the cortisone) is a common medication for Addison's. The aldosterone can be replaced by a daily oral medication called Florinef or a monthly injectable called desoxycorticosterone pivalate (DOCP). The injectable form is less expensive than the oral treatment, but neither is cheap (about $100 a month). Addison's dogs need careful monitoring, but if they get proper treatment, they can live a full and fairly normal life.

Tips for Living With an Addison's Dog

- Find a qualified specialist.
- Try to keep your dog stress-free.
- If stress does occur, you may need to adjust the medication.
- Keep a careful eye on your dog, and take note of any changes in weight.
- Keep an eye out for increased drinking and urination, which could signal a problem.

ALLERGIES

Most allergies affect dogs by attacking the skin rather than by making them sneeze (as happens in

Most allergies affect dogs by attacking the skin rather than by making them sneeze.

condition in dogs. (Only flea allergies are more common.) Signs usually begin by the time the dog is a year old, often first appearing in the summer. As dogs age, they become more allergic to more substances, and the allergies may become year-round. Your vet will need to do diagnostic testing to make sure your dog is suffering from allergies, possibly including both skin and blood testing.

Another kind of allergy is contact allergy, where the animal has to make physical contact with the allergen, usually some sort of plant, although some experts put dust mites in this category too. (The highest concentrations of dust mites are found in homes with concrete basement floors, homes without air conditioning, and in dog beds with foam mattresses.) Contact allergies are not usually hereditary.

Dogs can also suffer from food allergies, but this is not the most common culprit. Food allergies account for only about 10 percent of all dog allergies. Dogs with food allergies often paw at their faces.

Care of Your Allergic Dog

For any kind of allergy, the most sensible course of action is to reduce exposure to the allergen. If it is fleas, you're in luck—fleas can be eliminated by the use of any adulticide flea killers. If it is dust or mold in the house, you'll need to get out the vacuum and the duster and get to work. It is also worthwhile to install a high-efficiency particulate air (HEPA) filter to reduce the amount of dander and pollen. Limit your pollen-allergic dog's outdoor exposure during high-pollen-count days, and stay indoors with the windows closed and the air conditioning on.

people). About 15 percent of all dogs suffer from allergies, but the percentage is higher in retrievers, terriers, Cocker Spaniels, German Shepherd Dogs, Irish Setters, Dalmatians, Bichon Frises, Chinese Shar-Peis, and Boxers. The most common culprits are pollen, mold, and house dust—just as with people. An allergic dog will paw, lick, scratch, or rub at the affected area (usually the face, ears, and belly). Allergies cannot be cured, but they can often be managed with shampoos, antihistamines, and fatty acids.

One common type of allergic reaction is called atopy, or inhaled allergy, which occurs in response to substances swirling around in the environment, typically pollen, house and dust mites, molds, and grass or weed pollens. Atopy is probably inherited and is the second most common allergic skin

Once you get the environment under control, check with your veterinarian about options. You may want to go whole-hog and try immunotherapy. It will definitely increase your dog's resistance to what's bugging him, but it's a long-term project, sometimes taking up to a year.

Some dogs respond well to corticosteroidal therapy, although these powerful medications must be used cautiously. Side effects may include increased thirst and urination and a higher susceptibility to infection. Others fare well simply with the addition of omega-3 acids from fish or flaxseed oil, or even antihistamines—all of these reduce itchiness. Antibiotics can reduce secondary infections. Some people have excellent success with acupuncture. Frequent medicated or oatmeal baths are also helpful.

Food Allergies Versus Food Intolerance

Food allergies and food intolerance are different conditions. An allergy is an immunologic reaction to food. Like atopy, it can cause reddened skin, and perhaps secondary skin infections. The ears are particularly likely to take a hit, and many cases of chronic ear infections signal an underlying allergy. Food intolerance occurs when an animal has trouble digesting a food but is not truly allergic. It signals a reaction to something in the food, but the reaction is not a response by the immune system, which defines a real allergy. Food intolerance is much more common than a true allergy. Food intolerance is more likely to produce vomiting or diarrhea than signs of a true allergy.

In December of 2003, the US Food and Drug Administration (FDA) approved Atopica (oral cyclosporine capsules) for treating atopic dermatitis in dogs. Cyclosporine blocks the release of certain chemicals from white blood cells that cause inflammation in atopic dogs. The cyclosporine in Atopica is specially formulated to provide consistent absorption from the digestive tract and is marketed as safer than the long-term use of corticosteroids. The most common side effects with Atopica are occasional mild, temporary vomiting and diarrhea. Improvement can be expected within four weeks after beginning full-dosage treatment. Once good clinical improvement is seen, the dosage may be slowly decreased.

If it's a food allergy, go for the elimination diet—start with highly suspect foods like beef, chicken, pork, lamb, milk, eggs, whey, fish, corn, wheat preservatives, and soy, and work your way down the list. You might also consider feeding your dog a "novel" protein like duck, venison, or something else you're sure he has never tried. Many commercial manufacturers produce anti-allergy or modified protein diets, including Hill's, Iams, Innovative Veterinary Care, Nature's Recipe, Old Mother Hubbard, Purina, DVM Pharmaceuticals, and Waltham. It has been shown that dogs fed a variety of foods from early on in life are less apt to develop allergies.

When You Are Allergic to Your Dog

If you are allergic to your dog, all is not lost—you don't have to give up your pet! Here are some hints to help you get by. For a severe case, consider getting immunotherapy yourself. A weekly shot (and even less often once you build up immunity) can make the presence of your dog tolerable again. You can expect results in three to six months. Less severe allergies often respond well to simple antihistamines. Cromolyn-sodium nasal sprays may also help. You may want to consider corticosteroids if you are willing to deal with the side effects.

Once you settle on a course of treatment for yourself, start with the dog. Get him bathed at least once a week (coerce a family member or friend to do it if you have to), and keep his coat clipped. Try to isolate yourself from the dog to some extent. At the very least, reserve one room for yourself, such as the bedroom, where you can keep the door shut and where the dog is simply not allowed. Use a HEPA filter in every room. Get rid of carpets and install tile or wood floors. Vacuum frequently and change the bags often. Wash linens, curtains, and couch coverings frequently. (Use plastic covers under the fabric for added protection.) There are also products that can be applied to the pet's fur with a cloth that claim to neutralize the allergens found on the coat. They make take several weeks before becoming effective, though.

"Hypoallergenic Dogs"

Certain dog breeds, such as Poodles, Bichon Frises, Miniature Schnauzers, Soft Coated Wheaten Terriers, and the like, are touted as hypoallergenic. Actually, there is really no such thing because all dogs produce the villainous proteins found in dander and saliva. However, it is true that these dogs are probably easier on the allergic owner.

Tips for Living With an Allergic Dog

- Find out what type of allergy your dog has.
- Control your dog's environment as much as possible.
- Look into immunotherapy or corticosteroids.
- A change in diet may help.

AMPUTEES

Amputation, which can occur in the treatment of bone cancer or as a result of trauma, is usually not a life-altering event for a dog. Most dogs don't experience much loss of activity and can run and play as before. And while people often suffer psychological trauma from losing a limb, dogs don't care about apparent "disfigurement." They have a common-sense attitude about legs—they exist to move the dog from one place to another, and if three will do the job, that's fine with them. It's the human beings who need to adjust to the new way their dog looks.

How to Care for Your Amputee

- Don't baby your amputee dog—he's lovin' life.
- Replace steps with ramps where necessary (although many three-leggers handle steps just fine!)

- You can ask for a handicapped dog license (but you may not be able to get one).

ARTHRITIS AND OTHER DEGENERATIVE BONE OR JOINT PROBLEMS

If your dog has arthritis, he's not alone; in fact, he has ten million fellow sufferers. Arthritis (formally known as osteoarthritis) is simply the inflammation of a joint. Typically, arthritis occurs in the synovial joints (like the knee), which consist of two bones and a fibrous capsule (a sort of hinge) filled with synovial fluid that holds them together. The slippery cartilage that covers the surface of the bones helps the bones glide over each other during normal movement. In arthritis, the cartilage gets rough and worn. The joint capsule is inflamed, and the lubricating fluid it produces stops working well. Arthritis has many causes, including injury, normal wear and tear, bad conformation, joint abnormalities, and tick-borne diseases, so it's not just older animals who are potential victims.

The key signs are stiffness and a limited range of motion. However, never simply assume that a stiff dog has arthritis. A number of other more serious conditions, such as bone infections, tumors, fractures, and dysplasia, can mimic its signs. Get an accurate diagnosis from your veterinarian before proceeding with treatment.

Care of Your Arthritic Dog

NSAIDs: Care of an arthritic dog involves regular use of pain relievers, such as oral nonsteroidal anti-inflammatory drugs (NSAIDs) like Rimadyl (generic name carpofen), adequan (polysulfated glycoscaminoglycan, given by injection twice a week to help reduce pain and inflammation and rebuild damaged cartilage), palaprin (buffered aspirin formulated specifically for dogs), as well as newer generations of medications like Deramaxx (deracobix). Deramaxx is especially exciting, as it is designed to target the enzymes responsible for pain and inflammation without attacking the enzymes necessary for normal bodily functions (like platelet formation and gastrointestinal activities). Many of these medications come in chewable tablets. Side effects can include intestinal bleeding, and a few dogs may develop liver or kidney problems. Dogs on NSAIDs should be carefully monitored.

Supplements: Glucosamine/chondroitin supplements with manganese can do wonders for your arthritic dog. Studies show they are as effective as NSAIDs for arthritis and with very few of the side effects. (There is a concern that glucosamine may reduce the blood's ability to clot, which would be dangerous for a dog with von Willebrand's disease.) They do, however, take four to eight weeks to become effective. Glucosamine is produced naturally in the body; it is a building block for cartilage. Commercial glucosamine, which is derived from the shells of shrimp, comes in several forms, but the most effective for treating arthritis are glucosamine hydrochloride and glucosamine sulfate. Glucosamine is rapidly taken up by cartilage cells and helps in the synthesis of synovial fluid. Chondroitin is another naturally produced substance; it works to stymie enzymes that cause joint pain. This substance works especially well for older dogs, whose natural production of chondroitin has declined with age. Glucosamine and chondroitin together help reduce swelling and improve circulation, in addition to their other benefits. Be sure to get a product that includes manganese; it is a necessary cofactor for the biosynthesis of glycosaminoglycans. As a bonus, look for a product with ascorbate, a necessary cofactor for collagen biosynthesis.

Research seems to indicate that green-lipped mussel contains a supplement that may help both osteoarthritis and rheumatoid arthritis. It contains

natural anti-inflammatory agents and building blocks to rebuild certain joint components.

Supplements of shark cartilage have also been found to help with arthritis. However, I cannot advise using this treatment because of the serious effects the rage for shark cartilage is having upon the shark population. At the present rate, soon all these majestic and awesome creatures will have vanished. Furthermore, shark cartilage, however well it may work, is unnecessary—glucosamine/chondroitin supplements do the same job.

Methylsulfonylmethane (MSM) is a natural sulfur-containing compound produced by kelp in the ocean. Sulfur is stored in almost every cell in the body, particularly in the joints, hair, skin, and nails. MSM is said to boost the structural integrity of connective tissue and to help reduce scar tissue. It is reported to have strong anti-inflammatory and pain-reducing properties, blocking the pain perception in nerve fibers before the pain impulse reaches the brain. It is closely related to DSMO but without the side effects of that drug. It comes in

The key signs of arthritis are stiffness and a limited range of motion.

pill and caplet form.

Corticosteroids: Corticosteroids, which are natural anti-inflammatory and pain-relieving drugs, are sometimes prescribed for an arthritic dog, but over time, these drugs can make dogs put on weight, which increases the pressure on the joints. In the long run, they may be worse than no treatment at all for arthritis because they decrease collagen and proteoglycan (another component of connective tissue) synthesis. Long-term side effects can include high blood pressure, hair loss, and glaucoma. Aspirin in small doses (about 81 milligrams per 10 pounds [4.5 kg] of body weight) can also be used in dogs—but not cats! Note that aspirin can have bad effects on the digestive tract of some dogs (and people, too!).

Diet and Exercise: Diet control is also critical for arthritic dogs. The best thing you can do is to help your obese dog lose weight. Obese animals have

Obesity is a leading cause of arthritis.

Essential fatty acids like omega-3 and omega-6 are anti-inflammatory. Omega-6 fatty acids are found in many vegetable oils, but omega-3 acids are harder to obtain, though there are lots in fish oil and flaxseed oil. Vitamin therapy, consisting of daily supplementation of A, E, and ester-C, or mineral supplementation of selenium may be useful, but work with a holistic veterinarian before embarking on a program of vitamin/mineral supplementation, as overdoses can be dangerous. Dogs can make their own vitamin C, but they aren't very good at it; some studies show that supplementation is very helpful in this regard. Vitamin E helps protect cell membranes; however, too much may lead to further inflammation.

Many holistic vets now recommend the spice turmeric, in powder form, as a supplement to the diet. Turmeric has cortisone-like anti-inflammatory properties. It is much safer and cheaper than synthetic drugs and may give positive results. If your dog doesn't like the stuff, even when mixed with his favorite dinner, you can put it in a gelatin capsule wrapped in a piece of cheese. The therapeutic dose is a teaspoon every day. Other botanicals that may help include boswellian extract, devil's claw, alfalfa, bromelain, yucca, and granular greens like wheat sprouts.

much more stress on their joints; large dogs are at an even greater risk. In fact, obesity itself is a leading cause of arthritis—and there are about 15 million overweight dogs in the US. Your vet can recommend a diet for weight loss, but the basic principles are the same as for humans: fewer calories and more exercise. Unless your dog is on a top-quality diet, you may need to supplement with vitamins if you reduce his intake. Some commercial foods supply only the minimum amount of nutrients in the recommended, weight-sustaining portions. Once you dip below this amount, as you need to in order for the dog to lose weight, you risk losing nutrients as well.

Arthritic dogs need plenty of rest and plenty of the right kind of exercise—be sure to follow your veterinarian's advice in this regard. In general, exercise for arthritic dogs should be both regular and moderate. The curse of arthritis has been that it often hurts the dog to exercise—even though that is just what the animal needs. This is where the new pain-relieving medications come in handy. If you have the opportunity, swimming (hydrotherapy) is excellent. Swimming allows the joints to gain strength without bearing weight; there are even underwater treadmills available at canine rehabilitation places (which have heated pools, too). While I'd like to recommend that everyone who has an arthritic dog install this device, they are costly, running between $15,000 to $50,000. (You can stop laughing now.)

Holistic Therapies: Gentle massage is very helpful, as is chiropractic care by a trained veterinary chiropractor. Magnetic therapy and acupuncture have also yielded good results. In magnetic therapy, either static or pulsed electromagnetic field magnets (which use a low-frequency pulsing current) are used. Magnets appear to remove inflammation and encourage circulation by increasing blood flow to a particular site. Acupuncture has been used to reduce muscle spasms around affected joints.

Tips for Living with an Arthritic or Otherwise Joint/Bone-Impaired Dog

Caring for an arthritic dog can be a bit of a challenge.

- Ideally you should modify your house (or your dog's lifestyle) so that stair climbing is unnecessary.
- It is a good idea to keep water in several places so that the patient does not have to travel too far to get it. It is true that the exercise might help him, but too many dogs just forgo the idea and do without the water—to their detriment.
- Some people install ramps to help their dogs in and out of the house.
- If your dog is not at risk for bloat, raised food and water bowls can ease stiff joints. However, in breeds that are subject to this deadly disease, it's better to keep the feeding dishes at their natural, ground level.

BLINDNESS

While blindness can be a tragedy for a person, for many dogs it's only an inconvenience. After all, dogs don't care about fine art, glorious sunsets, or reading books. Most of their main interests in life—eating, playing, digging, barking, and being petted—can be accomplished rather well by a blind dog. My friend Melinda Brown of Charlottesville, Virginia, had a blind dog, Chelsea, who achieved her Canine Good Citizen certificate so easily that the judge was not even aware she was blind.

Tips for Living With a Blind Dog

- Be conservative about moving furniture around, since it will take your blind dog a while to orient himself to it.
- Be neat; put your chairs neatly under the table after use so that your blind dog won't wander into them.
- Stairs require special help and should be closed off from the blind dog. However, when you are with the dog, you can help him negotiate stairs by saying "Step" at each riser.

Continuous Glucose Monitoring Systems

Veterinarians at the College of Veterinary Medicine, University of Missouri, examined the feasibility of using continuous glucose monitoring systems (CGMS) in dogs, cats, and horses. A sensor inserted under the skin is attached by wires to a recording device hooked onto the dog's harness that continually monitors the level of glucose in the fluid beneath the skin, which reflects the level of glucose in the blood. The dogs seem to feel no discomfort. There are many advantages to this system; most importantly, the dog does not need to have multiple blood samples drawn. Glucose levels can be obtained every five minutes.

- Sprinkle fragrant cedar chips around the property line to let your dog know when he is approaching the fence.
- Cover spas or hot tubs—but this is a smart idea even for a sighted dog!
- Toys for blind dogs should have squeakers that continue squeaking for a while after being squeezed; this will help the blind dog locate the toy. Many toys and chews are scented as well, giving dogs another way of locating them .
- There is an excellent web site for owners of blind dogs: www.blinddogs.com, which includes tips as well as a support group.

CANCER

In cancer, normal cell division has gone haywire. Most normal cells (excepting skin, bone marrow cells, and intestinal cells) stop dividing when an organism matures. Cancer cells keep on dividing and eventually crowd out the normal cells. In dogs, the most common cancer types are lymphoma, soft tissue sarcomas, mast cell tumors, mammary cancer, and oral cancers. Most types of cancer occur spontaneously, as a result of exposure to radiation, toxins, viruses, and so forth, but some, like osteosarcoma, certain skin and soft tissue cancers, mammary tumors, and melanomas, are thought to be hereditary.

Signs of cancer in dogs may include:
- Persistent abnormal swellings
- Sores that do not heal
- Weight loss and loss of appetite
- Bleeding or discharge
- Foul odor
- Difficulty eating
- Exercise intolerance
- Persistent lameness or stiffness
- Difficulty breathing
- Problems urinating or defecating

It is not surprising that cancer is common in dogs, just as it is in people, especially when we consider that we live the same kind of lives and that every cell in the body is capable of turning into cancer. In fact, some studies show that cancer is three times more likely to occur in dogs as in people (other studies put the risk at about the same) and that fifty percent of older dogs will develop the disease. However, cancer is no longer a death sentence, and even when it cannot be completely cured, today's dogs, with the help of a combination of contemporary and ancient medicine, can live much longer with cancer than heretofore suspected.

Care of Your Cancer Patient

Common treatments for cancer include the following:

Surgery is often the first line of defense against cancer. Because there is always a worry that some cancer cells might remain, surgery is usually followed by chemotherapy or radiation.

Chemotherapy is an option for many dogs with cancer. It can have a positive response of 80 to 90 percent in cancers involving multiple sites or those cancers not suitable for radiation or surgery. Chemo drugs are extremely toxic to rapidly growing and dividing cells—and that's what cancer is. Forget about the horror stories you may have heard, most of which apply to human beings and are long outdated. Very few dogs become nauseated, bald, or extremely weak from this treatment. The few dogs who do have side effects like nausea or weakness usually only experience them for a day or two, and there are medications like Zofran that can greatly reduce even this discomfort. As a rule, chemotherapy, either alone or in combination with radiation, is used as a precautionary measure even after a mass has been removed. In general, chemotherapy doesn't resolve the cancer completely, but it can produce a

If your dog has a terminal illness, it's up to you to make his remaining time pleasant and comfortable.

long remission. The most common chemotherapy drugs are doxorubicin (Adriamycin), vincristine, cyclophosphamide (Cytoxan), L-aparaginase, mechlorethamine, cisplatin, carboplatin, lomustine, ifosfamide, and cytarabine (Ara-C). Costs for treatment vary according to the region of the country and the complexity of the treatment. Dogs on chemotherapy usually need to be monitored weekly. In some cases, bone marrow transplants are used after chemotherapy. This is because bone marrow tends to be particularly affected by chemo; the bone-marrow transplants allows doctors to be more aggressive.

Radiation, often used as an adjunct to surgery, is the treatment of choice for invasive tumors that are rapidly spreading, or do not have well-defined borders. Radiation therapy uses high energy X-rays to kill cancerous cells while saving as many normal surrounding cells as possible. It can also be used to reduce pain in affected animals whose cancer is not treatable. A new kind of radiation equipment called linear acceleration expands the kinds of

tumors treatable by radiation. Brachytherapy implants radioactive beads into the tumor, where they release a low but continuous dose of radiation. This kind of treatment is available at most veterinary schools as well as in certain large referral clinics.

Herbal treatments have been used successfully as an adjunct to regular cancer treatments. Essiac tea (the name is a backwards formulation for the developer of the tea, Caisse) is one of the most frequently used of such remedies. It is a combination of burdock root, slippery elm, sorrel, Turkish rhubarb, and other plants and can be purchased commercially. While some folks use herbals as alternative curative therapy for cancer patients, others use them as supplements only. Always consult with your veterinarian before adding herbals to prescribed treatment. Some herbs and drugs do not interact well.

Experimental therapies, including gene therapy and immunology, are showing us new ways to deal with cancer. Kinase-inhibitor therapy for dogs with mast cell tumors, trace mineral (copper) and anti-angiogenesis therapies (to prevent the growth of new blood vessels needed to nourish the tumor), vaccines using the enzyme tyrosinase against malignant melanoma, and genetic research to find a cancer "gene" have all given hope to those dealing with cancer. Gene-based therapy has been used to treat soft-tissue sarcoma and oral melanomas. Nonsteroidal anti-inflammatory drugs (NSAIDs), such as COX-2 inhibitors, are being tried out for the prevention or elimination of certain bladder, kidney, and prostate cancers, as well as certain squamous cells cancers. *Salmonella*, a noxious bacterium, has also been tried against melanoma and sarcoma.

Hyperthermia, which "burns out" the cancer, is being used with radiation and chemotherapy as an adjunctive treatment. The other extreme, cryotherapy, which uses freezing, is also being tried. Other therapies such as photodynamic (exposure to light) therapy are being tried for superficial tumors.

Feeding Your Cancer Patient: One of the great challenges for the cancer-patient owner is cancer cachexia, a condition characterized by weight loss, weakness, and dehydration. Some tumors physically interfere with the ingestion and digestion of food. Additionally, chemotherapy may cause nausea. In some cases, the cancer patient has no appetite, but others lose weight even when eating normally. If you are offering a good-quality food, resist the temptation to coax the dog to eat. Even the old advice about warming the food may have a counterproductive effect, since the stronger smell may

You must be your dog's biggest champion when it comes to dealing with an illness.

make the dog sick. You will have to experiment and see what works for your pet. In some cases, a feeding tube may be necessary. Some dogs lack appetite because of "learned food aversion," a condition that develops when the patient associates the act of eating (or even of smelling the food) with nausea. He may then refuse to eat. In that case, speak with your vet about anti-emetic drugs. There are also some drugs that can stimulate the appetite, but they are best used when the animal actually starts to feel better.

Interestingly, cancer cells selectively grow on carbohydrates in the diet. As a result, most cancer patients do better on a very low carbohydrate, higher fat, and better-quality protein diet. Cancer cells prefer certain amino acids to others, and they hate fat. Arginine, cysteine, glycine, and glutamine are amino acids in particular disfavor with cancer cells. Omega-3 fatty acids, such as those found in fish and flaxseed oils, are also very desirable in the diet. Hill's Pet Nutrition has developed a commercial diet specifically for cancer patients that I highly recommend.

You may wish to supplement your pet's diet with vitamins A, C, D, and E. Green tea and garlic may also have anti-cancer properties.

Tips for Living With a Dog With Cancer

- Find a low carbohydrate, higher-fat, high-quality protein diet that's right for your dog.
- Check out herbal supplements.
- Work to keep your dog eating well.
- Research the latest cancer-fighting therapies.
- Make sure your dog sees the vet often for examinations.

To learn more about your dog and cancer, go to the Veterinary Cancer Society's website (www.vetcancersociety.org), which lists specialists by region. The American College of Veterinary Internal Medicine (www.acvim.org), the American Veterinary Medical Association (www.avma.org), and Tufts University School of Veterinary Medicine (www.tufts.edu/vet) can offer help regarding care options.

CUSHING'S DISEASE (HYPERADRENOCORTICISM)

Cushing's disease is sometimes called "the great pretender," since it can mask itself as so many different ailments. (Its mirror image is Addison's, which is called "the great imitator.") Cushing's usually strikes dogs who are over six years old and occurs when the adrenal glands, which are located right next to the kidneys, produce too much glucocorticoid (cortisol). (In Addison's, by contrast, not enough is produced.) Cushing's develops so slowly that most owners are not aware the dog is ill until the disease is well advanced. Signs include panting, excessive drinking, lethargy, a swollen abdomen, and seeking of cool surfaces. Breeds most often affected include Beagles, Boxers, Poodles, and Golden Retrievers. (My own Basset Hound, Mugwump, died of complications from this disease.)

The disease can occur in two forms. In the most common form (about 85 percent of the cases), a very small, nonmalignant tumor develops in the pituitary gland. This is called pituitary-dependent hyperadrenocorticism (PDH). In this case, the tumor makes the pituitary gland secrete too much ACTH, a hormone that causes the adrenal glands to produce excess cortisol. The other kind occurs when a tumor forms in the adrenal gland itself. In some cases, insulin-resistant diabetes can develop. Other complications can include urinary tract infections, pulmonary embolisms, and blindness.

Care of Your Cushing's Dog

When the tumor is in the adrenal gland, surgery is the most usual course of action, although it requires a very skilled practitioner. If, as is more common, the tumor is in the pituitary gland, medical treatment or radiation is the usual therapy. The point of both practices is to reduce the cortisol levels as quickly as possible. With pituitary-dependent Cushing's, veterinarians usually prescribe Lysodren, which destroys the outer layer of the adrenal glands and so cuts down on the amount of cortisol they can produce. A newer treatment therapy uses Anipryl for milder forms of the disease, which has fewer side effects than old medicines, although it is not recommended for dogs with heart or kidney disease. Ketoconazole, an anti-fungal medication, also works on Cushing's for some dogs by blocking the production of cortisol; however, this is a very expensive option and can damage the liver.

The owner's challenge is to carefully monitor the dog's food and water intake, as well as his general attitude. If the cortisol level drops too low, it can be life threatening. Because of the frequent testing and monitoring necessary, Cushing's can be an expensive disease to treat. One well-liked supplement is Azmira's Stress and A'Drenal Plex, whose manufacturers say helps to restore integrity to the adrenal glands and promote a greater sense of energy and stamina while also building up the body's response to stress. These herbs are also nutritive and tonic to the adrenal glands, as well as to nerve cells and tissues. They also are said to reduce the stress on a body constantly exposed to excessive physical or emotional strain.

Tips for Dealing With Cushing's Disease

As with Addison's (or indeed, any hormonal condition):
- It's important to keep your dog as free of stress as possible.
- Make sure you take your dog to the vet as regularly as is recommended to have his cortisol levels checked.

- A good diet for Cushing's is one that is high protein, low fiber, low fat, and low purine. Do not oversupplement calcium. Hills i/d diet (prescription only) is one way to meet this requirement.
- Don't restrict water in any way, even if your dog seems to be drinking a lot of it.

DEAFNESS

Deafness can be genetic or acquired. Breeds prone to deafness include Dalmatians, English Setters, white Bull Terriers, Cavalier King Charles Spaniels, Australian Cattle Dogs, Australian Shepherds, Catahoula Leopard Dogs, English Cocker Spaniels, Parson Russell Terriers, and white Boxers. (For many of these breeds, the culprit is a gene associated with the white coat, transmitted by the gene responsible for the merle, dapple, or piebald color. Unfortunately, the same gene responsible for the attractive color of these breeds also produces genetic defects.) Mixed breeds seldom suffer from congenital deafness. Acquired deafness usually occurs as a result of chronic ear infection, chemicals, or from trauma, as when an eardrum ruptures. (If the rupture heals properly, hearing usually returns.) And of course, many dogs gradually become deaf as they age. Veterinarians can check your dog's hearing by a test usually referred to as the BAER (brain stem auditory evoked response), which records brain responses to sounds.

Care of Your Deaf Dog

Deaf dogs can live a rich, full life. They are not suffering pain and in fact are relieved from many of the sounds that alarm, annoy, or overexcite other dogs, such as vacuum cleaners, fireworks, violin practice, and screaming kids. The most important challenge for owners of deaf dogs is to keep lines of communication open. This means sign language, and believe it or not, many dogs pick up the vocabulary of American Sign Language with relative ease. (In addition to its being accessible to dogs, a rather large number of human beings know this language as well, so they can communicate with your dog, too.) You can pick up a paperback of ALS, highlight the major signs you use with your dog, and leave the book with your vet or boarding kennels so that the vet or dog sitter can use them as well.

Training a dog to use sign language works much the same way as teaching him to recognize voice commands does. The secrets are patience, praise, and practice. Dogs are oriented to body language anyway and will quickly pick up your meaning. For example, the sign for "cookie" is to make the letter C with your right hand and then make a cookie-cutting gesture on the palm of your left hand.

(Dogs learn that one right away.) You can also use signs of your own devices, of course; they are to some extent arbitrary, although they should make sense to us, at least. Pat Miller, a dog behaviorist and positive reinforcement trainer, suggests some of the following signals:

- Down: Move your open hand, palm down, towards the floor.
- Sit: Move your open hand towards your chest, palm up.
- Come: Pull your arm back from your side (parallel to the ground), then bend your elbow and bring your open hand in towards your chest.
- Stay: Place your hand in front of the dog's nose.

Because deaf dogs can startle easily if you approach them from behind, it's a good idea to make big stomping noises when you approach the dog from behind so that he will feel the

vibration. Even so, you must keep in mind that strangers or kids may not always remember

your dog is deaf—children especially need to learn how to conduct themselves properly around a deaf dog. For your dog's safety, it's probably a good idea to desensitize him by practicing silent approaches. If you are patient, he may soon learn to accept the fact that surprises are a part of life and not necessarily anything to worry about. However, owners still need to be careful not to startle their dogs, as the startle reflex can evoke a bite.

Puppies born deaf need lots of extra socializing and lots of opportunities to meet people, smell them, and recognize them as friends. Overprotecting a deaf dog can make him unduly shy and skittish. Let your deaf dog have the same opportunities for play and other enjoyments as hearing dogs.

Tips for Living With a Deaf Dog

- Write the word "DEAF" on his nametag so that if he gets lost and is picked up by someone else, they will have a better idea about how to handle him.
- Flashlights and vibrating collars can also be used to signal commands.
- Deaf dogs can learn to respond to hand signals as easily as dogs with hearing answer to your voice.
- Keep your deaf dog on a leash when you're off your own property.
- Find a safe vibrating collar.
- Add a new (hearing) dog to the household who can act as a "leader" to the deaf dog.

To learn more, go to the Deaf Dog Education Action Fund (DDEAF) at www.deafdogs.org.

DIABETES MELLITUS

Diabetes, formerly known as the "wasting disease," comes in two forms. Type 1 diabetes is a condition in which the body lacks insulin, an important hormone made by the pancreas that makes it possible for body tissues to absorb blood sugar (glucose). (Much of the food we eat is broken down into glucose.) Type 2 diabetes occurs when the pancreas makes enough insulin, but the cells in the body are resistant to it. Symptoms of diabetes, including extreme hunger and thirst, weight loss, and weakness, are caused by excessive levels of glucose in the blood. Some of the glucose leaks past the kidneys into the urine and can be detected by a urine test.

Most dogs get Type 1 diabetes (just the opposite of people). No one knows the cause, but experts think it is due to an autoimmune problem or inflammation in the pancreas. Obesity increases the risk, and there is a definite genetic component involved. Some dogs can develop diabetes from overtreatment with corticosteroids for Addison's disease. Most diabetic dogs are females, with initial onset beginning at about six to nine years of age. Without treatment, diabetic dogs die in a matter of weeks. Diabetes is not curable, but it can be treated and controlled. Breeds most susceptible to diabetes include Poodles, Miniature Schnauzers, Golden Retrievers, German Shepherd Dogs, Keeshonden, and Dachshunds.

Treatment is usually with insulin injections into the fat beneath the skin once or twice a day; owners can learn how to do this themselves. (Dogs can't take insulin in pill form, since it would break down during digestion.) A new kind of insulin designed especially for dogs is now on the market. Recently, Generex, a Toronto biotechnology firm, has developed a spray pump similar to an asthma inhaler. Here, the insulin passes through the oral membranes, so the dog does not even have to inhale. While it is developed for human use, veterinarians will soon be able to recommend it. The odd thing is that human medications have to pass through animal trials first, and the device was used on Beagles with great success.

Diet regulation and proper exercise are also important for your diabetic dog. Diabetic females should be spayed because the hormone levels are disrupted by the heat cycle. In any case, what responsible breeder would want to breed a diabetic dog?

While diabetic dogs can live a normal life, up to 90 percent develop cataracts as a common result of the disease, which is caused because blood sugar is higher than normal for long periods. Unfortunately, it is practically impossible, with the current state of therapy, to regulate the blood sugar so that cataracts do not occur. This is because activity level, other hormone activity (several others are involved in regulating blood sugar), and diet changes (even slight ones), affect the level of sugar in the blood. When cataracts do occur, they seem to appear overnight, causing immediate blindness. However, if the optic nerve is not damaged, the cataract can be removed surgically by a veterinary ophthalmologist, and the dog will regain normal vision.

Another concomitant of diabetes for many dogs is infection of the urinary tract, due to the sugary nature of diabetic urine. Regular urine cultures are critical because the bladder infection may not be readily apparent to the owner. In addition, the pancreas can also become irritated, and diabetic dogs can develop skin problems, including bacterial and yeast infections.

Care of Your Diabetic Dog

Feeding: The key challenge for owners of diabetic dogs is scheduling. The patient needs the insulin dose at the same time every day. In like manner, meals should be consistent in amount, substance, and time. Twelve hours apart is ideal. Although I usually recommend variety in a dog's diet, a diabetic dog does better on a uniform, closely monitored diet. Most diabetic dogs require a high-fiber diet. Dietary fiber slows glucose absorption, as do complex carbohydrates, another plus for diabetic dogs. If you can't be home to feed your dog on a regular schedule, you can purchase an automated feeder that will do the trick. (Some even have refrigerated compartments to keep the food fresh.) Some veterinarians recommend a chromium supplement as well a vitamin supplement (especially the antioxidants C, E, and beta-carotene) and essential fatty acids.

Insulin: Insulin comes in many types. Humulin L or N, intermediate-acting insulins, are the most commonly used forms and are usually used twice a day in pets. There are very slight differences between the insulins of different species. In the US, insulin is almost exclusively of the human type and is manufactured via genetic engineering. (In the past, insulin was extracted from animal tissues for human use.) A new insulin developed specifically for dogs is now on the market. It's called Vetsulin.

Giving injections is the biggest part of caring for a diabetic dog. Syringes come in 0.5 cc and 0.3 cc sizes. The smaller the volume, the easier it is to give the injections. Ask your vet about which is right for your dog.

Giving injections is the biggest part of caring for a diabetic dog.

Follow the bottle directions about storage of insulin. Roll the bottle gently (do not shake it) in

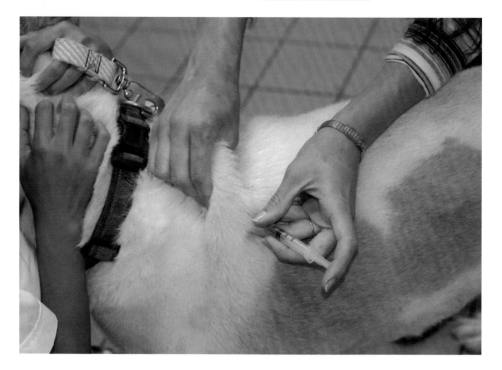

your hands before you administer it. Storing the vial on its side in the refrigerator will help mix the contents. When you are ready for the injection, hold the bottle vertically to lessen the possibility of bubbles forming. If you do get bubbles in the syringe, flick the syringe with your fingers until the bubbles rise to the top; then simply push the air out of the syringe with the plunger.

Draw the prescribed amount into the syringe and pull up the scruff of the dog's neck skin, making a triangle. Place the needle into the center part. Pull back slightly on the plunger to make sure you are not injecting it directly into a vein. (That would cause the insulin to be absorbed too quickly and possibly lead to hypoglycemia.) Most dogs do not even seem to notice they are getting a shot—these subcutaneous injections are much less painful than those in the muscle.

What if you aren't sure the insulin actually got there? (Sometimes the dog scoots off before you're finished.) In that case, most veterinarians recommend skipping that dose—overdosing on insulin is more dangerous than underdosing and can result in life-threatening hypoglycemia. Signs of hypoglycemia include incoordination, weakness, and confusion. (If this occurs, apply corn syrup to the dog's gum, then feed him.) Of course, contact your veterinarian immediately. In the early stages after detection, you should carefully monitor your dog for about eight hours after the last shot; that's when hypoglycemia (low blood glucose) is most likely to occur.

Some dog owners are able to do glucose monitoring at home by using a single drop of blood from the ear. This saves the dog the stress of the vet's office. While you can use a conventional "lance" to get the blood, a new device called a Microlet Vaculence may be easier on the dog. You will need also to buy a portable blood-glucose meter to determine the dog's glucose level. Some owners use urine test strips to calculate the level of sugar in the blood. If ketones (an intermediate product of glucose metabolism) are present for more than three days, contact your vet.

Tips for Living With a Diabetic Dog:

- Buy emergency medical ID tags for your diabetic dog so that if he is found, the finders will know he needs insulin. To order, go to www.gotags.com.
- Your diabetic dog needs a veterinary checkup at least four times a year.
- If your dog needs diabetic surgery, your vet will probably want to follow a special protocol.

To learn more about caring for a diabetic dog, go to www.petdiabetes.org; the Society for Comparative Endocrinology at www.compendo. org; or the Auburn University College of Veterinary Medicine at www.vetmed.auburn.edu/sac/mededu/diabetes/home.html.

EPILEPSY

Simply described, epilepsy is a neurological dysfunction, an uncontrolled electrical state inside the brain in which the circuitry of the brain is disrupted. The causes are often unknown, in which case the disorder is called idiopathic or primary epilepsy. Sometimes the seizures are not caused by epilepsy but by electrolyte (blood levels of sodium, potassium, and chloride) imbalance, low thyroid function, tick-borne diseases, encephalitis, or toxic substances. (These conditions should be ruled out before diagnosing "epilepsy.") Most of the time, however, the disease is inherited, with multiple genes involved. It usually does not occur until a dog is at least two years old.

All too often people hear the word "epilepsy" and decide that the next step is euthanasia. Perhaps this stems from the days when people thought victims of epilepsy were possessed by demons, but nowadays it's certainly not necessary. Although epilepsy is not curable, it is not generally life-threatening to the dog and can be controlled.

Anticonvulsant medications for epilepsy include phenobarbitol, potassium bromide (or a combination of the two), primadone (Mysoline), Valium (diazepam), dilantin, and gabapentin. In addition, some dogs respond to gold bead implants and acupuncture. For these treatments, find a veterinarian skilled in alternative medicine.

Caring for Your Epileptic Dog

Knowledge is power and comfort when dealing with this disease. Owners of epileptic dogs should learn the four stages of a seizure and be able to recognize them in their dogs.

- Stage One is the prodome, which can occur hours or even days before the seizure itself. You may notice mood swings or changes in your dog's behavior, but they can be very subtle.
- Stage Two is the aura, which indicates the beginning of the seizure itself. The dog may whine, tremble, salivate, or get restless.
- Stage Three is the ictus, or seizure itself. The seizures associated with the disease may be very brief (five to ten seconds) or continue for three to five minutes or more. In some cases, there is no loss of consciousness. In mild events, the dog may not even lose control of his posture. In other cases, the dog may lose consciousness, fall to the ground, paddle his feet, lose bowel control, and vocalize. (During the seizure stage, some

Most of the time, epilepsy does not occur until a dog is at least two years old.

owners have found four drops of Bach's Rescue Remedy [placed on the tongue] to be helpful.)

- Stage Four is the post-ictus stage, in which the dog may pace, drool, seem blind or deaf, or exhibit other signs of confusion.

A major challenge for the dog owner and the treating vet is deciding on the right dosage of anticonvulsant medications. Each drug has a different way of "acting." For example, potassium bromide is eliminated slowly from the system, while phenobarbital is eliminated relatively quickly. Dose-dependant side effects, including drowsiness or weakness, are quite common. Usually lowering the dose can eliminate these. In other cases, the dog has a reaction to the drug itself.

Diet can play a part in controlling epilepsy. Feeding fresh meat and perhaps green vegetables is recommended, and many practitioners suggest a diet free from preservatives and dyes. In the same vein, keep the environment as clean as possible, but avoid pine-scented cleaners, which have been known to induce seizures in some dogs. In some cases, vaccinations can trigger seizures, so ask your vet to split any required vaccinations rather than giving them all at once. Some people recommend supplementation with vitamins A, C, E, and choline. Herbs like skullcap, rosemary, rue, comfrey, garlic, seaweed, nettles, elder, couch grass flour, senna, and valerian root may also be used as adjunctive therapy.

Tips for Living With an Epileptic Dog

- Try an all-natural diet.
- Female dogs with epilepsy should be spayed, since estrogen is found to increase susceptibility to seizures.
- If your dog needs surgery, be sure to notify the surgeon that your dog has epilepsy. Certain phenothiazine tranquilizers like acepromazine and ketamine should not be used with an

Cluster Seizures and Status Epilepticus

Cluster seizures, defined as more than one seizure during a 24-hour period, and status epilepticus, a seizure (often a series of seizures in rapid sequence) lasting more than five or ten minutes, are both exceedingly dangerous and require veterinary treatment immediately. The first can cause brain damage and the second can result in death, often because the dog "overheats" during the seizure.

epileptic dog. In all cases, epileptic dogs need special monitoring during surgery.

- Reduce the stress in your dog's life as much as possible, since stress can trigger a seizure.

HYPOTHYROIDISM

The thyroid gland is an H-shaped organ in the throat that produces two kinds of hormones that affect the entire body. The thyroid regulates metabolism, and a thyroid malfunction can result in weight gain, poor skin and coat, and more serious internal changes. The two hormones are T3 (triiodothyronine), the "active" form, and T4 (thyroxine), an "inactive" form that circulates through the bloodstream. How much T4 is produced is regulated by the pituitary gland, the "master" gland at the base of the brain. The pituitary gland secretes thyroid-stimulating hormone (TSH) that tells the thyroid how much T4 to make.

In hypothyroidism, there is simply not enough T4 produced. Usually the cause is an atrophy in the thyroid gland itself, although the disease may be caused by a lack of iodine in the diet. In a few cases, the disease is congenital. Hypothyroidism usually strikes during middle age. Signs include skin problems and hair loss (including a rat-like, hairless tail), poor coat, obesity, lethargy, and possibly anemia. Many dogs exhibit tissue thickening around the face and head. Problems may also develop in the cardiovascular system, or more rarely, in the nervous system. In addition, dogs with a tendency toward aggression may become even worse.

To diagnose the disease, a laboratory will measure the T4 level circulating in the blood. The active hormone, T3, fluctuates too much to measure easily.

Care of Your Hypothyroid Dog

Hypothyroidism is easy and inexpensive to treat. Hypothyroid dogs are simply given a thyroid supplement once or twice a day. The treatment must continue for the remainder of the dog's life. Your dog's vet will want to monitor him at regular intervals.

INFLAMMATORY BOWEL DISEASE (IBD)

Inflammatory bowel disease is a chronic inflammatory disease that may occur anywhere along the gastrointestinal tract, especially the duodenum (the first part of the small intestine). It is actually a group of various conditions, but most result from activation of the immune system that affects the lining of the GI tract. Cocker Spaniels, German Shepherd Dogs, and Yorkshire Terriers seem particularly affected by this disease. It is frequently associated with a bacterium called helicobactor, but the relationship between the disease and the bacterium is not well known. Vomiting, diarrhea, and weight loss are characteristic of the condition.

Care of Your IBD Dog

Some recent studies target dietary hypersensitivity as a factor, especially sensitivity to soy isolate hydrosylate, a frequent source of protein in commercial food. Beef and horsemeat may also be culprits. Other suspects include milk, food additives, parasites, and stress. The disease may also have a genetic component. The best foods for an IBD dog contain a single source of hypoallergenic protein, possibly rabbit, duck, or venison. Insoluble fibers in the food may also be helpful. Immunosuppressive drugs, antibiotics, anti-inflammatory drugs, and corticosteroids like prednisone are also frequently used.

LYMPHOMA

Lymphoma is a rapidly growing cancer of the lymphatic system and is unfortunately very common in middle-aged dogs. Since the lymph system goes everywhere in the body, the disease itself can occur anywhere. You will probably not even be aware that anything is wrong until you discover a large, firm lump (or lumps) near the lymph nodes, most prominently the ones found in the neck and hind legs. (Keep in mind that most dog lumps are harmless.) Your vet will probably do a blood panel, a needle biopsy, or perhaps a bone marrow aspirate to make a diagnosis.

No one knows exactly why some dogs get lymphoma. It's partly a matter of genetics, but other factors may also be involved. If your dog does have lymphoma and it goes untreated, he may only live about two months. However, chemotherapy is an option for many lymphoma patients, depending on the stage of the disease. Classical lymphoma is divided into five stages. In the first stage, only one lymph node is involved; in the second, several lymph nodes in the same area are involved; in the third, all peripheral lymph nodes are involved; in the fourth, all peripheral lymph nodes as well as the spleen, liver, or anterior mediastinum in the chest are involved; in the last, everything previous is present, plus the bone marrow is involved. Chemotherapy can help most dogs, except those in the last stage.

Care of Your Lymphoma Patient

Dogs usually have few side effects or complications from chemotherapy. Your dog's whiskers may fall off, but the rest of his hair will probably stay where it is. A few breeds, such as Poodles, Shih Tzu, Lhasa Apsos, and Old English Sheepdogs, may have a hair-loss problem—but that's an improvement over cancer.

About three-quarters of dogs with lymphoma undergoing chemotherapy experience remission, often for two years or even more. It is definitely an option worth considering, if your finances permit.

For tips on taking care of a dog with lymphoma, see the section on cancer.

MEGAESOPHAGUS

The esophagus is a tube that connects the mouth and stomach. Normally, the esophagus contracts and relaxes rhythmically to force food to pass down the tube. Sometimes, however, the esophagus loses its muscle tone and does not contract properly. This will cause regurgitation of food and is especially dangerous because the dog can develop aspiration pneumonia from inhaling regurgitated food particles. Most victims of this disease are young puppies; there is also a genetic component, with Great Danes, Irish Setters, and German Shepherd Dogs the most predisposed. In some cases, the esophagus will develop some tone as the puppy matures.

Another kind of congenital megaesophagus is vascular ring anomaly. In this case, a band of tissue constricts the esophagus. Most of the time, surgery is necessary to correct it. In adult dogs, nerve damage resulting from myasthenia gravis, hypthyroidism, Addison's disease, or trauma are sometimes associated with the condition. All too often, however, no cause is found, and the disease simply has to be treated without finding the underlying cause.

Care of a Dog With Megaesophagus

Managing the disease includes determining the proper kind of diet—liquid or solid. (This depends on the individual.) In any case, the dog needs to eat with his food dish elevated and ideally should be kept in this position for ten minutes or so after eating. This requires a huge commitment on the part of the owner! Without great care, food particles can go down the windpipe, producing pneumonia in the dog. The drug Reglan (metoclopramide) and a motility modifier (Cisapride) may also be administered,

> Consider a mobility cart for your paralyzed dog if he has good strength in his front legs.

as may antacids and medication for nausea.

Handling this disease requires a great commitment from the owners. It can be expensive to treat because the dog may require frequent trips to the veterinarian. Dogs must also eat food in small quantities in an "abnormal" feeding position, almost always requiring the help of their owners.

Tips for Dealing With a Dog With Megaesophagus

- Elevate your dog's food bowl.
- Talk to your vet about the proper diet (liquid or solid).
- Be sure to supplement any missing nutrients.

PARALYSIS

Damage to the spinal cord can lead to paralysis, often permanent. This does not mean the affected dog must be euthanized. Quite the contrary—with a committed owner and a spirited dog, a close, happy relationship can continue, just as with people. It's important to remember that dogs don't take a global view of things. To them, paralysis does not mean an assault upon their psychological well-being but rather a simple obstacle separating them from their food bowl, bed, favorite person, or activity. Your goal as an owner of such a dog is to remove the obstacle. This may require a cart, some carrying, or a major remodeling of your house—but it can be done!

Care of Your Paralyzed Dog

One of the main challenges in caring for a paralyzed dog is keeping him clean, especially since these animals frequently suffer urinary or bowel incontinence. This means frequent wipedowns (baby wipes work fine) of affected areas, as well as baths every few days. Dry shampoos, pet diapers, and underpads are also available. You can buy beds with waterproof covers, and it helps to place the bed on a piece of flexible plastic such as an office chair floor protector. Paralyzed dogs often have trouble emptying the bladder completely, which in turn can lead to infections, perhaps even traveling up into the kidneys, which is very serious indeed. Luckily, bladder infections are easy to cure with ordinary antibiotics. Owners can often tell by the smell or color of the urine that something is wrong; at this point, a trip to the veterinarian is in order.

In the most difficult cases, where the paralysis is towards the front, owners may have to learn to express the bladder themselves. A veterinarian can teach you this simple procedure, but it will need to be done several times a day. This may also be necessary if the dog has a leaky bladder, which can occur sometimes with lower-back paralysis. The leaks may mean the bladder is overflowing, which makes it doubly important to empty it.

Bedsores, especially at pressure points such as elbows and hips, are a common worry. Although most paralyzed dogs can manage to change their position to some extent, the very fact that they are paralyzed means they might not be aware of bedsores. It is your job to look out for them on your dog's behalf. In some cases, you may need to apply special padding. Certainly you will wish to purchase a machine-washable, orthopedic bed designed to protect the pressure points.

Tips for Living With a Paralyzed Dog

- Your may want to consider a mobility cart (you can check out www.k9carts.com for samples) if your dog has good strength in his front legs. Carts will help him exercise and give him the psychological boost that only self-propelled mobility can bring.
- Never allow a paralyzed pet to be outside alone. Not only is he vulnerable to the usual attacks from the neighborhood bullying dogs, even more dangerous are the noxious flies that have the habit of heading right underneath his tail and doing nasty things there.
- For many dogs, physical therapy is very beneficial. Under the direction of your veterinarian or qualified veterinary physical therapist, you can learn to help your dog with many of the flexing and stretching motions, which may help him regain some use of his limbs.

15

ACTIVITIES, SPORTS, AND TRAVEL

Keeping in step with your dog starts with keeping your dog fit. Even more so than human beings, dogs need exercise to stay healthy, happy, and out of mischief.

f your dog is elderly, out of condition, or stricken with arthritis or hip dysplasia, consult your veterinarian about the amount of exercise that is right for him. Always start slowly, and take frequent breaks to allow your dog to drink water. (It's also a good idea to encourage him to drink before the activity starts, as long he doesn't get waterlogged.) You can even purchase special made-for-dogs sport refreshment drinks, which help keep electrolytes at a proper level.

Exercising your dog regularly tires him out in a positive way, so he will be less inclined to destructive behaviors like eating your couch or excavating your yard. It also produces more

> Dogs need exercise to stay healthy, happy, and out of mischief.

serotonin (a neurotransmitter), which helps prevent anxiety and depression and also reduces appetite.

Before embarking on any canine sport, your dog should be reliable on several commands—come, sit, and stay at the very least (more on these commands in Chapter 8).Your dog should also be fairly immune to distractions.

BASIC ACTIVITIES FOR YOU AND YOUR DOG
Biking

Many dogs love to tag along while their owners ride. Because it can be dangerous to allow your dog to run free, you can buy bicycle attachments like the Springer or Canine Cruiser that attach the dog to the bike while preventing him from running too close behind and getting hurt.

Don't get carried away during your ride, however. Stop frequently for breathers, and don't go too fast or too far. Dogs will exert every ounce of energy to keep up with you, and more than one has died of heatstroke or exhaustion in his gallant efforts. Remember that dogs suffer more from heat than we do and can wilt at temperatures we find quite pleasant.

> When bicycling with your dog, stop frequently for breathers and don't go too fast or too far.

Camping

If you'd like to take your dog camping, you can buy a real "pup" tent—a portable, lightweight "crate." Like human tents, they can be staked into the ground. I wouldn't use one of these for inveterate diggers or chewers, but for the well-behaved camping dog, they are ideal. They can be purchased through many pet supply stores.

Dog Parks

A real boon for urban dwellers is the dog park. Dog parks allow formerly leash-bound animals to romp and play in the open air not only with their owners but also with other dogs. As long as the park is filled with well-socialized dogs and dog-savvy owners, it's a real blessing. The best parks are large enough to allow unlimited running but are also strongly fenced, for overexcited dogs can run off, even if previously recall-perfect. However, the park can be disappointing (and unhealthy) if owners do not pick up after or watch over their charges carefully. Many do provide poop bags! For a partial list of parks around the country, visit www.i-love-dogs.com/search/directory/Dog_Parks/.

Fetch

Most dogs get fun and enjoyment out of a simple game of fetch. (Hounds and certain other breeds typically aren't wild about it—too proud to fetch—but every dog is an individual.) Fetch has a triple function, actually; it gives your dog needed exercise, it helps strengthen the bond between you, and it gets him into the habit of returning to you.

First Off-Leash Dog Park
The first off-leash dog park, Ohlone Dog Park, opened in 1979 in Berkeley, California.

Jogging

For the more athletically inclined, dogs can be wonderful running partners—if yours is in the same condition as you are! (Mismatches can be exhausting for both of you.) Be sure you have a dog whose type and temperament make him suitable as a running partner. Consult a vet before starting.

For the best running experience, do not use a regular leash unless you enjoy getting your arm pulled out of the socket. Buy or make a hands-free running leash that ties securely around your waist. Commercial types have a 360-degree range of motion so that they can swivel all around your body. Some have a bungee section, too, and some are reflective for night jogging. One great advantage of such a device is that it lets you keep your regular running form.

Swimming

Swimming is another great exercise for dogs. It's low impact, so it doesn't stress the joints of older or arthritic animals. It also works many muscles at the same time. While not all dogs are natural swimmers, most can learn to enjoy it. By the way, it's perfectly fine for dogs to swim in chlorinated pools, just as you do—just make sure they are supervised. The chlorine may do a number on their fur, just as it does with your hair, but you can just bathe the dog afterwards. It won't hurt them to drink the stuff either. (Remember, pool water is designed not to make children who accidentally swallow it ill.) The ocean is a different matter. I would never allow a dog in the ocean. It's full of jellyfish, riptides, and sharks, all of which are lying in wait for your pooch.

Walking and Hiking

Walking is a great exercise for both you and your dog as long as you walk together. Use a leash unless you're in a safe, fenced-in area.

Remember—if you are attached to your Poodle, keep your Poodle attached to you. If you're a hiker, consider getting a lightweight nylon backpack for your larger dog. That way your dog can haul his own food and water. On the other hand, if you have a toy dog, it wouldn't be a bad idea to get a special pack to carry him in.

For nighttime strolling, you can buy a leash with a combination retractable lead and flashlight.

For more information about hiking with your dog, visit: Hike With Your Dog (www. hikewithyourdog.

Walking is a great exercise for you and your dog as long as you walk together.

com), the American Hiking Society (www. americanhiking.org), or the Partnership for Animal Welfare (www.paw-rescue.org/PAW/PETTIPS/DogTip_Hiking.php).

ORGANIZED SPORTS FOR YOU AND YOUR DOG
Agility

Agility is more than a sport; it is a passion among its adherents. It is also one of the few dog sports that's equally thrilling to spectators. In agility, a handler is given a set time to guide a dog (off lead) through an obstacle course consisting of jumps, tunnels, chutes, A-frames, weave poles, teeter-totters, and other interesting objects. Handlers are not allowed to touch the equipment or the dog during the trial. Like everything else in the dog performance world, your dog can win one of several titles. In the American Kennel Club (AKC), it's NAD (Novice Agility Dog), OAD (Open Agility Dog), ADX (Agility Dog Excellent), and MAX (Master Agility Excellent). Dogs must be at least one year old to be entered in the AKC event; spayed and neutered dogs are welcome.

In agility, a handler is given a set time to guide a dog through an obstacle course.

While most dog can participate, breeds that truly excel include Shetland Sheepdogs, Belgian Tervurens, Border Collies, Australian Shepherds, Golden Retrievers, Labrador Retrievers, Cocker Spaniels, Welsh Corgis, and among the small fry, Papillons. The age at which your dog is allowed to compete varies by club—6 months for United Kennel Club (UKC) events, 12 months for AKC events, and 18 months for the North American Dog Agility Council (NADAC) and the United States Dog Agility Association (USDAA). Once he gets started, an agility dog can compete successfully until he is eight or even ten years old.

Before participating in this exciting sport, get some veterinary pre-screening done on your pet. Hips, elbows, and eyes especially need to be in good shape. Explain to your vet why you want the exam and what kinds of physical stresses will be placed on the dog. (Although I feel like a lone voice crying in the wilderness, I maintain that certain breeds, such as Dachshunds and Bulldogs, simply should not compete in agility due to their physical peculiarities.) You can even bring along a short video to show your vet what goes on!

In addition to the initial vet check, you'll need to do regular continual conditioning for your dog. Weight-bearing exercises, short sprints, and games of Frisbee will all help build up the dog's cardiovascular system. Bone building exercises that are essential for jumps are a slow, painstaking process—expect to spend half a year or more working on low jumps before progressing to higher ones. Patience is the real name of the agility game.

If you proceed too fast, you can do irreparable harm to your dog.

In addition to physical conditioning, a basic amount of obedience training is essential. To work agility, your dog must be reliable off lead. He should sit, down, stay, and recall at your command. Most agility instructors say that dogs who have been taught to fetch have additional advantages as well. Your dog should also be sociable and under control around other dogs.

To get started in agility, contact your local kennel club. They probably have classes or can direct you to the right place. Warning—this sport is habit-forming.

Carting

Carting is a great sport that's open to dogs of all sizes, although traditional

Traditional carting breeds include the Bernese Mountain Dog.

carters are Rottweilers, Saint Bernards, Bouviers des Flandres, Bernese Mountain Dogs, and Greater Swiss Mountain Dogs. Unlike many other events, it is actually useful. In carting, you hook up your big dog to a cart and join a parade, sell vegetables, or just have fun. I first saw these dogs in Switzerland, and I was truly amazed! There are several carting clubs all across the country to help you get started. Go to www.cartingwithyourdog.com for complete information.

Coonhound Events

These specialized events for the six breeds of coonhounds include "nite hunts" and water races. Check out www.akc.org for more details.

Coursing

This event is designed for sighthounds, but I can tell you from experience that nearly all dogs love it if given a chance to participate. Officially, eligible breeds for this event are Whippets,

During a lure coursing event, the dog must chase the lure.

Basenjis, Greyhounds, Italian Greyhounds, Afghan Hounds, Borzois, Ibizan Hounds, Pharaoh Hounds, Irish Wolfhounds, Scottish Deerhounds, Salukis, and Rhodesian Ridgebacks. There are two basic types of coursing: open coursing, which involves chasing live game (rabbits) and is usually performed in the West, and lure coursing, which involves a couple of white plastic bags (that honestly do look like rabbits) tied to the back of a machine and pulled. The lure is zipped along at pace that suits the participating dog. Usually the course is 500 or 600 yards (457 or 548.5 m) long. This sport requires no real training on the part of the dog and no effort on the part of the owner, either (which makes it even more fun). No bothersome commands to train for—just sit back with a lemonade or hot chocolate and enjoy yourself. You can find out more at www.akc.org.

Dog Shows (Conformation)

The first requirement in succeeding at dog shows is to have what is called a "worthy" dog. This means that your dog comes close to the official standard for the breed, which can be found on the breed's website or at www.akc.org. Read the standard carefully and examine the illustration if one is provided. If you bought your dog from a reputable show breeder, she has already probably told you whether the puppy is "show quality." (Even if he isn't, don't worry. There are lots of events you can enter with your dog that require ability rather than looks; many are described in this chapter.) If you have a show-quality dog, you should talk to your breeder or local kennel club about how to proceed. The best way is to find a mentor, someone who will guide you through the showing world.

In a conformation show, dogs are judged against the standard for the breed.

If your dog has show potential, you must make sure he will be able to meet the rudimentary behavior requirements. Show dogs should be able to walk on lead, allow themselves to be "stacked" (or posed), and hold the position while being checked over by a judge. This checking over involves having the judge feel the contours of the body, examine the "bite" (the way the teeth meet), and in males, checking the testicles. You can help your dog by socializing him well and taking him to conformation classes at your local kennel club.

Dog shows are really giant beauty contests. If you decide to participate, your goal is to have your dog awarded a championship, which means he will have accumulated 15 points. He can earn between one and five points per show, depending on how many other dogs of his breed he beats. Included in the 15 championship points must be those won at two "majors," big shows that award three to five points. To earn the points, he has to win; you get nothing for second place except a red ribbon. Males and females compete separately, so the top dog of each sex can get points. If your dog excels and wins Best of Breed, he'll go on to compete against others in his "ground" (other hounds, say). If he wins there, it's on to Best of Show, where he competes against the other group winners. The Best in Show dog may be the victor of more than 2,000 other dogs at a big show!

If you decide to show, you'll probably start off by entering your puppy or young dog in a "match," which is sort of like a rehearsal for a real dog show. You don't acquire points at matches but get something just as important—experience. Match shows are cheaper to enter than dog shows, and the judges don't expect fully ready dogs; they know the animals are there for practice. Unlike shows, you can enter your dog on the day of the match.

Full-fledged dog shows are much more complicated and competitive. You need to send your entry form in advance—no exceptions. (Fill out the form carefully!) The day before the show, be sure to bathe your dog and dry and groom him according to the breed standard. Once at the show, make sure to get to your class on time, since they don't hang around waiting for people. Showing dogs can be a lot of fun, but if you expect to win a top spot (or an invitation to Westminster), it's time consuming and expensive. Most top-rated dogs are shown every weekend, which means spending a lot of money not only in entry fees but also for gas, hotels, and restaurants. There is also "campaigning" involved, which means running all over the country every weekend and advertising in

Senior Exercise

Don't neglect the importance of exercise for seniors! Not only is it fun, it's also important for your pet's health. It is true that an older dog has a lower exercise tolerance than one in his prime. He may also have problems in hot or humid weather (very few dogs of any age like it, in fact). But that does not means he needs no exercise— quite the contrary. Exercise will help him keep at a good weight, for one thing. This will reduce the stress on his heart, lungs, and bones. It will also keep him mentally fit, since exercise gets plenty of glucose and oxygen into the brain.

an attempt to sway the judges even before they've seen your dog. Some people simply hire a handler for all this. However, the owner-handler of a show dog obtains a much higher level of satisfaction for having done it herself.

A special subdivision of dog shows is Junior Showmanship, designed for the children in your dog's life. Here kids learn the ins and outs of dog shows, gain self-confidence, and learn to bond with their dog. To get the best results, your child can attend handling classes at your local all-breed kennel club. And so can you!

Earthdog Trials

Earthdog trials, begun in 1994, are open to all small terriers and Dachshunds. Like other performance events, earthdog trials are noncompetitive, meaning that each dog needs only to qualify—not win. So, theoretically, every dog can be a winner! In these events, dogs are expected to follow the "game" to ground, then work the quarry. The AKC is eager to let you know that the quarry is not harmed during an earthdog trial. (It is protected by a cage.) Your Scottie can win three earthdog titles: Junior Earthdog, Senior Earthdog, and Master Earthdog. Dogs must be one year old to compete, and they can be spayed or neutered. You can find more details at www.akc.org.

Field Trials

AKC field trials are held for hounds, pointing breeds, retrievers, and spaniels. They are designed to test whether your dog can perform the tasks for which his breed was designed. Hounds chase rabbits or hares and either run in packs or braces (pairs). Pointing breed trials evaluate the dog's ability to locate and indicate game by pointing. Retrieving events ask the dog to retrieve shot game. Spaniel trials test the dog's ability to find birds within shotgun range and to flush and retrieve the game when commanded. These events are highly competitive and difficult to master. Competitive dogs often go to a professional trainer to get them in shape.

Flyball

Flyball is a high-speed sport that requires eye-paw coordination. It is also a team sport with 6 to 20 dogs per team. It involves four wooden jumps set 10 feet (3 m) apart, a "flyball box," and a whole lot of tennis balls. Mixed-breed dogs are welcome at these events. Hundreds of flyball tournaments are held around the country each year. For more information, contact the North American Flyball Association (NAFA) at www.flyball.org.

Flying Disc

The flying disc is another name for the Frisbee. Various sorts of competitions are held, including the "catch and retrieve" or the "toss and fetch," a timed round in which teams (each consisting of

a throwing human and catching dog) attempt to make as many successful catches as possible. They usually get to use only one disc. More advanced competitions consist of "freestyle" or "free flight," "accuracy events," and long-distance events. Although this is not yet an AKC event, it is becoming increasingly popular. Mixed breeds are welcome at most competitions. For more information, go to www.skyhoundz.com or www.discdog.org.

Herding Tests and Trials

This is a sport mostly for dogs in the Herding Group, such as Border Collies, Old English Sheepdogs, and Collies. Different herding groups offer different events and different titles. The American Herding Breed Association (AHBA) offers two types of trial classes, each with three levels. They also have a test program. Dogs can

examination, and perform a recall, long sit, and long down. There are three levels of competition, and a title is award at each level, when the dog earns three "legs," or qualifying scores (170 points out of a possible 200).

- The more advanced title of CDX (Companion Dog Excellent) requires additional heeling exercises, drop on recall, retrieve on the flat, retrieve over high jump, broad jump, long sit (with the handler out of sight), and long down (handler out of sight).

- The next rung on the obedience ladder is UD (Utility Dog). To earn this title, a dog must complete a signal exercise, scent discrimination, directed retrieve, moving stand and examination, and directed jumping.

- The highest regular title in obedience is UDX (Utility Dog Excellent). A UDX dog must qualify ten times at high-level obedience shows.

- After a dog has won his UD, he is eligible for OTCh (Obedience Trial Champion). This prized title is awarded when the dog has won 100 obedience championship points. Further, there are special rules about what shows a dog must qualify in to complete the title. The placements must be won under three different judges at all-breed obedience trials.

be tested on sheep, ducks, or cattle. The AKC Test/Trial Program offers tests, pre-trial, and trial classes, again using ducks, sheep, or cattle. All AKC Herding Group breeds, plus Samoyeds and Rottweilers, are eligible.

Obedience

The AKC awards more than good looks or brilliant field ability—your dog can also win an obedience title. Unlike conformation, spayed and neutered dogs can be shown in obedience, as can dogs who may have a fault that disqualifies them from showing. These events are also not strictly competitive, since all the dogs who appear that day could gain a title.

- To win the title of Companion Dog and get the initials CD after his name, your dog must pass several required test elements, including his ability to heel on and off lead, stand for

Rally Obedience

In addition to classical obedience, there's a new sport on the horizon: rally obedience. Rally is a sport, held in conjunction with obedience, where the dog and handler proceed at their own pace through a course of directional signs in a manner similar to rally car racing. The signs are numbered sequentially in the ring to indicate the course the handler must take. The dog and handler team heel from sign to sign and perform the exercises indicated on the sign at each location. Each sign contains an exercise illustrated with symbols.

Dogs are expected to heel at different paces, make turns, do recalls, and jump. (Two levels are currently available—Level One is an entry-level course that is performed on lead, while Level Two calls for more advanced exercises off lead.) Dogs can earn 200 points for a perfect score, with point penalties assessed for errors. But unlike regular obedience competitions, rally allows the owner to repeat commands, and even more importantly, allows owners to verbally assure and praise their pets for succeeding. This is not allowed in regular obedience classes.

Rally obedience seems to be a lot more fun for both owners and dogs and even for spectators, who find it an enjoyable change of pace. Unlike regular obedience, rally is a fast-moving event wherein the dog and the owner follow a predetermined course; they don't wait for a judge to give commands. There are about 45 possible different exercises, and each specific course uses 25-28 of them.

In 2005, rally became a titling event with the AKC. A title may be earned in each of three levels—Novice, Advanced, and Excellent. In addition, a dog may continue to compete in the Advanced and Excellent classes to earn a Rally Advanced Excellent title.

Talk to Your Vet

Always discuss a prospective exercise program for your senior with your vet before starting. Keep an eye on him during the exercise, watching especially for breathing and gait problems. And remember, never force a dog to exercise—it should be fun for both of you.

Schutzhund

Schutzhund is a performance event that tests intelligence, athleticism, tracking, obedience, and protection ability. There are three levels: Schutzhund I, II, and III—a dog must score a minimum of 70 out of a possible 100 points at each phase of each level. While Schutzhund was originally developed in Germany for German Shepherd Dogs, the sport is open to all athletic dogs with correct working abilities, including Dobermans, Rottweilers, Airedale Terriers, Bouviers des Flandres, and others. The United Schutzhund Clubs of America has more information for people working with German Shepherds. Check out www.germanshepherddog.com.

Skijoring

Skijor is a Norwegian word that means "ski-driving." It combines cross-country skiing with drafting, using dogs as the draft animals. The main challenge in this event is teaching your dog to pull (just after you have spent all that time teaching him not to). However, most natural skijor dogs have an instinct to pull anyway. To participate, you will need a skijor line at least 7 feet (2 m) long that includes a bungee section. And skis—don't forget the skis. Traditionally people have used northern breeds

Lost Dogs

If you are traveling to a sports event and have the misfortune of losing your dog, go to Pets 911 (www.pets911.com). The site contains a nationwide list of animal control facilities, humane societies, and veterinarians and is searchable by zip code.

like Alaskan Malamutes and Samoyeds, but there's no reason you can't hook up the family Labrador. Go to www.sleddogcentral.com/skijoring.htm for more information.

Skijoring combines cross-country skiing with drafting, using dogs as the draft animals.

Tracking

Tracking is a noncompetitive event that's open to all breeds. All your dog needs is a harness and a 20–40-foot (6-12 m) lead, and you're set to go. AKC tracking events are sort of like canine search and rescue, only in this case the main object is not a human being but an "article," usually a human-scent-impregnated leather wallet (empty, unfortunately) laid by one person. Unlike agility and obedience events that require a dog to qualify three times, a dog only needs to complete one track successfully to earn each title. To get started, you must have your dog certified by an AKC judge. An experienced tracklayer or AKC judge will lay a regulation TD track for your dog. If he successfully completes the track, the judge will issue four tracking certificates. The certificates are good for one year, and each time you enter a test, you must provide one certificate with your entry form. If you are not accepted into the test, you should request your certificate be returned, since you will only receive four certificates on one dog. The point is to ensure that only dogs with a reasonably good chance of passing will be competing. (Tracking takes up a lot of room, as each entrant needs his own field.)

Three titles are available. A dog who earns all three titles is a Champion Tracker. At the Tracking level, a dog follows a 440–500-yard-long (402.5-457 m) track that is between 30 minutes and 2 hours old and contains three to five turns.

Therapy Dogs

This term usually refers to dogs who visit people in hospitals, nursing homes, and other facilities. Their job is simply to make people feel better just by being there. (Another term, "animal-assisted therapy," is often reserved for more formal treatment programs.)

Pet therapy helps enhance the deep connection between mind and body. Having an animal visit someone in need helps relieve depression and loneliness. For elderly people, the gentle stretching movements involved in petting the therapy dog are healthy and strengthening. A dog also serves as a conversation piece—many elderly people will often recall the dogs of their youth, which is a great way to start a conversation. And of course, sick kids like nothing better than a furry friend to

confide their troubles to. Even inmates of prisons are helped by the presence of these friendly, nonjudgmental visitors.

Good therapy dogs should be friendly but not overexuberant. A calm dog who is not afraid of odd smells, wheelchairs, and oddly dressed people is ideal. And of course a therapy dog is clean, pest-free, and well groomed (with short nails). And while this job may seem totally enjoyable, therapy dogs can get stressed just like any other athlete or worker. Keep a careful eye on your best pal and give him a break from being on his best behavior—this can get the best of even the most calm, polite, and happy dog.

Good therapy dogs should be friendly but not overexuberant.

For more information, contact Bright and Beautiful Therapy Dogs at www.golden-dogs. org; the Delta Society at www.deltasociety. org; Therapy Dogs at www.therapydogs.com; or Therapy Dogs International at www.tdi-dog.org.

TRAVEL

This is a mobile society, and both dogs and their owners must be prepared to travel, move, sojourn, and at least in the case of the dog, bide awhile in a kennel or day care facility. Luckily, it's all possible—and even easy! Whether you're off for a weekend jaunt or have decided to tour the country, maximize your chances for a safe trip and do the following:

- Clip your dog's nails. You don't want him ripping up the upholstery in the car—or the carpet, or the bed in the hotel, or your leg. It's safer for everybody.
- Make copies of your dog's rabies certificate and vet records, and take them with you in case of emergency.
- Be sure all your dog's ID tags are attached. If your dog is not microchipped and/or tattooed, do it now.
- If your dog is prone to carsickness, get out the over-the-counter motion sickness medication (like Dramamine or Benadryl), or for a natural cure, try ginger or peppermint. They all work fairly well.
- Pack the travel kit. It should include: dog food (including a can opener, if necessary); dishes; bottled water (exposing your dog to strange water could give him diarrhea—no fun on a trip); dog toys and treats; a dog bed; paper towels and cleaning supplies; a pooper scooper; and plastic bags.

By Car

Fido secured? Be sure he's in his crate or seatbelt for the ride. Some countries, like Germany, actually require dogs to wear seatbelts. They safely restrain your dog, keeping both you and him safe. As a rule, your dog should ride in the back seat. Do not allow him to ride in the front seat; in case of an accident, the airbag could kill him. (Airbags deploy at 200 miles [322 kph] an hour!)

You can also purchase a net or metal barrier to insert between the front and back seats. These barriers are adjustable both vertically and horizontally and are pressure mounted for quick installation. Some versions are net-like, which is fine if don't think your dog will chew yours to pieces.

Please don't let your dog run loose in the car—he'll jump in your lap or insert his head between your foot and the brake pedal or your hand and the steering wheel. Having a 100-pound (45.5-kg) dog leap into your lap while you're negotiating a difficult turn is not as much fun as it sounds. Unanticipated sharp stops can also hurl a dog into the windshield. Nor should you allow your dog to stick his head out the window. As much as dogs love it, it puts their eyes and nose at risk from flying debris. And yes, dogs do leap out of windows, even dogs who have "never done anything like that before."

Keep the car cooler than you like it. Dogs react badly to heat; they're not tropical animals like us. You can wear a sweater, after all. Stop frequently to exercise your dog and let him drink or eliminate, but keep him on a leash at all times. All you need is to have the dog escape while you're on vacation.

And of course, never leave your dog unattended in the car, ever. Warm weather (65°F [18.3°C] and over) is very dangerous—even opening the window "a crack" is not sufficient to save him from overheating. You also risk having your dog stolen.

The European Way

Europe has fewer boarding establishments than the United States does; one reason is that dogs are welcome in more places and Europeans commonly take their pets wherever they go! This includes restaurants, where it's not uncommon to see a well-mannered dog lying quietly at his owner's feet while the latter is having lunch or dinner.

Motion Sickness: You turn on the ignition, and there is that telltale "Urghierrh" and then the unmistakable odor of vomit filling your car. It is a dispiriting way to start a trip, and all too common. Fortunately, most cases of motion sickness in dogs can be controlled.

The first step, however, is understanding why the dog is getting ill. There are two, possibly interrelated, causes for carsickness.

Your dog may have physical motion sickness. In this case, an over-the-counter motion sickness medication that contains dimenhydrinate (like Dramamine) can reduce or halt canine carsickness. Simply follow the weight directions given for human beings. (You can't always do this with a medication, but in this case, you may.) The usual dosage is between 25 to 50 milligrams (or 2 to 4 milligrams for every pound (.45 kg) of body weight) three times a day. Give it about an hour before traveling. Most dogs tolerate this drug best

When traveling with your dog by car, make sure that he is safely restrained in the back seat.

if you give it to them with a little food. The medication won't help if your dog is already sick, however. Also don't give the motion sickness medication if your dog has bladder problems, hyperthyroidism, seizure disorders, or glaucoma. The effectiveness of the medication diminishes with repeated use. For a more natural remedy, try ginger. (A couple of ginger snaps will work fine.)

Your dog's carsickness also may be psychological or at least originate in logical causes, such as a traumatic experience. If your dog exhibits signs of anxiety (panting and drooling) even before getting in the car, the cause may be psychological. This can get complicated because if the dog has a physical reason for getting sick, the sight of the car might set up anticipatory stress—he knows he might get sick again. In that case, you'll have to deal with both physical and psychological causes. Maybe you're a bad driver and the dog fears for his life. More likely, however, he associates car rides with trips to the vet, groomers, or boarding kennels. If he is a rescue dog, he may think he is being returned to the pound or shelter.

To make the trip more pleasant for a dog prone to carsickness (and thus for yourself), keep the car as chilly as you can stand it, open some windows, and allow the dog to face front.

By Plane

Over half a million dogs and cats fly every year in our country, and like most people, fly in safety and comfort. But this is not always the case. In fact, the Humane Society of the United States (HSUS) charges that 5,000 animals are killed, injured, or lost on planes every year.

Here are some tips to help you keep your dog safe and comfortable on his flight:

- If your dog isn't accustomed to a crate, practice with him before you travel. Traveling dogs unused to crates are subject to increased stress; they're also apt to annoy airport personnel— something you definitely don't want.
- Have your dog vet-checked within ten days of the flight. She will issue you the required health certificate.
- Identify your pet. He should wear a collar and tags bearing your name, phone number, and where you can be reached. It's wise to include a family member's contact information as well.
- Book a direct flight. This reduces both stress on the animal and the risk of "misplacement." If possible, don't plan to arrive on the weekend—if something goes wrong, there's never anybody around who can take charge. In the summer, try to get an early morning or evening flight. It will be more comfortable for your pet.

- Feed your dog about four hours before flight time, and allow him to drink water freely. You don't want to feed him right before a flight if he is prone to motion sickness, but the law requires that the animal be fed within four hours of a flight, in case there is a delay and he misses a meal. Use your best judgment, taking into account possible mishaps. Attach further feeding and watering instructions to the kennel. Adult dogs must be given water at least every 12 hours and fed (at minimum) every 24 hours. Food and water must be supplied to puppies (under 16 weeks) every 12 hours. Puppies under 8 weeks are not permitted to fly.
- Your dog should be checked as excess baggage, not as freight! If he gets checked as freight, he may end up on a different plane.
And here are a few "don'ts":
- Don't travel during extreme weather conditions; both heat and cold can kill your dog.
- Unless specifically instructed by your vet, don't tranquilize your dog before a flight, especially if he is traveling as baggage. The medication interferes with his cardiac functioning and heat

regulatory system. In addition, no one is there to monitor him. If your Lhasa has breathing problems, leave him home.

Booking a direct flight will reduce both the stress on your dog and the risk of misplacement.

- Don't lock the crate. Airline people may need to free your animal from it in case of emergency.

The Carrier

Here are some basic carrier rules, but make sure you always check with your airline beforehand.

- Most airlines require that wheels on the container be removed or made immobile prior to the flight.
- Kennels must be ventilated, and the rules are quite specific about it: at least 14 percent of the total wall space must be ventilated, with at least one-third of the opening located in the top half of the kennel.

- Secure your dog in an enclosed fiberglass kennel large enough for the dog to stand, sit, turn around, and lie down.
- The kennel must have a solid, leak-proof floor covered with absorbent bedding. Pegboard flooring is not allowed.
- The carrier must have grips for the convenience and safety of cargo handlers. The kennel should bear a sign saying "LIVE ANIMAL" and "THIS SIDE UP" in 1-inch (2.5-cm) letters.
- Put a familiar toy or an article with your scent in the kennel to keep your dog calmer.

Some airlines allow your pet to travel with you in the passenger compartment. Check with the airline. He must be in a crate, and you'll need to buy a separate ticket for him. Most airlines charge about $50 for a pet ticket. In nearly all cases, his crate must be able to fit under the seat, so that leaves out a Saint Bernard. Because of crowded schedules and heat, some airlines won't transport your dog in the summertime. Be sure to check.

Other requirements may include a limit to the number of pets per cabin. (Book early.) These differ from airline to airline, and a few do not accept any pet transportation.

Even the federal government is waking up to the idea that pets are not baggage. The Department of Transportation's Federal Aviation Administration (FAA) has provided a new rule that will help pet owners gauge the level of safety that airlines provide for pets. This ruling requires airlines to report any incident in which a pet being transported aboard a flight is lost, hurt, or killed. The reports will be published regularly in the Air Travel Consumer Report. Until now, pet owners haven't been able to get information about the number of these occurrences because transported pets were considered the same as baggage.

Lodging

According to the American Animal Hospital Association (AAHA), 41 percent of pet owners take their pets along on vacations. Some hotels allow pets, but you need to inquire first. Expect to put down a deposit or even an extra fee, since motels take a dim view of having their carpets and furniture eaten or urinated on by pets. (It's bad enough when people do it.) The number of motels and hotels that do accept dogs has dropped by 25 percent in recent years. If your dog is not well behaved in every way, it's best to leave him at home.

Ask for a first floor room, if one is available; it's more convenient when it comes to those late night strolls. (And wipe off the dog's feet before re-entering the room.) If you have to leave your dog alone in the room while you have dinner, put him in his crate with a chewy. (If he's a whiner or barker, you'll have to call room service or send out for a pizza.) Put a "Do Not Disturb" sign on the door if you do go out.

Big Business
Day care and pet sitting have become big business in the United States—Americans shell out about 500 million bucks a year to have someone look after our pooches.

If You Can't Take Your Dog With You
Boarding Your Dog

In some cases, you must leave your precious pooch at home. This is not the end of the world—some dogs find traveling scary and stressful. And while you may enjoy visiting your Aunt Enid's Rottweiler, don't assume your Toy Poodle will find it an equally pleasant experience. Sometimes the best thing you can do is simply leave the dog home with a pet sitter or at a good boarding kennel. If you decide to board, get recommendations from your friends or vet, and visit the facility before committing. Be sure to book ahead; most kennels are swamped all the time. Many kennels offer grooming services, special playtimes, swimming, and other activities for your dog, usually at an extra fee. Be sure to inquire.

Ask yourself the following questions when choosing a kennel:
- Is the kennel licensed and inspected? Ask for proof.
- Is it clean? Check out the walls, the floors, and the food bowls. Food should be kept in airtight, pest-proof containers.
- Is there sufficient noise control? Although a kennel will never be as quiet as a library, you don't want your dog subjected to 24 hours of nonstop barking, either. He may become stressed with the noise—or he may pick up

- How are the animals separated? Good kennels do not allow nose-to-nose contact between animals, both for fear of spreading disease and to prevent barrier fighting.
- Does the kennel have adequate quarantine facilities? This is an important consideration if a boarded dog should develop symptoms of a contagious disease.
- Can you pick up your pet on Sunday? Many boarding kennels are closed on Sunday, and pets are unavailable for pickup. Sunday, of course, is the very day when most people want to pick up their pets.
- Is the kennel accredited by the American Boarding Kennel Association (ABKA)?

the habit himself. You don't want either of these things to happen.

- Is it spacious? Some kennels provide individual runs for each dog, while others bring dogs into a common area for play. (This is good for socialization but can pose health risks.) Discuss how the kennel plans to ensure your dog's safe exercise. If you don't want your dog associating with others, make that clear.
- Is the kennel heated and cooled according to the season? This is not a luxury but a necessity.
- Is there a vet on call?
- Does the kennel employ veterinary technicians on its staff?
- Are there both indoor and outdoor runs?
- Is the kennel secure? If your dog is an escape artist, let the kennel manager know in advance.
- Is the kennel safe, with fire alarms, sprinkler systems, and double doors? All staff should be trained in CPR.
- Is the indoor area well ventilated?
- What kind of bedding is provided? (Most kennels will allow you to bring your dog's own bed for him, if you'd like.)

Doggy Day Care

Boarding your dog while traveling on vacation is one thing, but what do you do when you travel every day to work? Dogs are social creatures who do much better when they have human and (usually) canine company. But most people have to work for long hours every day. For many, the answer lies in doggy day care.

You have a lot of choice when it comes to canine day care. Some places offer nothing more than rudimentary runs and water, while others are state-of-the-art facilities that can include basic obedience classes, grooming services, and even canine "spas." Climate-controlled play areas, wading pools, and doggy gyms are commonplace. A few even have "petcams" on at all times so that you can observe your dog from afar (and make sure that he is getting everything he deserves).

Of course, if your dog is not a social animal, he may not be permitted to attend day care. Obviously, the proprietors don't want to deal with fighting dogs all day long—even more reason to socialize your dog. Good day care facilities also expect your dog to be up to date on his vaccinations and on a regular flea/tick preventive. You may be asked to fill out a questionnaire about your dog's temperament, level of training, and preferences. He may also be evaluated before being accepted into a day care program.

You too should be looking around and doing some evaluating of your own. Many of the same criteria apply here as those relating to kennels. Visit the day care facility before you enroll your dog. It should obviously be clean, nice smelling, and well cared for. It should also be safe. Safety measures may include double doors or other "decompression zones" to keep dogs from escaping. Most good day cares have a connection with a nearby vet in case an emergency happens. Good day care centers put dogs of similar size together and separate overly boisterous animals. Regulations should be written down for your perusal.

Take time to meet with and interview the staff, and ask specifically what the staff-dog ratio is. (It shouldn't be more than ten dogs per one staff person.) Ask the staff what their procedure is when introducing new dogs. Most offer playgroup sessions—after all, the point of day care is to give your dog activity and company, not to lock him up. In a few cases, a fight may break out (they are dogs, after all), but good operations do everything they can to minimize quarrels. Extra benefits may include massage or a limousine pickup or drop off service, but there will be an extra charge.

Observe the staff's interactions with the dogs. They should be attentive, friendly, and knowledgeable about their charges. Try asking them about a few of the dogs in their care and see what they know. Good day care facilities provide references.

Rates vary considerably, largely depending on the size of the dog, what is offered, and what part of the country you live in.

Pet Sitters

For a more personal at-home solution while traveling or at work, try a pet sitter. References are a must, of course. Ask for them. And experience counts as well. One way to gauge experience, or at least expertise, is to pose a couple of likely problems that might come up and ask how the sitter would deal with them. Good pet sitters are also bonded and insured.

For more information, check with The National Association of Professional Pet Sitters (NAPPS), www.petsitters.org; or Pet Sitters International (PSI), www.petsit.com.

16

END-OF-LIFE ISSUES

All beings must pass away, and unfortunately, our wonderful dogs pass all too soon. The experience of losing a beloved pet is undoubtedly one of life's more painful moments, but it can be eased by knowing how well you cared for your dog, how much you loved each other, and how the memories will remain.

The most painful part of pet ownership is saying good-bye, and the most difficult part of that decision is deciding when the time has come. For a few lucky ones, the pet makes the decision himself and passes away quietly in his sleep. A friend of mine had her aged dog climb up on the bed (something he had not been able to do for many months), lay his head on her, and die. One of my dogs insistently tried to tell me it was time by going outside and lying against the fence in the freezing cold, no matter how often I attempted to keep her inside.

In most cases nowadays, you will know in advance that your dog's time to die is near, and it will be up to you to take him to the vet and be with him when that time actually comes. Some owners do not feel up to being in the room during euthanasia, and if you are one of these, rest assured that your dog's old friend, the vet, will make his passing easy and painless. On the other hand, you may want to brave it out and hold your dog until the last. Whatever decision you make, it will be the right one for you.

Most of the time, it is up to us to arrange our dog's death as we shared his life. When you learn that your dog has a terminal illness, you can assess the quality of his life at the present time and ask your vet for an outline of how the disease is expected to progress. As long as your pet is relatively pain-free and evinces an interest in life, it is to no one's benefit to hurry him to the Rainbow Bridge. Here are some criteria you may to use to judge your pet's interest in life.

- Food. It's an old axiom, but a good one—as long as your dog is hungry and enjoys his food, he is probably not ready to say good-bye. Typically, a dog eats less enthusiastically and becomes pickier as he gets sicker, and it's tempting to offer more and more favorite foods and treats as the illness progresses. However,

There's nothing sweeter than senior dogs with their kind, compassionate natures.

the day will come when your terminally ill dog may pass up any treat.

- Comfort. If your pet is suffering, you will need to decide if painkillers can adequately relieve his discomfort. You can assess this by watching his movement, appetite, and desire for petting and affection.
- Personality change. Many pets grow more distant as their time to die approaches. It is almost as if they know the time to part is coming and they are trying to ease you into it. They have their minds on higher things, and you may no longer be the center of their lives. This is very painful to many owners, who especially want to be close to their dog at this time.
- Psychological factors. Many pets become incontinent as they sicken, and I believe they suffer true embarrassment and shame at losing control of their bodily functions. My Irish Setter was of this kind, and it pained me to see the anguish on her face as she realized she had made a "mistake."

- Financial considerations. Only you know how much you can afford to spend. The progress of some diseases, notably cancers, can be slowed, or in some cases, cured with certain kinds of treatments. Only you know how much you can afford, but you should consider the pet's pain as well as your own. While no pet owner wishes to see an animal pass on before "his time," death itself is inexorable.

THE PASSING

When you have decided that the time is right, call (or ask someone to call) your vet to make the appointment. Most veterinarians will arrange a private time, and many will even come to your home if you feel that is less stressful for you and your dog.

Only you can decide if you will be present at the death of your dog. While most dogs draw peace and comfort from their owners at the final moments, you will not be able to help your dog if you are hysterical, terrified, or angry at the world. If you truly cannot be there, your dog will understand and will make his peace with the help of a gentle and caring professional staff.

Check With Your Vet

Don't decide on your own that your pet has a terminal illness. Many a suspicious lump has turned out be a harmless lipoma, a death-rattling cough simply kennel cough, and the like. And even if your trusted veterinarian declares an illness to be terminal, it never hurts to get another opinion and perhaps learn about other treatment options.

If you feel you can be there, the staff will place a catheter in the dog's foreleg for the procedure. (You don't have to watch this.) Then you will be able to take some time (as long as you want) alone with your pet. The procedure itself is very quick, a matter of seconds. Usually an anesthetic is delivered first, so the animal is actually asleep when death comes. (You may, if you wish, leave at this point in the procedure.) Modern euthanasia drugs are usually so good that some disturbing side effects such as twitching and "gasping" are repressed.

It is easiest if you have made arrangements for the disposition of your pet's body before the event. Cremation or burial is usual but not required. The veterinarian can dispose of the body if that is your wish.

Be honest with your child when explaining the passing of the family pet.

PET LOSS AND CHILDREN

For most children, their first experience of death is the passing away of a beloved pet. Part of our job as adults is to help them understand that death is a natural part of the life cycle, and if in concert with your beliefs, explain that death is not necessarily the end.

Be honest. Don't tell the child that the dog is away on a long trip or has been sent to a farm in the country. While such an explanation may lessen the immediate anguish, sooner or later the child will find out the truth and realize that you have not been honest. Even using words like "put to sleep" can be confusing and sometimes frightening; children have been known to have bouts of insomnia, fearing they too might go to sleep and not wake up again. If the family dog has had to be euthanized, gently explain why you made that choice. Children understand pain. Simply explain that the pain was not ever going to go away and

now the pet is at peace. If your religious beliefs permit, assure the children that they will see their beloved dog again in heaven.

Ideally, the death will not come as a total surprise, and you will have time to prepare your young one. If the pet has been ailing, explain that there is no cure for the disease and that the family needs to make a decision on behalf of the dog. Include the child in the decision-making process if possible.

Opinions differ about whether or not a child should be allowed to witness the euthanasia procedure or come back later to view the deceased pet. It depends on the age and maturity of the child, her wishes, and individual circumstances. You will have to use your best judgment.

Expect your child to ask questions about death, what will happen to the body, and so on. Answer them as honestly as you can, but don't be afraid to give your child comfort and hope. Very young

Only you can decide when it's time to add another dog to the family.

children may need to be reassured that the pet's death is unrelated to anything the child may have said or done. They may experience a temporary setback in bladder or bowel control or may develop sleep disorders. Some children also believe that death is "catching" and that they too will soon die. Understanding and patience will get you through this difficult time.

The First Pet Cemetary

The first official pet cemetery in the United States, the Hartsdale Pet Cemetery, was established in Hartsdale, New York, in 1896.

Questions will probably arise about whether or not to get another dog. Younger children may wish to get a new pet immediately; older ones may say they never want another dog. Explain your own feelings on the matter and let your child express hers as well. Everyone in the family should agree about when it may be right to add a new family member.

Don't hide your own grief, either. It is good for children to know that their parents have the same sorts of feeling that they do. It is proper to grieve over the death of a friend, and by showing your feelings, you are being a good role model. Being stoic in the face of death will only make your child wonder if you are human.

After the death, you may wish to make a memorial scrapbook for the dog, including pictures that your child may draw or a poem or story she may write. You may even want to write a letter to the dog in heaven! Planting a tree in your dog's

If you feel it might help, allow your dog to view a deceased companion.

honor or making a donation to the local animal shelter are other options.

If anyone in the family is having trouble dealing with the loss of a pet, call (217) 244-CARE. This helpline, based at the University of Illinois College of Veterinary Medicine, was developed to provide a supportive outlet for people experiencing the loss of the bond they shared with their beloved pet. The hotline is staffed by veterinary students who have received training by professional grief counselors and receive ongoing supervision by a licensed psychologist.

REACTION OF OTHER PETS

Pet owners are becoming increasingly aware of the emotional needs of their animals, especially when another pet dies. One question that sometimes arises is whether they should allow their living pets to view the body of the deceased animal.

No one can give a definitive answer, and cases probably vary from individual to individual. Many maintain that pets are not able to comprehend that death is final, although dogs surely know that a deceased animal has a different smell than a living one. It is well known that horses and donkeys seem better able to handle the death of a foal if allowed some time with it. And there are cases of elephants never leaving the bodies of their own dead young until decomposition alters the familiar smell.

I believe that dogs do understand something about grief, from a couple of experiences in our own family. In one case, our beloved English Springer Spaniel was killed in a car accident (as a rider). His Irish Setter companion, while she could not have known what happened to him, knew that something precious was gone from her life. For the next six months, she seldom left the couch except to go out to eliminate, and she showed signs of her former vivacity only if she heard his name mentioned—then she would jump up and look around expectantly for him. It was heartbreaking. In another equally wrenching case, our Gordon Setter was killed by a train. His best friend, a Basset mix, witnessed the accident and was never quite the same afterwards. She knew something horrible had happened.

Cognitive scientists are still wrestling with the concept that animals have self-awareness, let alone awareness of another creature's mental or physical state. The weight of opinion today is that a "viewing" is not likely to help a pet to understand the death of a companion. While the argument continues, I think you should give your pet the benefit of the doubt and allow him to view a deceased companion if you feel it might help.

GRIEF

Losing a precious dog is very hard. It is natural and right to grieve. After all, you have lost a dear member of your family. Nowadays, most people understand how painful the loss of a pet is and will be there for you, but there are also groups who will help you get through this period. Do not be afraid or ashamed to seek help if you feel overwhelmed or insupportably depressed. The UC Davis School of Veterinary Medicine, among others, has a Pet Loss Support Program, offering toll-free telephone support Monday-Friday, from 6:30 a.m. to 9:30 p.m. Pacific Time: 1-800-565-1526. You may also go to the following websites: www.petloss.com or www.in-memory-of-pets.com.

RENEWAL

You can commemorate your dog's passing in many ways. You might want to donate to a rescue or the SPCA in your dog's name. You might want to hold a service, take some time off, write a poem, or construct a memory garden. Your grieving period is both a tribute to your dog and a chance for you to heal. Take your own time.

Some people decide to get a new puppy or adopt an older dog very soon after the passing of their pet; others prefer to wait months or even years. Some vow earnestly they will never get another dog because it was too painful to lose the first. But for most dog lovers, life without a dog is not to be contemplated. Sooner or later, a pair of bright eyes will catch at your heart, and you will be ready to fall in love all over again.

One last thing—remember that your new dog will not be a clone of your old one. Every dog is an individual, a unique creation that has never been before and will never be again. Love and enjoy your new dog for the renewed spirit he brings to you. It is a priceless gift.

APPENDIX A:
KEEPING YOUR DOG OUT OF THE POUND

Dogs themselves don't really have any responsibilities, legal or otherwise. Your dog doesn't owe you an allowance. He doesn't have to sign over his worldly goods to you. Your dog will never get a job, get married, or go to college. He doesn't even owe you love, respect, or good behavior. (It's your responsibility to earn them.) In addition, you, as the owner, are responsible for his behavior towards other people and other people's property. You are also responsible to him and for him. Yet, because dogs are part of society, it is inevitable that they become entangled in legal proceedings of various sorts. They can be victims, villains, and points of contention. What if someone steals, tortures, or kills your dog? What if your dog bites another dog or a person? Can insurance companies decline home insurance just because you have a Rottweiler? Can you be forced to pay higher licensing fees because your dog happens to be a "pit bull"? Can you leave a dog money in your will? Are you your dog's owner or guardian? Can you sue your vet?

DANGEROUS DOGS AND BREED-SPECIFIC LEGISLATION

Legal problems with dogkeeping start with problems keeping the dog in the first place. Since dogs kill about a dozen people a year and inflict thousands of dollars of damage in the form of medical bills, insurance companies are understandably concerned over the issue. (The average claim for dog-related physical and psychological damage is $12,000.) In the past ten years, injuries have increased 35 percent. Many jurisdictions around the world are uniting in passing "dangerous dog" legislations. Most of them attempt to pass special laws applying to certain breeds, like Pit Bulls or Presa Canarios (the breed that killed Diane Whipple in January 2001). This is known as breed-specific legislation. It may include special licenses or increased fees for certain breeds, requiring owners of certain breeds to prove that dog is not dangerous, special confinement requirements for certain breeds, liability insurance, etc. Some laws state that dogs of certain breeds cannot be let off leash in a dog park or public place where children are likely to be present.

While most kennel clubs are united behind the "punish the deed, not the breed" motto, the movement to banish or restrict breeds perceived as dangerous is growing. For example, in Ireland, certain breeds (Bulldogs, American Staffordshire Terriers, Akitas, Rhodesian Ridgebacks, Rottweilers, and others) must be muzzled in public. Portugal is considering the same legislation. Sweden is more worried about wolf crosses. Germany requires dogs of certain breeds to undergo a personality test. If the dog fails, he can be euthanized. Germany is also considering banning certain breeds outright.

In America, although most dog groups oppose breed-specific legislation on various grounds, constitutional challenges to it are usually unsuccessful. (You have no constitutional right to own a particular breed of dog.) The law generally gives state and local governments the power to enact their own animal legislation. Opponents of this kind of legislation usually have better luck in attacking the laws on the basis of their vagueness.

However, some lawyers suggest protesting the law through the due process clause—if the laws subject owners to go through rigorous testing of their dogs without a court hearing. You might also have some luck protesting the harshness of some of the penalties exacted. Legally, the punishment must fit the crime. For example, a ten-year sentence for jaywalking would be considered unjust simply because the punishment is so out of line with the offense. The same case might be made for some breed-specific legislation.

Some people have had luck in overturning local laws if the state laws cover the same area and supersede it. Others have attempted to overturn the law, in particular regarding "pit bulls," on the grounds that the term is not well defined (at least it is not a recognized breed by the American Kennel Club [AKC]). Some have tried to make veterinarians responsible for distinguishing between breeds—something veterinarians resent, for the simple reason that they are not qualified to make such distinctions. They are healers, not experts on breed types.

For more information and ideas about preserving your rights, visit the American Dog Owners Association (ADOA) at www.adoa.org; Dog Watch at www.dogwatch.net; the National Animal Interest Alliance (NAIA) at www.naiaonline.org; the American Society for the Prevention of Cruelty to Animals (ASPCA) at www.aspca.org; the Humane Society of the United States (HSUS) at www.hsus.org; or the Royal Society for the Prevention of Cruelty to Animals (RSPCA) at www.rspca.org.uk.

Ultimately, of course, the best way to avoid breed-banning legislation is to make sure dogs of any breed don't bite people. The fact is that some breeds are inherently more aggressive than others. Since contemporary society does not require large numbers of vicious dogs, breeders need to be more proactive in softening the temperaments of their breed. Doberman Pinscher breeders have been very successful in this regard.

BAD-ACTING DOGS

States like Indiana have ruled that if your dog bites a mail carrier or a police officer, you are more liable than if he had simply attacked the neighbors. The Indiana Supreme Court also ruled that it didn't make any difference if it was the first time or the thirtieth that the dog had attacked the officer or if the owner had made any attempts to control it or not. (Most of the time, people get a break under the "one bite" rule. But not always, and it's not a law.) Justice Theodore Boehm wrote in the ruling, "The Indiana statute gives the postal delivery worker the same protection from dog bites that the common law gives all citizens from tiger maulings." This is probably smart because dogs kill more people than tigers do (at least in the US).

In addition, some (not all) states make a distinction between a dog biting an invited guest and an intruder, usually holding that a dog biting a trespasser is less serious than a dog biting a visiting neighbor. Other states, like Oklahoma, make a distinction between rural dogs and urban dogs, with rural dogs being given more freedom to bite than urban ones.

DOGS AND HOME INSURANCE

Most states permit insurance companies to charge higher premiums or even to refuse to renew a policy based on the breed of dog owned (regardless of whether said dog has been in any trouble with the law). Owners of the following types of dogs are most likely to be targeted by insurance companies with restricted coverage: Pit Bulls, Rottweilers, German Shepherd Dogs, Huskies, Alaskan Malamutes, Doberman Pinschers, Chow Chows, Great Danes, and Saint Bernards. Not coincidentally, these are the same breeds most involved in dog-bite fatalities. For dog owners, it's patently unfair. From the viewpoint of insurers, it's a smart business decision. Most of the restricted policies apply to new owners. However, some companies take a middle of the road position, and instead of asking for the breed, merely inquire about the dog's biting history. Another option is to ask your insurance company to exclude your dog from coverage and then buy a separate liability policy.

If you need help finding insurance simply because you own the wrong breed of dog, go to the canine legislation department from www.akc.org. They have compiled resources to assist you.

RENTING WITH A DOG

The bad news is that no-dog clauses are perfectly legal. A landlord can decline to rent an apartment to people with a certain breed of dog, a certain size of dog, a certain number of dogs, or in fact, with any dog at all. They can allow one person in the building to have a dog and not anyone else. Or vice versa. Unless the landlord is discriminating against you based on race, sex, religion, national origin, or disability, you are out of luck. One loophole is the "disability." People with recognized disabilities who need the help or even, in some cases, the "companionship" of an animal can sometimes coerce the landlord into renting to them. This is not usually a problem for blind people or others with obvious physical disabilities. (The Fair Housing Act specifically excludes guide dogs from no-pet restrictions.) But for those people who need a pet for companionship, the road is much tougher. You will need to provide an established need for the service dog; even then, the landlord may try to get a second opinion. For more information, go to www.nupplegal.com/pets.html.

At any rate, before you rent, make sure your landlord or her authorized agent (not the maintenance person) knows you have a pet and is agreeable to it. And get it in writing. You don't want to be thrown out on the street just because your landlord suddenly changes her mind. And never, ever try to sneak a pet into a no-pet zone.

If your landlord seems flexible, you can provide references from previous landlords or pet sitters. If your dog has been to obedience school or participated in the Canine Good Citizen Program (and passed), you might also present the certificate.

For more information about renting or leasing with pets, visit Renting with Pets at www.rentingwithpets.com or People with Pets, a free nationwide apartment locator service, at www.peoplewithpets.com.

HOMEOWNERS ASSOCIATIONS

About 50 million Americans live in housing that is privately "governed." Most of them have protocols (usually restrictive rules) about pets. And most of the restrictive rules concern dogs. No one seems to care how many guppies you have. It's hard to fight these restrictions unless you have a documented disability for which the pet is a medical or psychological aid. Service dogs, for example, are usually seen as a reasonable accommodation. The average pet owner, however, seems to be stuck, although some effort has been spent in getting legislatures to enact laws that would override unreasonable restrictions.

THE CHANGING LEGAL LANDSCAPE OF DOG GUARDIANSHIP OR OWNERSHIP

In the past several years, several jurisdictions (including the state of Rhode Island) have enacted legislation reclassifying pet owners as pet guardians. Some jurisdictions have simply added the word "guardian" to "owner"; others have considered replacing it. Proponents of the change regard "guardian" as a term that puts in the correct light the relationship between owners and their dogs. For centuries, dogs have been considered chattel, like chairs or vacuum cleaners. Obviously that doesn't describe the way most owners feel about their pets. The word "guardian" implies a degree of responsibility and respect for animal welfare that "owner" does not. The dog becomes a ward, rather than merely property. Even the US Department of Transportation included the word in a recent proposal to force airlines to notify the Department when such an animal dies in transit or in custody of the airline. Some states have considered allowing emotional distress damages to be awarded to the owners of injured animals. This can apply to problems that occur in transit as well as deliberate acts of cruelty by the guy next door. And even where states don't allow this officially, the courts have stepped in. In the year 2000, Tennessee became the first state to give pet owners rights to pain and suffering damages as well as punitive damages for abuse and neglect. Other versions of this bill have passed or are being considered in other states. In many ways, this seems like a great idea. If someone wantonly kills a pet, caring owners suffer agonies of grief and rage. However, some people worry about what this will do to veterinarians, who may be subject to pain-and-suffering lawsuits. Insurance premiums are bound to skyrocket, and clients will be footing the bill.

The AKC and some other organizations oppose the use of the word "guardian" and prefer "owner," fearing that guardianship does not adequately protect either the owner or the dog, in some cases making it unclear as to who has authority to do what.

BY THE NUMBERS

Communities may also create legislation that limits the number of pets per household. In most cases,

courts have upheld these limitations, forcing some rescues into a panic. The law designed to prohibit animal "hoarding," a pathological activity in which people, possibly thinking they are "helping homeless animals," collect large numbers of them, far more than they can possibly care for. However, as is often the case with this kind of arrangement, the responsible, law-abiding citizens and rescue groups are penalized, while the hoarder keeps hoarding. (Already all states have laws against animal cruelty and the police power to remove such animals.) It's not clear that another law would help the situation.

YOUR DOG AND YOUR WILL

Currently, 14 states legally recognize dogs and cats as beneficiaries, allowing the owner to leave them both money and property. In most places, however, you'll have to leave the pet to a friend or relative, along with a bequest. Or you might be able to include a provision that leaves a certain amount of money with a humane society or rescue. You might even be able to set up a trust fund, at least in some states. This is something you need to research very carefully and discuss with your lawyer.

BREEDING CONTRACTS

Buying a dog is a legal transaction, one in which you need to protect yourself. Be sure that you receive all the appropriate documentation, including the names of the parties, pedigrees, and payment amount and provisions. Special features, such as the buyer's obligation to breed (or not breed) the dog, and the seller's take-back policy should also be spelled out.

Often the buyer and seller don't live in the same legal jurisdiction. In that case, what is called a "forum selection clause" is usually included in the contract, which states that legal disputes will be settled in the jurisdiction of the seller.

CO-OWNING A DOG

Many people, especially those in the dog show world, "co-own" a dog. While this arrangement can be delightful for all concerned, it is fraught with legal hazards. Before signing a co-owning contract, make sure it is well understood who is responsible for showing the dog (or paying the handler). If you are purchasing a show dog primarily as a pet, make sure the contract does not required you to be parted from the animal when he is on the show circuit.

Who pays for veterinary expenses, genetic testing, stud fees, advertising, transport? The contract should say. Co-ownership means co-responsibility. That is, you can be held liable for any damage the dog does, even if you are in another state. This includes dog bites. Be careful!

Divorce

Legally, pets are usually viewed as personal property or chattel, like a DVD player. This is why, until very recently, even if someone shot your dog on purpose, your civil damage awards pertained only to the monetary, not the emotional, value of your pet. Things are different in the divorce courts, though. In custody battles, family law courts increasingly recognize that animals occupy a special place in the hearts of their owners. You can buy another DVD player, but your dog is irreplaceable.

The best cure is prevention: Get it in writing in a pre-nuptial agreement! That's right. "Always, always, always put clear, concise language in prenups that covers your pet," counsels one divorce attorney. "Abuse, abandonment, homelessness, and possible euthanasia are real risks when families forget to protect their pets from life's most unpredictable circumstances."

APPENDIX B:
A CLOSER LOOK AT BREED-SPECIFIC LEGISLATION

Currently, about 200 cities and towns throughout the United States restrict or prohibit ownership of certain breeds of dogs. Banned dogs include Akitas, Chow Chows, Dalmatians, Dobermans, German Shepherd Dogs, Great Danes, Pit Bulls, and Rottweilers, as well as mixes of these breeds. In places such as Miami, Florida; Pawtucket, Rhode Island; and Cincinnati, Ohio, certain breeds deemed vicious are banned outright. Or localities place certain restrictions on owners, such as requiring that they carry liability insurance or muzzle their pets in public. But the US is not acting alone.

Here is a brief glimpse of some recently imposed bans or restrictions on dogs in Europe. These restrictions are constantly being challenged, however. If you are planning a visit to one of these countries with your dog (of whatever breed), check with the authorities before you go!

(Please note: The current situation in regard to breed-specific legislation is extremely fluid. Courts are constantly overturning legislation, and new laws are constantly being proposed. It is important to keep abreast of current events in the dog world.)

FRANCE

France has recently restricted Pit Bulls and is considering further breed controls, and there is also talk of expanding Germany's breed bans and restrictions to all the countries of the European Union. Currently the Pit Bull Terrier is heavily restricted, with a special license required, and several other breeds are on a specially controlled list, including the American Staffordshire Terrier, Rottweiler, and Japanese Tosa.

GERMANY

Germany attempted to enact specific legislation to ban what proponents of the measure label as "all fighting dogs." At one time, this list included American Staffordshire Terriers, Pit Bulls, and Staffordshire Bull Terriers, or crossbreeds containing these mixes (and well over a dozen other sorts of dogs), some of which were not even recognized as breeds! Laws differ in Germany's 16 states, but in Hesse, Lower Saxony, and North Rhine-Westphalia, they contained some version of the following provisions:

Category I dogs—dangerous breeds that cannot be imported, bred, or sold—include the American Staffordshire Terrier, Pit Bull Terrier, Staffordshire Bull Terrier, Bull Terrier, Neapolitan Mastiff, Spanish Mastiff, Dogue de Bordeaux, Dogo Argentino, Fila Brasiliero, Roman Fighting Dog, Chinese Fighting Dog, Bandog, and Tosa Inu. These dogs must be registered and sterilized.

Category II dogs—potentially dangerous dogs who can be owned, imported, bred, and sold if they pass a temperament test and are free of aggressive actions for three years—include Akbash, Briard, Beauceron, Bullmastiff, Doberman, Komondor, Kuvasz, Maremma, Pyrenean Mountain Dog (Great Pyrenees in the US), Rhodesian Ridgeback, Rottweiler, Tibetan Mastiff, and more than 15 other breeds that are not well known in the US.

Category III dogs—dogs who weigh more than 20 kilos (44 pounds) or are taller than 40 centimeters (15.75 inches). These dogs must be on a leash in developed areas and will be moved to Category II if they show aggression.

Cooler heads prevailed, however, and the Senate of the Supreme Administration court in Berlin canceled the directive of the state of Niedersachsen (Lower Saxony), along with its list of "dangerous" dog breeds. The judges said that the content of the directive went too far for a directive that is made by a single minister.

Although this one piece of legislation was overturned, Germany continues to restrict and ban certain breeds.

HOLLAND

Holland has banned the American Staffordshire Terrier, Fila Brasiliero, Dogo Argentino, and Neapolitan Mastiff.

ITALY

The Italian government has listed 92 kinds of "threatening" canines in Italy, including not only the larger breeds such as Dobermans, Bull Mastiffs, German Shepherds, Newfoundlands, St. Bernards, and Pit Bulls but Border Collies—and Corgis.

Under Italian law, minors, delinquents, and criminals who have caused harm to people or animals will be banned from owning a dog on the "dangerous" list. (I have no objection to persons who have harmed others being forbidden to own animals—but I think the ban should be extended to all animals.) Individuals who are not banned from owning one of the listed dogs must still keep any dogs in the "dangerous" category muzzled and leashed in public. The law also requires owners of the dogs on the "dangerous" list to obtain insurance—expected to cost approximately 150 euros—in case their pet inflicts harm on anyone.

NEW ZEALAND

There is movement on breed-specific legislation that would ban any dog with "bull" or "pit" in the name.

POLAND

Poland has required owners to obtain permits, provide reinforced fencing, and display "Beware of Dog" signs for American Pit Bull Terriers, Perro de Presa Mallorquins, American Bulldogs, Dogo Argentinos, Canary Dogs, Japanese Tosas, Rottweilers, Akbash Dogs, and Anatolian Karabash.

PORTUGAL

Portugal has banned the Staffordshire Bull Terrier, Rottweiler, American Staffordshire Terrier, Fila Brasiliero, Dogo Argentino, Tosa Inu, and the American Pit Bull Terrier.

UNITED KINGDOM

The UK has virtually banned or severely restricted the Dogo Argentino, Fila Brasiliero, Japanese Tosa, and the Pit Bull Terrier. The Home Secretary has the right to add any other breed at any time if he believes it is a threat to the public.

In 1991 the UK introduced the Dangerous Dog Act, which was followed by a "muzzling order" in Ireland that affected nearly 40 breeds. England has also had to deal with various attempts to ban the usual suspects, plus various other breeds including some perhaps unexpected examples, such as Rhodesian Ridgebacks and Maremma Sheepdogs, as well as Akitas, Dogue de Bordeaux, various mastiffs, and the usual bull breeds. The laws are often passed after a fatal dog attack has occurred in which there is public pressure to "do something."

THE RATIONALE

The movement to ban certain dog breeds from certain jurisdictions is all about aggression. People do not wish to ban breeds because they are too small, too big, too hairy, or bark too much but because they fear being bitten. And while dogs don't kill nearly as many people every year as bees do, they can and do bite people (mostly children) with unsettling frequency.

Certain breeds and types of dogs are on record as being more likely to inflict a dangerous bite than are others. German Shepherds, just to take one example, are more likely to bite someone than English Setters are. That's a fact. Aggression is largely inherited. It can be made worse by neglect and cruel treatment, but the basic pattern for a dog to develop an aggressive attitude is handed down in the genes. Dog breeding is also an enterprise in genetics, and many breeds have some well-established ingrained behaviors. Labrador Retrievers were bred to retrieve, Greyhounds were bred to chase, and Border Collies were bred to herd. In like manner, certain "fighting breeds" were bred to fight other dogs, and certain guardian breeds were trained to be fearless, and when instructed, aggressive to human beings.

However, aggression is not irretrievably linked to any breed type. What is bred in can be bred out. Part of the problem stems from unscrupulous people who actually breed dogs to be aggressive in a world where aggression is largely an unneeded and indeed undesirable trait. And in activities where aggression may be needed for police work and similar activities, certain lines of dogs can be bred who retain ancestral aggression. It can simply be bred out of the other dogs, as has been done, for instance, with the Bulldog—once a ferocious creature, now a perfect family dog.

As long as the general public perceives certain breeds as being unsafe, continued efforts will be made to ban breeds. And even if all the so-called dangerous breeds were officially banned tomorrow, a truly vicious breed could be recreated in only a few years of intensive breeding from random stock.

So-called Pit Bulls, for example, can be among the most loving and friendly of dogs—especially if they do not come from "fighting lines." Early on, even "fighting" Pit Bulls were perfectly safe around people and dangerous only to other dogs. In the same way, a well-trained guard dog is trained to attack on command, not randomly wander around seeking victims. Now, however, human-directed aggression is allowed by all too many people. In some cases, this happens simply because a breed becomes too popular. High popularity can result in expanded, careless breeding with little or no regard for sound temperament. This is especially dangerous in dogs who have a genetic predisposition for aggression. In the early 1990s, Rottweilers were the victims of such overpopularity, and their own sound temperament began to disintegrate. The same thing happened to Dobermans in the 70s, but conscientious Doberman breeders regained their hold, and today, Dobermans are of a much more stable disposition than 25 years ago.

A natural, if overhasty, response is simply to ban the breeds involved in fatal attacks. Yet this approach plainly does not work. In Cincinnati, Ohio, the police department spent over $160,000 per year during a ten-year period trying to enforce their Pit Bull ban. Since many people don't know a Pit Bull when they see one, they seized Boxers and even Golden Retrievers as examples of the dreaded Pit Bull. (The Cincinnati law was eventually overturned.) In Prince George's County, Maryland, the Pit Bull ban did not decrease Pit Bull bites. And German Shepherd Dogs, who were not banned, continued to bite as many people as before.

We have seen the "dangerous dog wave" pass from German Shepherd Dogs to Dobermans to Rottweilers to Pit Bulls—because these dogs were bred, at least partly, for aggression, abuse or neglect is more likely to produce an aggressive response. But keep in mind any dog can bite. Studies published in the *Journal of the American*

Veterinary Medical Association revealed that more than 25 breeds of dog have been involved in human fatalities, including Dachshunds, Golden Retrievers, Labrador Retrievers, and a Yorkshire Terrier (okay, the Yorkie had some help).

Irresponsible pet owners must take part of the blame. "If a specific breed is banned, irresponsible owners intent on using their dogs for malicious or illegal purposes will go underground with their dogs or switch to another breed and continue to jeopardize public safety," said Gina DiNardo Lash, director of club communications for the American Kennel Club (AKC). The state of New York agrees and has outlawed breed-specific legislation.

The answer, of course, is public education and stern judicial measures taken against owners who permit their dogs to bite someone—either because they deliberately "sic" the dog on someone or because they simply allow the animal to get out of hand. And I am not talking about lawsuits, although lawsuits play their part in keeping people under control. I am talking about criminal action. It is up to lawmakers to attach strong criminal penalties against owners who allow their dogs of whatever breed or mix to bite someone. "Punish the deed, not the breed!" Indeed.

But before punishment, we need education. Only when people learn how to select a breed that is truly right for them, how to care for it, train it, and properly restrain it, can we look to a halt in tragedies involving dogs and people. In about a quarter of the cases involving human fatalities, the culprit dogs were not restrained or even on their own property! In another quarter of fatalities, the dog was kept chained, a cruel practice that only serves to increase aggression. Further, in most cases where the attacking dog was male, the animal was not neutered, a simple surgical procedure that makes a dog a better pet and keeps him in better health.

WHAT YOU CAN DO

Contact your local legislators and explain why you are opposed to breed bans. But don't be negative. Instead, suggest that communities take steps to make it easy (or even required) for owners of all dogs to get educated about how to train, restrain, and care for their pets—regardless of breed.

Insist that people who allow their dogs to bite or who are convicted of cruelty to animals pay the legal price for their actions. Many cases of dog aggression can be halted by simply taking good care of our pets. And since one cannot completely rely on the purity of human nature to do the right thing, people must be required to do so, or lose the privilege of owning a dog.

Take personal responsibility for your own pet, particularly if it is one of the proposed "banned breeds." Show everyone what a friendly and excellent dog a well-socialized American Staffordshire Terrier or Rottweiler really is.

	US UNITS	MULTIPLIED BY	EQUALS METRIC UNITS
Length	Inches	2.5400	Centimeters
	Feet	0.3048	Meters
	Yards	0.9144	Meters
	Miles	1.6093	Kilometers
Area	Square inches	6.4516	Square centimeters
	Square feet	0.0929	Square meters
	Square yards	0.8361	Square meters
	Acres	0.4047	Hectares
Weight	Foot-pounds	1.3830	Newton-meters
	Pounds	0.4536	Kilograms
Volume	Cubic feet	0.0283	Cubic meters
	Cubic yards	0.7646	Cubic meters
	Gallons	3.7854	Liters
Temperature	Celcius to Fahrenheit: Multiply the Celcius temperature by 9. Divide that answer by 5. Then, add 32. Fahrenheit to Celcius: Subtract 32 from the Fahrenheit temperature. Divide the answer by 9. Then, multiply that answer by 5. Celcius°=5/9 (F°-32°) Fahrenheit°=9/5 C° +32°		

RESOURCES

PUBLICATIONS
Books
Anderson, Teoti. *Puppy Care & Training*. New Jersey: TFH Publications, Inc., 2007.

Anderson, Teoti. *The Super Simple Guide to Housetraining*. New Jersey: TFH Publications, Inc., 2004.

Becker, Susan C. *Living With a Deaf Dog: A Book of Advice, Facts and Experiences About Canine Deafness*. Ohio: S.C. Becker, 1997.

Boneham, Sheila Webster, Ph.D. *The Multiple-Dog Family*. New Jersey: TFH Publications, Inc., 2009.

Boneham, Sheila Webster, Ph.D. *Training Your Dog for Life*. New Jersey: TFH Publications, Inc., 2008.

Copeland, Sue and John A. *Hamil. Hands-On Dog Care*. California: Doral Publishing, 2000.

Dainty, Suellen. *50 Games to Play With Your Dog*. New Jersey: TFH Publications, Inc., 2007.

DeGioia. *The Mixed Breed Dog*. New Jersey: TFH Publications, Inc., 2007.

DeVito, Russell-Revesz, Fornino. *World Atlas of Dog Breeds, 6th Ed.* New Jersey: TFH Publications, Inc., 2009.

Downing, Robin. *Pets Living With Cancer: A Pet Owner's Resource*. American Animal Hospital Association, 2000.

Gagne, Tammy. *Designer Dogs*. New Jersey: TFH Publications, Inc., 2008.

Gagne, Tammy. *The Happy Adopted Dog*. New Jersey: TFH Publications, Inc., 2009.

Gagne, Tammy. *Living Green With Your Dog*. New Jersey: TFH Publications, Inc., 2009.

King, Trish. *Parenting Your Dog: Complete Care and Training for Every Life Stage*. New Jersey: TFH Publications, Inc., 2010.

Knueven, Doug, DVM. *The Holistic Health Guide for Dogs*. New Jersey: TFH Publications, Inc., 2008.

Lee, Laura and Martyn Lee. *Absent Friend: Coping with the Loss of a Treasured Friend*. Bucks, England: Henston Press, 1992.

Mammato, Bobbie and Susie Duckworth. *Pet First Aid: Cats and Dogs*. Missouri: CV Mosby Publishing Company, 1997.

Morgan, Diane. *Feeding Your Dog for Life: The Real Facts About Proper Nutrition*. California: Doral Publishing, 2002.

Morgan, Diane. *The Living Well Guide for Senior Dogs*. New Jersey: TFH Publications, Inc., 2007.

Morgan, Diane. *The Simple Guide to Choosing a Dog*. New Jersey: TFH Publications, Inc., 2003.

Smith, Kymberly, ed. *Healing the Pain of Pet Loss: Letters in Memoriam*. Pennsylvania: The Charles Press, 1997.

Tousley, Marty and Katherine Heuerman. *Final Farewell: Preparing for and Mourning the Loss of Your Pet*. Arizona: Our Pals Publishing Co., 1997.

Magazines
AKC Family Dog
American Kennel Club
260 Madison Avenue
New York, NY 10016
Telephone: (800) 490-5675
E-mail: familydog@akc.org
www.akc.org/pubs/familydog

AKC Gazette
American Kennel Club
260 Madison Avenue
New York, NY 10016
Telephone: (800) 533-7323

E-mail: gazette@akc.org
www.akc.org/pubs/gazette

Dog & Kennel
Pet Publishing, Inc.
7-L Dundas Circle
Greensboro, NC 27407
Telephone: (336) 292-4047
Fax: (336) 292-4272
E-mail: info@petpublishing.com
www.dogandkennel.com

Dog Fancy
P.O. Box 6050
Mission Viejo, CA 92690-6050
Telephone: (800) 365-4421
E-mail: barkback@dogfancy.com
www.dogfancy.com

Dog World
P.O. Box 6050
Mission Viejo, CA 92690-6050
Telephone: (800) 365-4421
E-mail: dogworld@dogworldmag.com
www.dogworld.com

Dogs Monthly
Ascot House
29 High Street, Ascot
Berkshire, SL5 7JG
United Kingdom
Telephone: 1344 628 269
Fax: 1344 622 771
E-mail: admin@rtcassociates.freeserve.co.uk
www.corsini.co.uk/dogsmonthly

ORGANIZATIONS
Animal Welfare and Rescue
American Humane Association (AHA)
63 Inverness Drive East
Englewood, CO 80112
Telephone: (800) 227-4645
Fax: (303) 792-5333
www.americanhumane.org

American Society for the Prevention of Cruelty to Animals (ASPCA)
424 E. 92nd Street
New York, NY 10128-6804
Telephone: (212) 876-7700
www.aspca.org

Canadian Federation of Humane Societies (CFHS)
102-30 Concourse Gate
Ottawa, ON K2E 7V7
Canada
Telephone: (888) 678-CFHS
Fax: (613)723-0252
E-mail: info@cfhs.ca
www.cfhs.ca

The Humane Society of the United States (HSUS)
2100 L Street, NW
Washington, DC 20037
Telephone: (202) 452-1100
www.humanesociety.org

Partnership for Animal Welfare
P.O. Box 1074
Greenbelt, MD 20768
Telephone: (301) 572-4729
E-mail: dogs@paw-rescue.org
www.paw-rescue.org

Royal Society for the Prevention of Cruelty to Animals (RSPCA)
Wilberforce Way
Southwater, Horsham,
West Sussex RH13 9RS
United Kingdom
Telephone: 0300 123 4555
Fax: 0303 123 0100
vetfone: 0906 500 5500
www.rspca.org.uk

Behavior

American College of Veterinary Behaviorists (ACVB)
Dr. Bonnie V. Beaver, ACVB Executive Director
Texas A&M University
College Station, TX 77843-4474
E-mail: info@dacvb.org
www.veterinarybehaviorists.org

Animal Behavior Society (ABS)
Indiana University
402 N. Park Ave.
Bloomington, IN 47408-2603
Telephone: (812) 856-5541
Fax: (812) 856-5542
E-mail: aboffice@indiana.edu
www.animalbehaviorsociety.org

BREED CLUBS

American Kennel Club (AKC)
5580 Centerview Drive
Raleigh, NC 27606
Telephone: (919) 233-9767
Fax: (919) 233-3627
E-mail: info@akc.org
www.akc.org

Canadian Kennel Club (CKC)
200 Ronson Drive, Suite 400
Etobicoke, Ontario
M9W 6R4
Canada
Telephone: (416) 675-5511
Fax: (416) 675-6506
E-mail: information@ckc.ca
www.ckc.ca

The Fédération Cynologique Internationale (FCI)
[World Canine Organization]
13 Place Albert 1er
B-6530 Thuin
Belgium
Telephone: 32 71 59 12 38
Fax: 32 71 59 22 29
E-mail: info@fci.be
www.fci.be

The Kennel Club
1-5 Clarges Street
Picadilly, London
W1J 8AB
United Kingdom
Telephone: 0844 463 3980
Fax: 020 7518 1058
www.thekennelclub.org.uk

United Kennel Club (UKC)
100 E. Kilgore Road
Kalamazoo, MI 49002-5584
Telephone: (269) 343-9020
Fax: (269) 343-7037
www.ukcdogs.com

GROOMING

The International Society of Canine Cosmetologists (ISCC)
2702 Covington Drive
Garland, TX 75040
Fax: (972) 530-3313
E-mail: iscc@petstylist.com
www.petstylist.com

National Dog Groomers Association of America, Inc. (NDGAA)
P.O. Box 101
Clark, PA 16113
Telephone: (724) 962-2711
Fax: (724) 962-1919
E-mail: ndgaa@nationaldoggroomers.com
www.nationaldoggroomers.com

HEALTH

The American Animal Hospital Association (AAHA)
12575 W. Bayaud Ave.
Lakewood, CO 80228
Telephone: (303) 986-2800
Fax: (303) 986-1700
E-mail: info@aahanet.org
www.aahanet.org

American Kennel Club Canine Health Foundation (AKCCHF)
P.O. Box 37941
Raleigh, NC 27627-7941
Telephone: (888) 682-9696
E-mail: caninehealth@akcchf.org
www.akcchf.org

Canine Health Information Center (CHIC)
2300 E. Nifong Blvd.
Columbia, MO 65201-3806
Telephone: (573) 442-0418
Fax: (573) 875-5073
E-mail: chic@offa.org
www.caninehealthinfo.org

Canine Eye Registration Foundation (CERF)
VMDB/CERF
1248 Lynn Hall
625 Harrison St
Purdue University
W Lafayette, IN 47907-2026
Telephone: (765) 494-8179
E-mail: CERF@vmdb.org
www.vmdb.org/cerf.html

Orthopedic Foundation for Animals, Inc. (OFA)
2300 E. Nifong Blvd.
Columbia, MO 65201-3806
Phone: (800) 442-0418
E-mail: chic@offa.org
www.offa.org

PET SITTING

The National Association of
Professional Pet Sitters (NAPPS)
15000 Commerce Parkway, Suite C
Mt. Laurel, NJ 08054
Telephone: (856) 439-0324
E-mail: NAPPS@ahint.com
www.petsitters.org

Pet Sitters International
201 East King Street
King, NC 27021
Telephone: (336) 983-9222
Fax: (336) 983-5266
E-mail: info@petsit.com
www.petsit.com

SPORTS

Agility Association of Canada (AAC)
RR#2
Lucan, Ontario N0N 2J0
Canada
Telephone: (519) 657-7636
www.aac.ca

North American Dog Agility Council
(NADAC)
P.O. Box 1206
Colbert, OK 74733
E-mail: info@nadac.com
www.nadac.com

North American Flyball Association
(NAFA)
1400 West Devon Avenue, #512
Chicago, IL 60660
Telephone/Fax: (800) 318-6312
E-mail: flyball@flyball.org
www.flyball.org

United States Dog Agility Association
(USDAA)
P.O. Box 850955
Richardson, TX 75085-0955
Telephone: (972) 487-2200
Fax: (972) 231-9700
E-mail: info@usdaa.com
www.usdaa.com

THERAPY

The Bright and Beautiful Therapy
Dogs, Inc.
80 Powder Mill Road
Morris Plains, NJ 07950

Telephone: (888) PET-5770
Fax: (973) 292-9559
E-mail: info@golden-dogs.org
www.golden-dogs.org

Delta Society Pet Partners Program
875 124th Ave. NE, Suite 101
Bellevue, WA 98005
Telephone: (425) 679-5500
Fax: (425) 679-5539
E-mail: info@deltasociety.org
www.deltasociety.org

Therapy Dogs Incorporated
P.O. Box 20227
Cheyenne, WY 82003
Telephone: (877) 843-7364
E-mail: therapydogsinc@qwestoffice.
net
www.therapydogs.com

Therapy Dogs International
88 Bartley Square
Flanders, NJ 07836
Telephone: (973) 252-9800
Fax: (973) 252-7171
E-mail: tdi@gti.net
www.tdi-dog.org

TRAINING

Association of Pet Dog Trainers
(APDT)
101 North Main St., Suite 610
Greenville, SC 29601
Telephone: (800) PET-DOGS
Fax: (864) 331-0767
E-mail: information@apdt.com
www.apdt.com

Certification Council for Pet Dog
Trainers (CCPDT)
1350 Broadway, 17th Floor
New York, NY 10018
Telephone: (212) 356-0682
E-mail: administrator@ccpdt.org
www.ccpdt.org

VETERINARY

Academy of Veterinary Homeopathy
(AVH)
P.O. Box 232282
Leucadia, CA 92023-2282
Telephone/Fax: (866) 652-1590
www.theavh.com/contact/index.php

American Academy of Veterinary
Acupuncture (AAVA)
P.O. Box 1058
Glastonbury, CT 06033
Telephone: (860) 632-9911
Fax: (860) 659-8772
E-mail: office@aava.org
www.aava.org

American Animal Hospital
Association (AAHA)
12575 W. Bayaud Ave.
Lakewood, CO 80228
Telephone: (303) 986-2800
Fax: (303) 986-1700
E-mail: info@aahanet.org
www.aahanet.org

American College of Veterinary
Internal Medicine (ACVIM)
1997 Wadsworth Blvd., Suite A
Lakewood, CO 80214-5293
Telephone: (800) 245-9081
Fax: (303) 231-0880
E-mail: ACVIM@ACVIM.org
www.acvim.org.

American College of Veterinary
Ophthalmologists (ACVO)
P.O. Box 1311
Meridian, ID 83680
Telephone: (208) 466-7624
Fax: (208) 466-7693
E-mail: office10@acvo.org
www.acvo.com

American Holistic Veterinary Medical
Association (AHVMA)
2218 Old Emmorton Road
Bel Air, MD 21015
Telephone: (410) 569-0795
Fax: (410) 569-2346
E-mail: office@ahvma.org
www.ahvma.org

American Veterinary Chiropractic
Association (AVCA)
442154 E 140 Road
Bluejacket, OK 74333
Telephone: (918) 784-2231
Fax: (918) 784-2675
E-mail: avcainfo@junct.com
www.animalchiropractic.org

American Veterinary Dental Society
(AVDS)
P.O. Box 803
Fayetteville, TN 37334
Telephone: (800) 332-AVDS
Fax: (931) 433-6289
E-mail: avds@avds-online.org
www.avds-online.org

American Veterinary Medical
Association (AVMA)
1931 North Meacham Road, Suite 100
Schaumburg, IL 60173-4360
Telephone: (800) 248-2862
Fax: (847) 925-1329
E-mail: avmainfo@avma.org
www.avma.org

International Veterinary Acupuncture
Society (IVAS)
1730 South College Ave., Suite 301
Ft. Collins, CO 80527-1395
Telephone: (970) 266-0666
Fax: (970) 266-0777
E-mail: office@ivas.org
www.ivas.org

US Food & Drug Administration's
Center for Veterinary Medicine (CVM)
Communications Staff (CVM)
Food and Drug Administration
7519 Standish Place, HFV-12
Rockville, MD 20855
Telephone: (240) 276-9300
E-mail: ASKCVM@fda.hhs.gov
www.fda.gov/cvm/default.htm

Veterinary Cancer Society (VCS)
P.O. Box 1763
Spring Valley, CA 91979
Telephone: (619) 741-2210
Fax: (619) 741-1117
E-mail: vcs@cox.net
www.vetcancersociety.org

WEBSITES

General
Animal Planet
www.animal.discovery.com
The domestic dog section has a
great guide to dogs, a breed selector,
training information, and more.

Digital Dog
www.digitaldog.com
Good information on choosing and
caring for a dog, as well as dog
training and behavior.

I Love Dogs
www.i-love-dogs.com
Numerous articles about dogs and
an extensive directory of dog-related
websites.

Nylabone®
www.nylabone.com
Nylabone premium chews, toys, and
other products promote good canine
dental hygiene, enhance overall mental
fitness, encourage positive behavior,
provide comfortable shelter, and allow
for safe, pleasant travel.

Peteducation.com
www.peteducation.com
Expert advice for all pets, with columns
updated monthly.

The Pet Place
www.petplace.com
A user-friendly website where pet
owners worldwide can go for complete,
up-to-date information on all pet
issues.

Planet Pets
www.planet-pets.com
A substantial pet directory, especially
for information about dog breeds.

The Senior Dogs Project
www.srdogs.com
Provides information on rescuing and
adopting older dogs.

TFH Publications, Inc.
www.tfh.com
Comprehensive and authoritative
animal reference books and learning
vehicles for pet owners that ensure the
optimum human–companion animal
experience.

Activities
Carting With Your Dog
www.cartingwithyourdog.com
Information and resources on carting.

DogPlay
www.dogplay.com

Excellent guide to activities that you
can do with your dog.

Dog Works, Inc.
www.dogworks.com
A great source for canine carting and
watersports equipment.

Hike With Your Dog
www.hikewithyourdog.com
Direct links to more than 2,000 dog-
friendly parks, plus dog regulations for
national parks in the US and Canada.

Skyhoundz
www.skyhoundz.com
Products and events for disc dog
enthusiasts.

Sled Dog Central
www.sleddogcentral.com
Sled dog information resource.

SportsVet.com
http://www.sportsvet.com
Website dedicated to athletic and
working dogs. A great site for health
and care information for your canine
athlete.

Behavior
Pet Behavior Resources
www.webtrail.com/petbehavior
A guide to all aspects of pet behavior.

Dumb Friends League
www.ddfl.org
Excellent advice for solving common
pet behavioral problems.

Integrative and Holistic Health
AltVetMed
www.altvetmed.com
The site contains information about
acupuncture, homeopathy, herbal
medicine, and many other alternative
methods of treatment.

Dr. Edward Bach Centre
www.bachcentre.com
The world center for information on Dr.
Bach's Flower Remedies.

Natural Rearing
www.naturalrearing.com
Provides information about holistic and
complementary health care for pets.

PetMassage
www.petmassage.com
Combines variations of traditional massage, acupressure, positional release, Healing Touch, and animal communication.

Lang Institute for Canine Massage
www.dogmassage.com
A canine massage school.

Legal

American Dog Owner's Association
www.adoa.org
Information and ideas about preserving dog owners' rights, and information about responsible dog ownership.

Animal Legal Defense Fund
www.aldf.org
Advancing the lives of animals through the legal system.

Dog Watch
www.dogwatch.net
Provides information on canine breed-specific legislation in North America and abroad.

National Animal Interest Alliance
www.naiaonline.org
Provides expert information on animals and public policy.

NUPP Legal
www.nupplegal.com/pets.html
Legal form for pet owners who are renting is available for purchase on this website.

People With Pets
www.peoplewithpets.com
A free nationwide apartment locator service for people with pets.

Loss

Petloss.com
www.petloss.com
Grief support website for those who have lost a pet.

In Memory of Pets
www.in-memory-of-pets.com
Support and memorials for those suffering from the loss of a pet.

Lost and Missing Pets

Last Chance for Animals
www.stolenpets.com
Learn about how to combat the problem of stolen pets who are sold to research institutions.

Missing Pet Network
www.missingpet.net
Website run by a group of volunteers sponsored by the USDA Animal Care Office, who help people find missing pet animals.

Pets 911
www.pets911.org
Contains a nationwide list of animal control facilities, humane societies, and veterinarians; searchable by zip code.

Medical

Arthritis and Glucosamine Resource Center
www.arthritis-glucosamine.net/pet-arthritis
Source for articles on all aspects of canine arthritis, including risk factors, signs, diagnosis, treatment, and diet.

Dog Genome Project
www.fhcrc.org/science/dog_genome
A collaborative study aimed at producing a map of all the chromosomes in dogs.

Pet Dental
www.petdental.com
Provides information about proper oral health care for dogs and cats.

Pets With Diabetes
www.petdiabetes.com
Provides educational information, Internet resources, personal experiences, and support for owners of diabetic pets.

Vetinfo
www.vetinfo.com/dogindex.html
An alphabetical listing and discussion of dog illnesses.

Special Needs

Deaf Dog Education Action Fund
www.deafdogs.org
Provides education and funding for the purpose of improving and saving the lives of deaf dogs.

K-9 Carts
www.k9carts.com
Manufacturer of "K-9 Carts," wheelchairs for mobility-impaired pets.

Owners of Blind Dogs
www.blinddogs.com
Provides support and information to blind dogs and their owners.

Training

Dr. P's Dog Training
www.uwsp.edu/psych/dog/dog.htm
A library of information about dog training and behavior.

Webzines

Dog Owner's Guide
www.canismajor.com/dog
A free online magazine that contains sections on choosing a dog, breed profiles, nutrition, health, training, travel, sports, and rescue.

Bark Bytes
www.barkbytes.com
Canine cyber magazine featuring breed profiles and many links.

Working Dogs Cyberzine
www.workingdogs.com
An international magazine for and about working and sporting dogs.

INDEX

Boldfaced numbers indicate illustrations.

AUTHOR

Diane Morgan is an assistant professor of philosophy and religion at Wilson College, Chambersburg, PA. She has authored numerous books on canine care and nutrition and has also written many breed books, horse books, and books on Eastern philosophy and religion. She is an avid gardener (and writes about that, too). Diane lives in Williamsport, Maryland, with several dogs, two cats, some fish, and a couple of humans.

PHOTOS